BRITAIN'S ANCIENT WOODLAND

WOODLAND HERITAGE

BRITAIN'S ANCIENT WOODLAND

WOODLAND HERITAGE

PETER MARREN

They shut the road through the woods
  Seventy years ago.
Weather and rain have undone it again,
  And now you would never know
There was once a path through the woods
  Before they planted the trees,
It is underneath the coppice and heath,
  And the thin anemones.
  Only the keeper sees
That, where the ring-dove broods,
  And the badger roll at ease,
There was once a road through the woods

from The Way Through the Woods
Rudyard Kipling

ESSO   NATURE CONSERVANCY COUNCIL

DAVID & CHARLES
Newton Abbot · London

No one who presumes to write about ancient woodland can fail to be indebted to Oliver Rackham, who virtually reinvented the concept of old woodland as a distinct entity and thereby added a fourth dimension – the past – to woodland ecology. Closer to home, George Peterken has succeeded in combining scholarly study of ancient woodland with practical realities and has written an influential book about it. In offering my own version of ancient woodland matters to the public, I acknowledge my debt to both masters. I am also grateful to colleagues and friends in the NCC for their comments on the draft and discussions on its content, particularly to Keith Kirby and Jonathan Spencer in the woodland section, and to John Bratton, Peter Clement, Steven Falk, Nick Hodgetts, Roger Key, Derek Ratcliffe and Paul Waring. The responsibility for any remaining errors is of course my own. I also thank Celinia Driscoll and Maureen Symons for their patience and exactitude in deciphering the manuscript and transforming it into type. And Libby Gluyas for teaching me elementary cartography. The following friends and colleagues have generously lent photographs: Stuart Ball, Sarah Fowler, Roger Key, Keith Kirby, John Mason, Steve Moore, Derek Ratcliffe, Jonathan Spencer and Peter Wakely. I thank Oliver Rackham for permission to reproduce his map of ancient and planned countryside.

British Library Cataloguing in Publication Data
Marren, Peter
 Woodland heritage – (Britain's ancient woodlands).
 1. Great Britain. Woodlands, history
 I. Title II. Series
 941′.009′52

ISBN 0–7153–9436–3

Typeset in Kennerley by
ABM Typographics Ltd., Hull
and printed in Portugal
by Resopal
for David & Charles Publishers plc
Brunel House   Newton Abbot   Devon

The pulp used in the manufacture of this paper was created
using environmentally friendly processes and comes from Sweden
where there is a strict policy of replanting.

CONTENTS

FOREWORD

Ancient woodlands have become part of the vocabulary of the countryside. Whereas in 1970 the ecologists had barely formulated the concept for themselves, by 1990 ancient woods have been debated in the House of Lords, have received special consideration in the national forestry policy, continue to be the subject of successful major appeals by an expanding Woodland Trust and have been explored by major research programmes in ecology, history and forestry. Their ecological importance, and the sense of history and place they impart, has made these remnants of the medieval and prehistoric landscapes a focus for conservation concern.

This interest has come not a moment too soon. Since 1945 the half million hectares of surviving ancient, semi-natural woodland in Britain has been greatly reduced. 10 per cent has been destroyed by clearance, mostly for agriculture; 30 per cent has been changed into plantations, many of them coniferous; 50 per cent has stood unmanaged – only 10 per cent survive under the traditional form of coppice, wood-pasture and high forest management. The Broadleaves Policy, initiated in 1985, may have arrested the clearances and the ingress of pure conifer plantations, but native woodlands are still being replaced by plantations.

Throughout the 1980s, the Nature Conservancy Council has been compiling a national inventory of ancient and semi-natural woodlands, and preparing maps showing the extent of ancient woodland in each county and district. Our inventory has shown that, while about 35,000 ancient woods survive, the great majority are very small. Moreover, most of the larger ancient woods are wholly or partly given over to plantation forestry. Only one ancient wood in ten receives protection as a Site of Special Scientific Interest or is owned by a conservation body.

The material from the inventory has been made available to conservation, forestry and land-owning organisations and government agencies, but the lists, maps and data-sheets do not by themselves convey the interest and importance of ancient woods, nor do they indicate how they might be managed. Accordingly, we have complemented our dry and dusty compilation of facts and figures with a trilogy of books under the series title *Britain's Ancient Woodland.*

These books have been made possible by the generous support of ESSO UK plc. For four years they have not only underwritten the work of the two authors, but have helped in many ways with technical advice and publicity. We would like to thank in particular Messrs John Peters, Martin Timms and Richard Bavister for their support and encouragement.

The volumes are:

Woodland Heritage by Peter Marren.
Woodland Management and Conservation by Charles Watkins
Discovering and Exploring Ancient Woodland by Peter Marren

Each book can be read independently. *Woodland Heritage* is an introduction to ancient woodland history and wildlife, emphasising the unique qualities that make these woods so special. *Woodland Management and Conservation* looks at the ways in which woodland management can be adapted to benefit wildlife. It also offers a do-it-yourself guide on how to find out more about your own local wood. The last volume presents, for the first time, a detailed survey of ancient woodland in Britain, emphasising the local character of our woods, and including a gazetteer of some of the finest woods open to the public.

We hope that the publication of these guides will encourage you to explore ancient woodland and to take part in helping to conserve these precious relics of yesteryear.

GEORGE PETERKEN
Peterborough

Woodland names mentioned in this book

• Mound Alderwoods

• Beinn Eighe
Rassal Ashwood

SPEYSIDE
• Abernethy
Rothiemurchus •
• Glen Tanar
Morrone Birkwood • DEESIDE • Birse
Ballochbuie

• Wood of Inglismaldie

• Ariundle
• Mealdarroch
Methven Wood •

Knapdale

• Dalkeith Old Wood
• Cadzow Park
• Ettrick Forest

• Glenlee and Garroch Woods

Borrowdale Woods • • Upper Teesdale

Roudsea Wood • • Star Carr
• Gait Barrows
Thornton Glen
• Colt Park Wood
• Willow Garth

Thorne Waste

• Lincolnshire Limewoods
Sherwood Forest •

• Swanton Novers Wood
Coed Crafnant •
• Coed Ganllwyd   Charnwood Forest •   Wothorp Grove
• Coed Afon Pumryd   Priors Coppice •   • Castor Hanglands   Wayland Wood
Gregynog Park •   Sutton Park •   Easton Hornstocks • Bedford Purlieus
Short Wood
Brampton Bryan Park •   • Pepper Wood   • Monk's Wood   • Bradfield Woods
• Tregaron   Wyre Forest
Moccas Park •   Salcey Forest •   • Hayley Wood   • Staverton Park
• Coedmore
• Coed Ty Canol   WYE VALLEY   Wychwood •   Woodstock •   • Hatfield Forest
Dynevor Park •   Wytham Wood • • Bernwood Forest   • Epping
Lady Park Wood •   Sydling's Copse   Forest
Brasenose Wood •
• Burnham Beeches
• Windsor Great Park

MENDIPS   • Scords Wood   • Blean Woods
Longleat Park • Bentley Wood   THE WEALD   • Sladden Wood
Horner Wood •   Selborne Common •   • Eridge   • Ham Street Woods
• Barle Valley Woods   Wealden Edge Hangers •   Park
Duncliffe Wood •
Melbury Park •   • NEW   • Abbot's Wood
Boulsbury Wood   FOREST
The Dizzard •   The Mens
Yarner Wood •   Kingspark Wood
West Dean Woods
Boconnoc Park •   • Wistman's Wood   Kingley Vale
• Arlington Park

N

0 kms   80
0 miles   50

© Crown Copyright

1

A WOODLAND WALK

You reach Short Wood by the bridleway to Tottonhoe Lodge, through the gate by the water tower and past a beanfield to where the first trees line the crest of the ridge. To the south you have a clear view across the fields to the village of Glapthorn with its Norman church, about a mile away. To the north, at about the same distance over the brow of the hill, lies Southwick (pronounced *Suth*-ick), and the lane to the village is enlivened by an avenue of whispering poplars. Our wood straddles the boundary of the two parishes and was once a source of firewood and common grazing for both of them. Short Wood is of no great size: you can walk round it in two hours, but even so it is as well to bring a good map with you, for it is easy to lose your way in its network of rides. And take your time, because this is no ordinary wood. Short Wood is said to be the best bluebell wood in Northamptonshire, but there are things in it to see and admire in all seasons. I come here to gape at wild maple at its biggest and best, sturdy spreading trees with multiple trunks and fan vaults of delicate leaves suspended fifty or sixty feet above the ground. There is a huge hollow service tree in which hornets have nested, a mysterious sunken lane far older than the trees that now puncture its surface, secret ponds and earthworks, and embossed, fissured ash trunks cut short abruptly ten feet above the ground. Late in the year you may find 'fairy rings' of pale umbrella toadstools and a beautiful frosting of clematis seeds over the russets and golds of autumn.

Like all old woods that have not been subjected to the planter or the plough, Short Wood is rich in meaning. It could be compared to a book in a foreign language, a great store of interesting information about its past and its living present – if only we could read it. You will probably enter the wood by the stile at its south-eastern corner. This part is called Hall Wood, separated by earth banks from the rest of Short Wood because it belonged to Glapthorn, while the rest was part of Southwick. Look about you. There are a few tall straight oaks and ashes present, but most of the trees have multiple stems arising from a common stump. The stems are known as *coppice* and the stump as a *stool*. If you know your common trees, you will have no difficulty recognising maple, ash and hazel, which make up most of the coppice at Short Wood.

They are worth a closer look, these coppice stools. The largest are about 7ft (2m) across, and some have wavy outlines and cavernous interiors, with all the lively coppice shoots sprouting outwards in a ring. They grow like this because for centuries the villagers of Glapthorn used to cut the coppice stems or *poles* regularly for firewood or to make useful

I belong to that half of humanity which, on confronting something new, first asks how it came to be as it is. (The other half asks how it works.)
George Peterken, *Woodland Conservation and Management*

9

A WOODLAND WALK

things like wattle hurdles, pea sticks and broom handles. At Short Wood this practice ceased about forty years ago, but something of its ancient history is known from a survey made of Crown woods in Tudor times and an estate map of 1635. The wood was slightly larger then, and divided internally by a network of rides and earthworks. The compartments and rides very likely bore individual names, just as farm fields once did, although the present names – Jackson's Ride, Middle Ride, Primrose Ride, Kepper's Ride – have a latter-day ring to them. The wood was organised in such a way that part of the underwood was cut over each year over a cycle of a dozen or so years. At any given time, therefore, there would have been several states of young regrowth present from recently cut clearings to mature coppice. The poles were cut from the stumps in winter by men armed with billhooks, collected up and bundled together in faggots, ready for transporting back to the village on waggons. Sometimes the poles were converted on the spot, the hazels split into flexible wattles, and the ash stakes into fence posts. A few trees, generally oaks, were left as *standards,* felled for timber after three or four rotations of coppice. We are used to woods as high forest, full of tall, close-grown trees, but most native woods were not like that in the past. Coppice woods like Short Wood consisted mainly of this regular cropped *underwood,* with just a scattering of taller trees, and often no more than a dozen of them per acre. It may seem paradoxical there are so few big trees in ancient woods, but rural communities found coppice poles much more useful than logs. And, since coppice needs plenty of light to grow well, the woods were generally warm, open and sunny, full of wild flowers and butterflies in summer. It was only with the expanding shipbuilding industry in the eighteenth century that the emphasis switched from underwood to timber trees and from coppice to high forest management, and even then its influence did not spread to small parish woods like Short Wood.

After cutting, the coppice compartments were enclosed by a paling fence and all deer and other grazing animals driven out to allow new shoots to grow up from the stumps. Most native British trees regenerate vigorously after being cut over. Some do so by coppicing, like hazel, maple, ash, birch, alder, lime, wych elm and, more slowly, oak, beech and hornbeam; others produce thickets of similar-looking *suckers* from their roots, like elms, cherry and aspen. These new shoots are usually immune to the nibblings of rabbits, mice and hares, but deer, cattle and sheep can eat them clean off and so must be removed until the growth is tough enough to withstand them. At Short Wood, the fences were removed after about four years, and cattle reintroduced after seven. A few more years after that, the wood-cutters moved in again, having cut their way round the rest of the wood in the interim, to begin the cycle anew.

Short Wood may contain no really big trees, but it has many very old ones. Regular cutting actually prolongs the life of a tree, providing that care is taken to prevent rainwater collecting on and eventually rotting the stump, and to ensure that overhanging boughs do not shade it. The biggest stools in Short Wood are ash and maple. They are typically-irregular rings of living wood with a decayed centre and are certainly several hundred years old: growth is slow since Short Wood is a wet

wood. The biggest coppice stools in England, like the 18ft (5.5m) wide lime stools of Boulsbury Wood in Hampshire and Duncliffe Wood in Dorset, were probably producing polewood as long ago as the battle of Hastings. Such giants may be our only living link with the Saxons, who founded our system of parishes and counties and helped to shape our woods.

But we are still at the very beginning of our tour through Short Wood. I shall have to skip a great deal of the first hundred yards, where Jonathan Spencer and I stumbled across a clump of the bottle-brush stalks of the rare wood-barley; past the secret shaded place where violet helleborines – miniature hot house orchids – grow, and the woodside field recently planted up with ash trees. We have reached a place where the boundary bank takes a sudden kink, an angular bite out of its otherwise gently sinuous outline. This is made by a field called Carvill's Stibbings, which is an *assart*, a portion of former woodland cleared for agriculture back in the Middle Ages. Hereabouts the shallow ditch that encloses the wood on most sides suddenly deepens into a hollow with raised banks, which looks as if it was once a lane or *holloway*. More reminders of the distant past lie in wait at the eastern end of the wood, known as Dodhouse Wood. If you look carefully at the grass along the ride you will see shallow corrugations, a series of wet hollows between drier ridges. This is *ridge-and-furrow*, and it proves that Dodhouse Wood was once ploughland, possibly cleared of its original vegetation in the lean famine years of the early fourteenth century, when there were

Wayland Wood, Norfolk, minutes before an April shower. There are three distinct layers of trees: the tall ash and oak standards; high coppice, here including a shocking pink wild cherry; and a low coppice, already in leaf and dominated by bird cherry

11

A WOODLAND WALK

more people than the land could comfortably support. Unlike the rest of the wood, Dodhouse Wood is *secondary woodland*, formed when the trees sprang back over the ploughed furrows once the villagers no longer needed them. The rest of the wood is much older, and there are no signs that it has ever been cleared since its origin, more than ten thousand years ago. If so then this is *primary woodland*. If you look carefully you will see differences between the two types: in Dodhouse Wood the coppice stools are smaller and there are fewer kinds of shrubs. Certain species, like wood-sorrel and spindle, are missing. A soil specialist would find more subtle differences, notably in the absence of a thin surface layer of sandy soil that is found elsewhere in the wood. The medieval ploughs obliterated all trace of it.

We are now standing by the north bank of the wood, overlooking Southwick, with its excellent pub and historic hall. Along the bank in front of the ditch are the curiously shaped ash trunks referred to earlier, all bosses and burrs, holes and underhangs. These are *pollards*, the name for trees whose tops are cut at 8–18ft (2.5–5.5m) above ground, leaving a thick permanent trunk or *boll* beneath. Roadside limes and planes in towns and villages are often pollards, as are riverside willows. The presence of pollards in a wood is almost a guarantee of ancient lineage, for pollarding in woods fell into decline nearly three hundred years ago, and had all but ceased by about 1870. They are commonest on wood boundary banks, as at Short Wood, where they served as markers of the legal boundary, or in old *wood-pastures* where timber and meat production were combined on the same patch of ground. Pity the poor woodman who had to clamber up a rickety ladder to swipe at the pollard shoots with his axe. Coppicing was safer by far.

Short Wood, then, is an old and interesting place, full of interactions between man and nature, acting as a reminder of how the land was

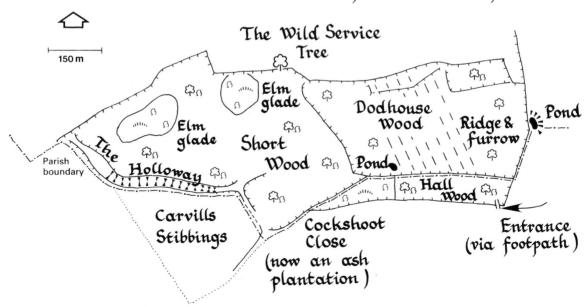

Short Wood, near Glapthorn, Northamptonshire

managed before trees became crops and fertility came out of polythene sack. It was the harvesting of *renewable* resources, the cropping of hay and sedge and the cutting of coppice wood, which produced that thread of continuity in which generation after generation made a living from the land without changing its fundamental nature. Short Wood may have been cut over a hundred times but its native trees, flowers and ferns persist, little changed. The Saxons who founded the village of Glapthorn doubtless saw the same spread of bluebells that we see there today.

A WOODLAND WALK

We know Short Wood is old partly because Tudor documents identify it, partly because it contains artefacts like old pollards and stools, and 'indicator' species like service tree and Midland hawthorn that are confined to ancient, stable places like this. It is an example of what naturalists have taken to calling *ancient woodland*. Perhaps it is time we defined this term more closely, for although it was used loosely more than a century ago to describe 'traditional' woods, it is only in the past fifteen years or so that people have started using the term to describe a very particular kind of wood. Ancient woods, then, are those that have been in existence for at least the past four hundred years, as proven by local maps made since that time. The year AD1600 is a convenient starting point since, until then, tree-planting was relatively unusual, while afterwards it became increasingly popular. Reasonably accurate maps, too, begin at about that time. This does not mean that there are necessarily any individual trees in the wood which are that old, only that the site has been continuously under trees since then.

Most of the woods that existed in 1600 were already old by that date. None of them are virgin forest – Britain is too small and densely populated to have retained any – but a significant number are almost certainly the direct descendants of the original prehistoric woods that covered the land before man became a farmer. These woods are precious. We shall come across many examples in the course of this book, but well-known areas of *primary woodland* are the New Forest, the Weald, the gorge of the River Wye, the woods of the East Anglian boulder clay and the Caledonian pinewoods of Scotland. *Secondary woods*, on the other hand, can be any age, but all of them grow on what was once open grazing land or crop fields. Dodhouse Wood is an example of an ancient secondary wood, and such woods are old enough to have accumulated a rich wildlife. There are much more recent secondary woods – in places like chalk downs, upland heaths and disused railway cuttings – which have formed in the past hundred years. Although at first sight it may be hard to tell the difference between these and much older woods, there is nearly always ample evidence on the ground that will separate the two. The table on page 14 rehearses the main clues.

Naturalists also distinguish between woods that formed naturally and those that were planted. Thus a wood can be secondary and natural, like the woods that have sprung up in the Cotswolds and the South Downs within living memory, or ancient but mainly planted, such as Salcey Forest in Northamptonshire, in which most of the original woods have been clear-felled and replaced by planted crop trees. The woods that are richest in wildlife and history are those which are both *ancient and natural,* and it is with these that this book is chiefly concerned.

WOODLAND HERITAGE

A WOODLAND WALK

An oak pollard at Lea and Pagets Wood, Hertfordshire. Unusually, this lies in the middle of the wood where it marks an ownership boundary. April 1987

Thanks to the detailed surveys undertaken by the Nature Conservancy Council since 1981, we now know roughly how many of these woods are left, where they are and what sort of condition they are in. Most ancient and natural woods are small – usually less than 20ha (50 acres). Larger blocks of woodland have usually experienced a greater degree of felling and replanting, although those on the sites of ancient woodland may contain islands of the original vegetation. Ancient woods are not scattered randomly about Britain but are concentrated in what the great woodland historian, Oliver Rackham, has called *ancient countryside*. The map on page 16 shows those parts of the country that are predominantly of this nature, characterised by irregular field boundaries, intricate lanes and paths, thick hedges and old farmhouses situated in the valleys. By contrast, *planned countryside*, typical of much of the Midlands, is essentially the product of enclosures during the past three hundred years, which have laid down a regular grid of rectangular fields with straight roads running past them. In counties like Kent, Sussex and Suffolk, where ancient countryside is the norm, the majority of woods are still ancient, albeit altered in varying degrees by forestry practices. Overall, there are about 300,000ha (750,000 acres) of ancient and natural woodland left in Britain: less than 2 per cent of the land surface. But they make an impact on the landscape out of all proportion to their area. Over much of lowland Britain you can still see trees dominating the horizon from the standpoint of a valley (although many of them may belong not to woods, but hedgerows).

Ancient woods	Secondary woods
Have names like 'wood', 'coppice', 'copse', 'dingle', 'dumble'. Have Welsh names in Wales and Gaelic names in the Scottish Highlands.	Often have names like 'covert', 'spinney', 'plantation', 'brake', 'heath', 'gorse', or no name at all.
Have an irregular boundary, often sinuous, and do not conform to the surrounding field pattern.	Tend to have straight angular boundaries, and fit squarely into the field pattern.
Are often near or on parish boundaries, or, especially in the uplands, occupy narrow river valleys or steep slopes.	Are often close to villages and country houses, or on cultivable land.
Are enclosed by an earthen bank and ditch.	Sometimes contain ridge-and-furrow, internal compartments or old habitations.
Contain old coppice stools, pollards or over-mature trees.	Are often even-aged (ie trees are all of same age), and lack these features.
Contain 'indicator species', like small-leaved lime, service tree and lungwort.	Lack these species.
Contain carpets of woodland flowers like wild daffodil, wood anemone, ramsons, lily-of-the-valley, sweet woodruff etc.	Often contain a jumble of colonist plants like ivy, nettles, elder, goose-grass and sycamore.
Are present within a recognisable boundary on first-edition Ordnance Survey maps (1800–30).	Are not marked on first-edition Ordnance Survey maps.
Are rich in wildlife, including rarities.	Are usually less rich in wildlife (though not without value).

A WOODLAND WALK

It is a sobering thought that most species of woodland wildlife depend largely on this tiny 2 per cent, one of the smallest areas of natural woodland in any European country. Only fifty years ago, Britain had nearly twice as much, but we have since experienced the loss of about 10 per cent of our ancient woods to clearances for agriculture and development and a further 30 per cent to plantations of non-native trees. What remains is all the more valuable. Nowhere else in Europe is there a mixture of medieval wood-pasture and heath to match the New Forest. Britain's bluebell woods and the steep, moss-laden woods of the Atlantic coast, the natural ashwoods of the Derbyshire Dales and the medieval deer-parks with their aged pollards are features of our landscape which are relatively scarce in Europe. Today many ancient woods are protected as nature reserves and Sites of Special Scientific Interest (SSSIs), although this does not necessarily guarantee their

Types of countryside and notable concentrations of ancient woodland. The distinction between ancient and planned countryside in lowland Britain follows that made by Oliver Rackham in The History of the Countryside, *1986*

16

survival against acid rain, the greenhouse effect or more mundane things like the grey squirrel or even sheer neglect.

This book is not specifically about conservation and management, which are more the subject of the volume in this series entitled *Woodland Management and Conservation*. Rather, it is an attempt to celebrate the life and meaning of ancient woods, an exploration of their roots in history and of their natural wonders in the present. I write this book as an employee of the Nature Conservancy Council, and I have tried to bring out some of that busy organisation's work in its pages. The NCC's single largest woodland project, its national survey of ancient woods, is the subject of the third volume in this series, *Discovering and Exploring Ancient Woodland*. My book also reflects the places where I have lived and worked, and whose woods I know best: Aberdeenshire, Oxfordshire and Rockingham forest in Northamptonshire. I hope that this will help to shift some of the current spotlight from East Anglia and the Home Counties to less well-documented, but equally fascinating, woods elsewhere.

A WOODLAND WALK

Before plunging once more into the forest, here is a brief guide to this book. We begin with a series of sketches of the building blocks of the wood – the native woodland trees and shrubs. Armed with a passing familiarity with these, we then approach the wood from the distant past, through its prehistoric beginnings to its gradual harnessing by man as a source of fuel, grazing and timber. The second part of the book concerns the wild inhabitants of specially ancient woodland; here I have tried to focus on the plants and animals, many of them rare and unfamiliar, which need the stability and continuity of habitat which only ancient woods can offer. I conclude with an account of the recent past, a sorry tale in the main of loss and alienation, but it is possible, at the time of writing, to end with a tentative suggestion of hope for a better future for our woods.

One last contemporary aspect of woodland deserves mention, because we take it so much for granted. Ancient woods today are often wild, overgrown places, and it is easy to assume that they have always been like that. It is a characteristic twentieth-century paradox that a place need not be natural nor particularly old to be very wild indeed. I would not like to be alone at night in the depths of Kielder Forest, one of the largest manmade forests in Europe, and even my friendly local copses can be tough going after rain, thongs of bramble lacerating your legs as you slop through the mud. Most woods are lonelier now than at almost any time in the past thousand years: that is why they are full of deer and foxes. As Nan Fairbrother put it in her evergreen *New Lives, New Landscapes* (1970):

> Already it is an unlikely concomitant of the population explosion that just as farmland is emptier, so the wilderness is wilder than it has been for centuries . . . It is only the popular places which have become more popular, the solitudes have never been more solitary.

Nan Fairbrother reminds us not to confuse wildness with age or with naturalness. A wood may well be all three, but they are not related. Ancient woods are studies in lost familiarity and, if they appear wild and unfriendly, it may be because we no longer understand them.

2
PRINCIPALS AND SUPPORTERS

There are only about a dozen trees that play a principal role in shaping our native woods, and, so far as we know, this has been so throughout the last twelve thousand years. They are, in no particular order, ash, maple, hazel, alder, and the two kinds each of oak and birch; and, more locally, beech, small-leaved lime, hornbeam, wych elm and Scots pine. Britain acquired most of the common trees of northern Europe before it became an island: only sycamore, Norway spruce and silver fir failed to make the crossing, and since then man has introduced all three; sycamore is now a plentiful tree in natural woods. The richest ancient woods contain most of the native trees, plus a fair proportion of the more numerous woodland shrubs, plants like dogwood, guelder rose and Midland hawthorn. Other ancient woods, generally those on upland margins or in rather extreme conditions, are dominated by just one or two: Glen Tanar in north-east Scotland, for example, is nearly all Scots pine and some Pennine woods on acid soil are almost solid sessile oak.

The native trees have played an important part in social development for at least five thousand years, and from the very start people sorted out the strengths and weaknesses of various types of timber and used different trees for different purposes. Woods dominated today by, say, beech or hazel are often the product of past silvicultural management to favour these particular trees. A large proportion of our wildlife – at least half in terms of species – needs woodland trees in general, and sometimes a certain species in particular. In this chapter a portrait is sketched of each of the common and less common woodland trees, and, as a codicil, a brief account made of how ancient woods can be classified using groups of trees or 'stand types'. More detailed accounts of trees and woodland vegetation are already in print; and for an account of how the NCC uses 'stand types' to define the different types of natural woodland for conservation purposes, the reader is referred to George Peterken's book, *Woodland Conservation and Management* (1981).

The tree as an ancient monument: the Major Oak in Sherwood Forest

Oak

The oak has long been a symbol of strength and, with the growth of the Royal Navy, also patriotic pride. It once fought our naval battles and carried our cargoes, framed our houses and spanned the roofs of cathedrals and barns, fed our pigs, tanned our leather and nourished our earliest industries. In Scotland, when traitors lost their head the best

oaks of their estate were chopped down. We prop up tottering old oaks and treat them as historic ruins: the Boscobel Oak which sheltered King Charles, the Major Oak of Sherwood, the vast shell of the Pontfadog Oak of Chirk, a full 43ft (13m) in girth, and the Shire Oak of Wentworth Woodhouse, which divides the counties of York, Nottingham and Derby. There is no denying the usefulness of a big oak in its prime. A single tree can provide 20 tons of timber, 15 cart-loads of wood, 3 tons of bark and 160 faggots of brushwood. But the mighty oak means a great deal more to the British than a mere timber tree.

Sessile Oak

There are two native oaks in Britain: the sessile or durmast oak, *Quercus petraea,* which is chiefly a tree of the western upland fringes from Cornwall to Inverness; and the pedunculate oak, *Quercus robur,* which grows all over Britain but is most at home on low ground with low rainfall. Sessile oaks can be slender, straight-boled trees with narrow crowns, as in the north Pennines, or bent, gnarled specimens with zigzag or corkscrew branches, as in Cornwall. The tallest oak in Britain, at Whitfield, Herefordshire, is a sessile oak. The pedunculate

19

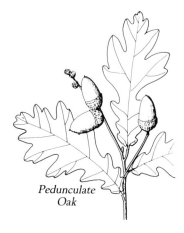

*Pedunculate
Oak*

oak is everyone's ideal oak, the stately oak of pub signs, with short boles and broad spreading branches. That is the sort of tree the navy wanted two hundred years ago: broad branchy oaks with plenty of crooks and 'knees' to fit the curved ships' hulls. Modern foresters, if they want oak at all, need the unbranched straight trunks of close-grown oaks for their power saws and processing machines. The botanical characteristics that separate the two species of oak will not be expounded here; they are not always as neat as the textbooks imply, and, in some places, like eastern Scotland, most oaks have characteristics of both.

Botanists once believed that oak was the natural 'climax' tree over most of Britain (see page 44). It is more likely that oak-dominated woods originally occupied deep, acidic loams, especially at the upland margins, and that elsewhere oak occurred in mixed woodland, taking second place to beech, elm, hornbeam or lime. But the oak has always been nurtured for its strength and durability. It was the most expensive timber tree and the most versatile, and all the attention devoted to it has exaggerated the role of oak in our woods leading to a misunderstanding of its natural place in woodland. But nature has benefitted, for oak, especially old oak, is the richest of all our trees in wildlife.

Today, for the first time in history, oak needs us more than we need it. Too many Highland oakwoods have been felled to make way for conifers, and the already small Welsh oakwoods continue to shrink, through heavy grazing, almost before our eyes. Oak coppicing is virtually dead as a craft, and the trees and their acorns suffer from a variety of mildews and blights, and grey squirrels that gobble up the acorns or nip off their growth points before burying them. Natural regeneration is failing, and so most young oaks have to be planted. Nevertheless the prospects for oak are still better than for most other native trees, for many people regard it as the obvious choice when planting native broadleaves, so much so that naturally mixed woods have sometimes been smothered by massed oaks. The main problem with oak is how to encourage more commercial production in ancient woodland without destroying the existing vegetation.

Beech

Three myths about beech are still widely believed: that it is essentially a tree of the chalk, that Julius Caesar did not see any and therefore it cannot be a native tree and, in apparent contradiction, that the Chiltern beechwoods are among Britain's most natural woods. In fact there is no doubt that beech is a true native in south-east England and South Wales, for pollen and other preserved bits of it have been found on prehistoric sites. Until the Bronze Age, however, when it suddenly increased, beech seems to have been one of Britain's least common trees. Its apparent liking for chalk is an artefact of forestry, for most beeches in the Chilterns and on the Downs are planted. Beech is a shallow-rooted tree, preferring free-drained soils, but its tolerances are broad. Some of the largest in Britain grow on acidic sand and gravel deposits in the New Forest. These trees are pollards, last cropped nearly four hundred years ago, but the well-known Chiltern beeches are the product of intensive management since 1800 to provide timber for the High Wycombe furniture industry. Beech predominates because there other kinds of tree were treated as weeds. Chiltern beechwoods are classed as ancient because they retain some elements of their indigenous vegetation, notably in the patches of mixed coppice found here and there on the steeper slopes, but their tall 'cathedral-like' beech trees are about the least natural thing about them. Nature retaliates now and again by blowing them over. Nearer to London, the famous trees of Burnham Beeches used to be lopped for firewood, and their misshapen trunks and contorted boughs make a striking contrast with the dull straight furniture beeches a few miles to the west.

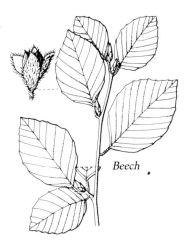

Beech

Beech is fast-growing for a broadleaf, and when close-grown on deep, brown forest soils it shoots up tall and straight. Beech can be coppiced, and formerly often was, but it requires a long rotation, the sprouts are often weak and the stools are easily infected by fungi or killed by shade. On thinner soils, beeches are smaller and are less vigorous competitors. On chalk slopes, for example, their translucent spring leaves can form a pleasing contrast with neighbouring dark yews and silver-flecked whitebeams.

Although, like oak, beech is a long-lived tree, really old specimens are confined to medieval wood-pasture or the boundaries of ancient woods, and nearly all of them are pollards. One such tree growing in Wakerley Spinney in Rockingham Forest a few miles from my house is possibly the northernmost medieval beech in Britain. It is surrounded by old limestone pits, for quarrymen, finding it in their way but too large to fell easily, simply dug around its roots. The beech responded by clinging to its pinnacle of stone with swelling root buttresses, as strong and massive as the rock itself. In its time, it must have witnessed change in its surroundings from pasture to roadstone quarry, to young coppice wood and latterly to conifers. And still, despite a multitude of ancient and modern grafiti, it shows no sign of decrepitude or decay.

Ash

Ash is the farmer's favourite tree, whose tough, elastic wood could be turned into tool handles, walking sticks, waggon frames, cart spokes and a hundred other uses. Such wood often came from hedgerow ashes or trees planted close to the farmhouse. In ancient woodland, ash usually grows with other trees, with wych elm in limestone dales or with hazel and maple on rich soils in the lowlands. Woods completely dominated by ash are a British speciality, and are almost always on limestone. Some are extraordinary places like Colts Park Wood in Yorkshire, where stunted trees spring from solid rock, or Rassal Ashwood, an oasis of greenleaf and birdsong in the wilds of Wester Ross. Ash rarely reaches a great age as a standard tree – hedgerow ashes often decay and fall to bits while still quite young – but it coppices well and ash stools of 6ft (1.8m) and more across are frequently the oldest living things in ancient woods.

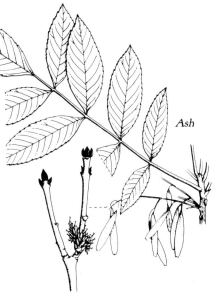

Ash

Like oak, ash is a good coloniser and it is by no means restricted to ancient woodland. But it looks after itself in present-day woodland better than most other native trees, producing dense thickets of poles in

open stands, and as a result some mixed woods are turning into ashwoods, especially in limestone districts. Ash is a tree of magic and mystery. The world-tree Yggdrasil of Scandinavian myth, which bound together earth, heaven and hell, was an ash. In Gilbert White's time, country people believed that a child who passed regularly through a cleft ash trunk would grow up in sound health, provided that the tree also did; no doubt this was a strong incentive to look after the tree.

Lime

Most native limes are the small-leaved species, *Tilia cordata*. This is the linden tree of old, least known of our forest trees, neglected alike by scientist, forester and countryman. And yet it is a singularly beautiful tree, honey-scented, delicately hued, with graceful heart-shaped leaves. It should not be confused with the planted lime of our streets and churchyards which is, by comparison, a vulgar object. The ancients knew and appreciated native lime, for place-names with *lynd* in them are scattered over much of England; and it was common enough to acquire local names like pry (Essex) and *palawyf* (Wales). Its timber, described in Gerard's *Herbal* as 'whitish, plain and without knots, very

The old beech pollard at Wakerley Spinney, Northamptonshire, described on page 21

Plants of ancient woodland: small-leaved lime and a regular associate, lily-of-the-valley. Hockering Wood, Norfolk

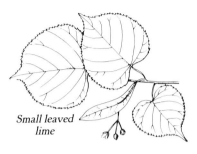

*Small leaved
lime*

soft and gentle in the cutting or handling', was used by Grinling Gibbons to create miracles of intricate wood-carving. The other well-known product of lime is the fibrous bast beneath the bark which was used to make matting and cheap rope. Better substitutes are available now, but the name survives in limewoods in the north of England, like Bass Wood and Bastow Wood. Coppiced limes are cut every fifteen to twenty years and, since the wood is still used for turning and pulpwood, some lime underwood continues to be managed commercially to this day. Standard trees of native lime are scarce, since the timber is of little value, but the coppice stools can seem immortal: those in Boulsbury Wood are said to be the oldest living things in Hampshire, and may be a thousand years old. In the Derbyshire dales there are some extraordinary lime stools, so old that the very rock has eroded away from their roots, leaving them as exposed 'trees on stilts'.

Lime is a gregarious tree and can dominate whole woods within its very localised range. There are mysterious, unexplained concentrations of lime woodland in the middling parts of England, from the Wye Valley to Norfolk, and a scattering elsewhere and in Wales, but not Scotland. I am fortunate enough to live in a lime district, and one ancient wood called Easton Hornstocks, growing next to a main road, presents nearly a mile of pure lime coppice, carpeted in the spring by bluebells, ramsons and lily-of-the-valley before the canopy closes. Good-sized lime stools are a reliable sign that a wood is ancient. They may very well also mean that the site is primary woodland, a direct descendant from the Wildwood (see Chapter 3), since in our present climate lime has trouble ripening its seeds and therefore does not readily colonise open ground. The distribution of limewood today seems to have changed little since Saxon times. Fortunately lime is a good survivor and those limewoods which have not succumbed to the onward march of the conifer since 1945 are mostly in good heart.

Hornbeam

Hornbeam

The hornbeam is a Home Counties tree, being commonest in Kent, Essex and Hertfordshire, and less so the further one travels away from London. Like limes, hornbeams are gregarious trees and most of them were routinely coppiced or pollarded, for the timber is too hard to work and shrinks as it dries. The standard tree moreover is a relatively feeble object, often decaying while still a stripling after a mere century. Among the hundreds of thousands of hornbeams in Epping Forest, only about twelve are mature standards, the others being the 'old, hideous, pollard, scarecrow trees' which past foresters regarded as an affront to their art. Epping and the other London hornbeam-woods supplied the capital with firewood in the days before the railways. 'Hornbeam', wrote Evelyn, three hundred years ago, 'burns like a candle' – brightly, with a steady flame and without crackling. Although its wood was too irregular for the timber merchant and too cross-grained for the joiner, its iron hardness made it useful for precision parts such as mill pulleys and cogs, and wood-screws, and it also produced fine charcoal and gunpowder.

Where hornbeam forms dense stands it casts as heavy a shade as beech and strews the woodland floor with its leaves. Many, perhaps even most, hornbeam coppices are ancient woodland and they have to be managed with care for the regrowth is slower than hazel or lime, while the stress of cutting can kill neglected old stools and pollards. The inevitable losses in managed hornbeam-woods used to be made good by planting saplings in the gaps. About half of our hornbeam woods have been replanted with other species since 1945, although the revival in demand for firewood has created a new market while the suburban sprawl of eastern London has, perhaps surprisingly, proved a force for woodland conservation. Fortunately hornbeam coppices are not in any case easily grubbed up or smothered, and since they provide a good refuge for the pheasant, our great-grandchildren will with luck still be able to recognise a hornbeam.

Elm

Common and small-leaved elms often invade ancient woodland from their bridgehead in the hedgerow and they are also an ancient feature of some woods. But it is the wych elm, whose switchy pliant wood made the Welsh bows that enabled the English to hammer the Scots, that is normally thought of as the 'true' woodland elm. Common and small-leaved elms reproduce by suckering to form stands of trees of the same genetic origin, and the bewildering array of local forms so produced in this country presents a study in itself, called pteleology – elm-naming. Wych elm on the other hand reproduces by seed in the usual way, and one tree is pretty much like any other. It hardly ever dominates a wood and usually occurs in mixed woodland, especially with ash, hazel or lime. Wych elm prefers well-drained, base-rich soils and is most at home along the sides of dales and glens in the North and West. Its solitary nature, and perhaps the greater abundance of hedgerow elms, must have prevented the wych elm from achieving a prominent role in woodland history, for it is a handy tree, coppicing well and providing tough, durable timber.

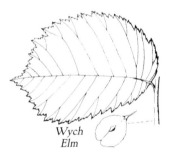

Wych
Elm

Since the mid-seventies the majority of British elms have of course become stricken by disease. No longer do the great towering hedgerow elms lend the countryside that 'rich, loaded, heavy personality' so well suited to oil painting. What is less well known is that half of the woodland elms had already been grubbed up or poisoned before Dutch elm disease struck; being less prominent in the landscape their loss was seldom noticed. Where no subsequent felling and planting has taken place, elm-rich woods now have a haunted quality, marked by clearings and gaunt barkless and leafless trees. Many elms remained still very much alive below ground however, and are now producing masses of leafy suckers, but those who like planting trees can be curiously blind to the fact. My own village elm hedges are bursting with growth and the adjacent grass verges are turning into elmwood. But, one supposes, elms have officially been declared dead; so the local authority has planted a row of expensive and irrelevant horse chestnuts on top of them.

Hazel

No native tree except oak has played so long and important a role in human affairs as hazel. Back in the Neolithic, or possibly even earlier, it was discovered that the marvellously pliant hazel rods could be split, twisted and bent without breaking, and that regular supplies could be obtained by cutting the tree every dozen years. This led to the ancient craft of wattle-work: whole or split rods were woven together to build hurdles and fences, or could be combined with timber and clay and used to build a house. Hazel rods were also used singly as pea and bean sticks, and as thatching spars and barrel hoops, while the brushwood was bound into faggots for fuel. Until fairly recently, hazel was a major rural employer: 3 acres (1.2ha) of hazel coppice was as much as one person could work in a year, and on the usual short rotation a mere 20 acres (8ha) provided a worker with permanent employment. And in 1945 there were about 114,000 acres (46,000ha) of hazel coppice in Britain, about a quarter of them in Hampshire alone.

Today the fortunes of hazel are waning, for it has lost most of its traditional commercial uses. The wattle fences of old have long been replaced by quick-set hawthorn hedges and barbed wire, the faggot trade has declined and hazel wood is too slender to be much use for pulpwood or firewood. In sad consequence, most surviving hazel coppice now lies derelict – even when managers have not tried to get rid of it, the bushes lie in permanent shadow and are failing to regenerate. Hazel is declining more rapidly than any other common tree and, unless new markets are found, it seems fated to decline further.

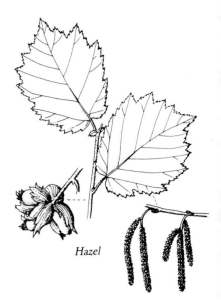

Hazel

Maple

Maple (ignore the modern name 'field maple' – its original name was plain 'maple') normally grows in woods and hedges, and is a sign of ancient lineage in both. Maple makes a beautiful tree, with its sturdy, spreading branches, furrowed bark and delicate leaves that turn glorious gold in autumn. The woodland maple is nevertheless easily overlooked since it is usually mixed up with other trees and, like them, cut over regularly as coppice. When neglected, as they usually are now, maple stools sprout clusters of corky-barked poles which blend in the branchy green shade with those of hazel, ash and other trees, and maple can easily be mistaken for oak at a distance. It lends its name to the ash-maple-hazel woods, which have more woodland flowers in them than any other kind of wood. We should rejoice that it is as frequent as it is, because maple wood is not of much commercial use except to the craftsman, and he only needs small quantities. In the Middle Ages its hard fine-grained wood was used for top-quality drinking vessels, the Saxon *masers*, and for musical instruments. Later, cabinet-makers used it as for inlaying.

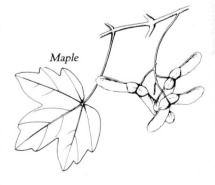

Maple

Sycamore

Sycamore is not a native tree, it just behaves like one. There is something faintly bogus about it. For a start, it is misnamed: *sycomorus* is biblical

Hornbeam in the spring at Wayland Wood, Norfolk, close to the northern limit of this tree in Britain. The multiple trunks spread like a fan from a common base – a century ago these trees were cut as coppice for the last time.

for the unrelated mulberry fig and, in the mistaken belief that the Holy Land was well populated with sycamores, medieval sculptors carved its leaves on bosses and capitals in churches and cathedrals. The Latin name is closer to the truth: *pseudoplatanus* – maple masquerading as plane. Evelyn hated it, particularly its big, clumsy leaves which 'fall early, turn to mucilage and noxious insects, and putrefy with the first moisture of the season, so as they contaminate and marr our walks'.

Sycamore has not lacked supporters, however, even among naturalists. It is damaged less by atmospheric pollution than most trees; because its leaves rot quickly they enrich the soil; and it produces nectar for the bees and bark for two hundred species of mosses and lichens – more than many native trees. It has forestry virtues too. Its fast growth and creamy, even-textured wood, well suited to turning and carving, make it one of the few presently profitable broadleaved trees. In a recent article entitled 'The Case for Sycamore', Esmond Harris found it 'strange that many people complain of sycamore as a weed. What man gets easily he does not want, but what he cannot obtain he strives for . . . Every forester or conservationist should accept the free gift of the sycamore . . . It offers itself to us freely, yet we despise and neglect it.'

The trouble is that by smothering the ground with seedlings and saplings, sycamore offers itself rather too eagerly when there are good reasons for preferring oak or ash.

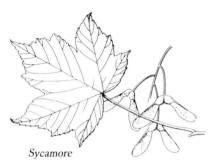

Sycamore

Alder

Alder likes to have its feet in water and its main haunts are swamps and fens (where the stunted, lichen-draped trees are known as carr), plus riverbanks and flushed slopes: in other words, places where the ground is always wet but seldom completely submerged. The conditions best suited to alder are seldom conducive to elegance. Geoffrey Grigson describes alderwoods thus: 'trees alive and dead, moss-bearded and lichen-bearded, the soil water like coal slack and blacksmith's water, in between the tussocks of sedge'.

The fresh-cut wood is bright orange, and dyes have been extracted from it, but it rots too easily to be worth much as timber, and burns reluctantly. So managed alders are almost invariably coppiced, and the turned wood is put to humble uses like brush-backs, clogs and underwater piles. In one thing alder excelled, and that was in providing fine black charcoal for making gunpowder, but this hardly amounted to a major use since a good alderwood could supply enough powder to win the battle of Waterloo several times over. Alder occurs as an occasional tree in ancient woodland, but pure alderwoods are usually fairly recent, having grown up over former reedbeds. One of the biggest and best in Britain, Mound Alderwood in Sutherland, occupies a stretch of former estuary which silted up after the head of Loch Fleet was embanked in 1816. But these are among the least-disturbed and wildest-looking of all woods, places of stagnant pools and biting insects, rotten logs and hummocks of sedge, where tall flowers and ferns can luxuriate in the damp without being instantly devoured by sheep or deer.

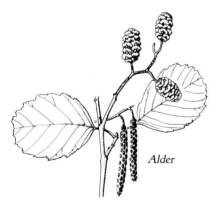

Alder

Birch

To some, birch is the 'Lady of the Wood', to others a large weed. This is a tree that comes into its own when no other kind is available, and in parts of the Scottish Highlands it was used for nearly everything. A forestry manual of 1828 noted that Highlanders used birch:

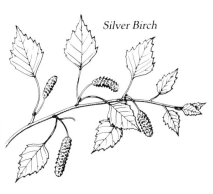

Silver Birch

> . . . for almost every purpose, domestic or agriculture. They cover their houses, they make their ploughs, harrows, sledges, panniers, pack saddles, fences, gates and even tables, chairs and bowls, trenchers and spoons of them. They also make ropes of Birch which are extremely strong. No part of the tree is wasted . . .

Hailing from more umbrageous southern climes, Evelyn thought less highly of birch but even he praised birch-sap wine and devoted several pages to discussing how to make it.

Over most of Britain, birch is a pioneer tree, colonising waste ground with its light windborne rain of seeds, but it is short-lived and soon replaced by other forest trees. In most ancient woods it is an occasional tree, moving into open spaces when the opportunity presents itself. On soils too harsh for most other trees birch woodland can be self-sustaining. The drying peat of Holme Fen in Cambridgeshire is densely covered with birch as are some of the light, sandy Bagshot commons of Surrey and Berkshire and they show no signs of yielding place to longer-lived trees.

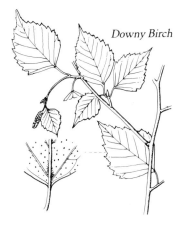

Downy Birch

In Highland glens beyond the upper limit of oak and elm, birch can probably hold its ground indefinitely, and here, if anywhere, are the true ancient birchwoods. The Highland birch is a blacker, more crooked tree than the southerner, its crown a mass of brushy twigs and lollipop-shaped from the deer browsing below. As its buds burst in the brief northern spring the tree gives off a delicious resinous scent which Highland lassies used to extract from the twigs and apply as hair-rinse.

In Sweden, Finland and (using a related species) Canada, birch is a commercially important tree, furnishing saw timber, peeler logs, pulpwood and plywood. British foresters seem to prefer conifers, which is too bad for our wildlife and scenery. Native birches are cut up for wood-burning stoves, or used to make brush backs and, until recently, cotton reels, but most birchwoods are presently in a state of silvicultural neglect and face an uncertain future.

Holly

Holly leaves are more edible than they look and were once valued as winter browsewood. Groups of old hollies, known as hollins, used to be pollarded regularly in wood-pasture to feed deer and, although this practice ceased nearly two hundred years ago, a few hollins survive in special places like Needwood Forest in Staffordshire, the Stiperstones in Shropshire and, above all, the New Forest, where holly forms a dense shrubbery beneath the oaks and beeches. Woods in which holly plays a dominant part are a British speciality, rarely found elsewhere. It is a frost-sensitive tree and perhaps for that reason is commonest in southern

Holly

Wilderness and wet. Alder coppice interspersed with hummocks of tussock sedge at Godstone, Surrey

Highland birch in woods at the pass of Killiecrankie, Perthshire. November 1971

and western counties or near the coast in the East. It is remarkably persistent and can survive for years as heavily browsed gnarled rootstocks – which burst into leaf again at the first opportunity. Today the biggest trees are often in hedgerows, for the holly is bewitched and it is unlucky to cut them.

Chestnut

The sweet chestnut has scarcely been given a fair deal by British naturalists, who regard it as an interloper. If so, it is scarcely a recent one for it has been part of the natural scene in southern England since Roman times, and the 60,000 acres (25,000ha) of chestnut-wood in Kent, Sussex, Essex and Hampshire are of interest for wildlife as well as of commercial value – one of the instances where the two coincide. So here it will be treated as an honorary native.

Chestnut grows in a spiral and its timber splits easily; so it is usually cut every twelve years or so as coppice. As underwood it excels, growing fast and producing sound, durable poles on rot-resistant stools, ideal for paling posts and hop poles. Chestnut woods are mostly on acid soils and a few years after cutting are often carpeted with bracken and bluebells. In mid-rotation they become shady places, a leafy shroud, prickly green above, prickly brown below.

Scots pine

There is nothing quite like a well-grown Caledonian Scots pine, with its stout trunk plated in reddish-grey, and spreading masses of blue-green needles, quite different from the spindly, high-crowned pine of southern climes. Unlike broadleaved trees, pine does not coppice or produce suckers, and regenerates only by seed. This it produces in plenty, but unless the ground surface is mineral soil, preferably acid sands and gravels, and fairly open and well drained at that, the seedlings do not take root. In the past, native pines were felled by the thousand for timber, and the logs sometimes floated many miles downriver towards the eventual market-place. Some of the biggest woods were 'saved' by landowners wealthy enough to value sport more than timber, but in many cases neglect has simply changed the nature of the problem from over-exploitation to lack of regeneration.

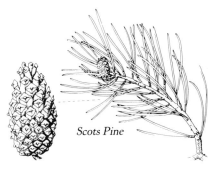

Scots Pine

Native pinewoods look very pretty against their magnificent mountain backcloth, but some are on their last legs. Foresters lend a helping hand by 'screefing' the accumulated layer of peat from the topsoil or planting pines 'of local provenance' *en masse* inside deerproof fences. Conservationists think they are overdoing it. Better would be fewer deer and a more restrained approach, leaving more of the healing process to nature. These rare, lovely woods surely deserve protection for their own sake, not merely to continue commercial production.

Yew

Wild yews live in dry places, especially windy downland, sometimes mixed up with other trees that can cling to poor, thin soil, like whitebeam or box, or otherwise as a massed uniform army as at Kingley Vale in Sussex, reputedly the largest yew-wood in Europe. Yew has the hardest coniferous timber in the world, hard as iron and longer-lasting, but even so the trees are of more aesthetic than commercial value. Even the longbows of Crécy and Agincourt were reputedly made from imported wood, since the English yews were too knotty and brittle. Geoffrey Grigson saw yew as 'one of the most tropical of English sights' with its 'black tufted density' and 'coral berries against a blue sky'.

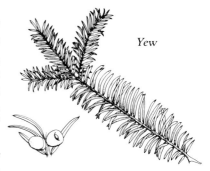

Yew

But despite appearances, the hard nut of yew inside its pink candy coat is deadly poisonous. The Ministry of Agriculture bulletin cheerfully notes the main symptom: 'sudden death'.

Juniper

It is arguable whether juniper is a tree and whether large groups of them are woods or shrubberies. Botanists seem to regard southern junipers as overgrown grassland but northern ones as woods! Since both types shelter woodland plants and animals, let us regard them as trees, capable of forming woods. Juniper offers a delightful mass of natural topiary, from billowing clouds to straight-sided columns and needles. Old bushes collapse outwards to form giant prickly doughnuts with herbaceous interiors. Hill sheep avoid dense juniper scrub and so it offers a refuge for grazing-sensitive plants like ferns and woodland flowers. There are small, often sick-looking, groups of juniper on chalk downs, but upland hillsides, especially in north-east Scotland, are now the places to see juniper at its best. In eastern Scotland, open natural woods of Scots pine and birch are sometimes underlain by dense, spiny juniper thickets, interspersed with golden-green moss cushions and blaeberry (bilberry). On the few natural tree-lines in Scotland, a narrow band of wind-cut juniper struggles for existence above the trees. The cut wood and berries of juniper are deliciously perfumed. Gin, not whisky, should be the toast of the Highlands.

Juniper

Supporting roles

Apart from trees that are common or gregarious enough to dominate a wood, there are numerous other native trees and shrubs which occur in smaller numbers, generally in the underwood or at the wood-edge. In coppices, the woodland shrubs used to be cut over more or less indiscriminately and bundled into faggots. Only box, cherry trees and, occasionally, spindle were more valuable and put to special uses. Box was far too valuable for its own good and was ruthlessly exploited in the past, but has always been rare in Britain for it needs exceptionally warm dry places, like Box Hill in Surrey, and is only really at home much further south.

Certain trees and shrubs are closely tied to ancient woodland in parts of their range in Britain, such as spindle in Lincolnshire and bird cherry in Norfolk, but are more ready to spread into hedges and recent scrub in other areas. Aspen in England and Wales is more often than not a tree of

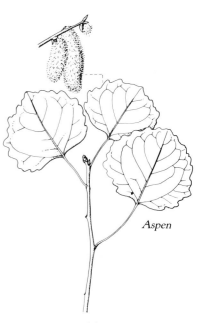

Aspen

33

A spray of leaves and flowers of the wild service tree, Sorbus torminalis

damp hollows in ancient woodland, but in Scotland it is an efficient coloniser of open fields and one of the few species to accompany birch in Highland woods. Everyone likes aspen, the 'trimmlin tree', whose quivering, shivering leaves were compared by the Welsh to the 'clack and gossip of women's tongues'. This is the only tree that you often hear before you see it. Aspen depends less on seed than on suckers growing up from its spreading roots, and a mature tree is often surrounded by a spinney of siblings. The shoots are sensitive to grazing, however, which stops the tree in its tracks. Fortunately they taste horrible.

Other trees and shrubs typical of ancient woodland are crab-apple, Midland hawthorn, wild service tree, wild pear and several kinds of whitebeam, all of which by a curious coincidence are related members of the rose family. Only the first two are at all common. Crab trees are scattered in ancient woods and along ancient field boundaries throughout lowland Britain, but usually only in ones and twos; this is one of the least gregarious forest trees. Midland hawthorn is an important understorey shrub in ancient woods lying south and east of a line connecting the Humber and the Severn but excluding Thomas Hardy's Wessex. This is a more spreading shrub than ordinary hawthorn and has several stems, big blunt spines and shallowly lobed, shining leaves, and it grows deeper inside the wood in denser shade. If you find Midland hawthorn, look sharp because you are probably standing in an interesting place.

Wild service is a beautiful and fascinating tree. Although its leaves have distinctive triangular lobes and it can attain a considerable size, service is easily overlooked for, like the crab tree, it is usually scattered among other trees in woods on limestone or clay. It should be sought along the wood-edge, particularly the boundary bank, where it spreads by suckering. Service has almost ceased to regenerate by seed in Britain, and it is one of the best indicator species of ancient woodland. By contrast, in the Dordogne it is a ready coloniser and an important constituent of secondary woodland. Unlike lime, service certainly ripens fruit regularly, and its pitted brown fruits or 'chequers' used to be gathered for the market-place. Evidently something is preventing all this ripe seed from germinating. The seeds are said to require a period of intense cold to germinate, by which time they may have already softened and rotted, or been eaten by mice. Or perhaps the service tree needs birds to spread its fruits, and the latter are already too surfeited with brighter berries from rowan and whitebeam to bother with the dull-coloured 'chequers'.

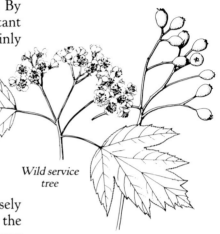

Wild service tree

Those who enjoy studying the minute differences between closely related and sexually confused plants could do worse than look at the whitebeams. The common ones are small trees that grow on limestone crags or chalk downs, and probably have no particular association with ancient woodland. But some of the rare ones, known only by delightful names like *Sorbus porrigentiformis,* are confined to mixed woods and wooded gorges on limestone in western England, Wales and Arran, while others are still more restricted to sessile oakwoods on the fringes of Exmoor. Although they are usually ignored, except by botanists, these closely related whitebeams are interesting curiosities and have probably occupied their limited haunts for a long time.

How many people have ever set eyes on a true wild woodland pear tree? Probably rather few, for it has been a great rarity since the Middle Ages, although the Saxons were evidently more familiar with it. Only four wild pear trees are known in East Anglia and they may be the last descendants of prehistoric trees; one blew down in a gale recently and was sold to a harpsichord maker, a traditional use of pear wood. Even rarer, indeed a good candidate for Britain's rarest plant, is the whitty pear of Wyre Forest, a strange tree with rowan-like leaves and pear-like fruits. There is only one, first recorded deep inside the Forest three hundred years ago when it was already old. This was a celebrated tree whose portrait was engraved at different stages in its life, but it came to a sad, if hardly untimely, end when vandals set it alight in 1862. Fortunately saplings from the original tree were in cultivation and one of them was planted by the stump of its parent in 1913. By 1968 it had become a flourishing tree 50ft (15m) tall. The origin of Britain's only whitty pear will always be a mystery, but its antiquity and remote location argue against its introduction and suggest that it is a true native.

Types of ancient woodland

Some kinds of ancient and natural woods are very distinctive. If you compare the Caledonian pine forests of Royal Deeside with those of Wester Ross you will find differences due to slope, exposure and rainfall, but you will be left in no doubt that you are dealing with the same kind of wood. Fifty years ago, Sir Arthur Tansley, the pioneer of natural vegetation studies in Britain, described Britain's woods on the basis of their dominating tree into oakwoods, beechwoods, ashwoods, pinewoods, birchwoods, alderwoods and scrub. Unfortunately this commonsense approach had a fundamental defect — it left out the majority of ancient woods which are composed of *mixtures* of trees and are not dominated by any particular species. Moreover Tansley underestimated the influence of trees like maple, lime and hornbeam, which are very important locally, and he believed that it was the fate of most woods to end up dominated by oaks. Today, ecologists believe that it is the *underwood* — the coppices and shrubs — which is the natural element of the wood, while the big oaks, beeches and other standard trees are very often the product of silviculture.

Ecologists who have tried to classify woods by their *ground* vegetation, which is less subject to the vagaries of planting and felling, find the opposite problem: ground vegetation is almost infinitely variable, and different 'communities' of plants often blend into one another without any obvious boundary. The whole exercise can easily seem like an arcane mathematical conundrum to non-specialists, although the more distinctive communities, like those on light soils dominated by bluebells, bracken and soft-grass, are obvious enough to the casual visitor.

The NCC uses two ways of classifying ancient woodland for its particular purposes. One is the Peterken Method, named after the NCC's own George Peterken. The other is the grandly titled National Vegetation Classification, inevitably referred to as the NVC. Sir Arthur Tansley would surely approve of the Peterken Method, since, being based primarily on the trees and the underwood, it has the merit of simplicity and can, with a little practice, be used by inexperienced people in all seasons. The NVC is the product of fifteen years of wrestling with the puzzles and complexities of both ground vegetation and underwood, using methods successfully employed by plant geographers in Europe. At the time of writing it remains unpublished, and is not yet fully field-tested. Both methods are based on sample studies from woods throughout Britain. Here they are merely summarised, to give an indication of the variation of ancient and natural woodland in Britain.

Methods of classifying natural woodland in Britain

THE PETERKEN STAND TYPES

1. *Ash-wych elm woodland.* Throughout Britain, but most widespread in the west. Mostly on valley sides on base-rich soil and managed

formerly as coppice. On free-draining soils the floor is awash with dog's mercury.

2. *Ash-maple woodland.* England and South Wales. Woods containing maple, usually with ash, hazel and oak, and typical of heavy soils in the Midlands and drier soils in east and south-west England. Traditionally managed as coppice. Complex, beautiful woods, often rich in wild flowers.

3. *Hazel-ash woodland.* Widespread except in north-east Scotland. Usually contains oak (often planted) as well as hazel and ash. Mainly on acid soils in the lowlands, but more often on alkaline loams in the North and West.

4. *Ash-lime woodland.* Local concentrations in England and Wales, especially the Welsh borders, Lincolnshire, East Anglia and north-west England. Mainly on acid loams in east England but on alkaline soils in north-west England and Wales.

5. *Oak-lime woodland.* Local concentrations in England and Wales, but rare in the south. These are woods that contain lime but not ash, lie on acid soils and are managed as coppice.

6. *Birch-oak woodland.* Throughout Britain. Woods on acid, mostly free-draining soils, dominated by pedunculate and/or sessile oak. Traditionally managed as coppice or wood-pasture.

7. *Alder woodland.* Throughout Britain. Always on wet soil, usually in valley bottoms and streamsides, but sometimes on flushed slopes and flat plateaux. Alders are often accompanied by pedunculate oak, hazel, ash and bird cherry.

8. *Beech woodland.* South England and South Wales. Beech-dominated woods on acid and calcareous soil, and generally managed as high forest or wood-pasture.

9. *Hornbeam woodland.* Mainly south-east England with a few outliers. Woods containing hornbeam, often with oak, on a variety of soil types. Usually former coppice or wood-pasture.

10. *Suckering elm woodland.* Throughout Britain as patches of common or small-leaved elm in woodland. Occasionally elm dominates the wood.

11. *Chestnut woodland.* Mainly south-east England, but locally in East Anglia and south-west England. Woods dominated by sweet chestnut, often on acid, light soils and usually planted. Managed as coppice.

12. *Pine woodland.* The native pinewoods of Scotland, plus or minus some birch or oak.

13. *Birch woodland.* Widespread throughout Britain on a variety of

WOODLAND HERITAGE

PRINCIPALS AND
SUPPORTERS

soils, but normally a temporary stage except in parts of upland Scotland. A local variant is birch-hazel woodland.

Most of these types of woodland have been further subdivided, according to soil type and degree of wetness, and according to the presence or absence of particular trees (see George Peterken's *Woodland Conservation and Management*, Chapter 8, which gives detailed descriptions and distribution maps).

The National Vegetation Classification

Brackets indicate that the woodland is more often recent and secondary than ancient.

A. WET WOODS

W1. (*Grey sallow – marsh bedstraw woodland*. Widely scattered in lowlands. Willow scrub on wet mineral soils)

W2. (*Grey sallow – downy birch – reed woodland*. Mainly recorded from East Anglian fens. Fen carr on wet peat.)

W3. (*Bay willow – bottle sedge woodland*. Local in upland Britain. Willow scrub on wet peat)

W4. (*Downy birch – purple moor-grass woodland*. Local throughout Britain. Wet acid birchwoods.)

W5. *Alder – tussock sedge woodland*. Widespread but local, mainly England. Alder thickets on wet peat.

W6. (*Alder – stinging nettle woodland*. Widely scattered in lowlands. Flood-plain alderwoods on moist, rich soils.)

W7. *Alder – ash – yellow pimpernel woodland*. Scattered throughout Britain but best developed in the uplands. Alderwoods on wet mineral soils.

B. ASH, OAK AND BEECHWOODS

W8. *Ash – maple – dog's mercury woodland*. Throughout lowlands on base-rich soil. This is the most common type of forest on the richer soils of Britain, and its many subdivisions include lime-rich and hornbeam-rich types.

W9. *Ash – rowan – dog's mercury woodland*. Replaces the above in the cooler, wetter parts of Britain. Ash-hazel woods, usually with birch and rowan, on rich soils.

W10. *Oak – bracken – bramble woodland*. Throughout lowlands. Oakwoods on less base-rich soils. This widespread and important type is often characterised by carpets of bluebell and includes the more acidic lime, chestnut and hornbeam woods.

The zigzag architecture of sessile oak coppice in Cornwall, pruned naturally by the salt laden *winds. Note the abundance of bark lichens in the clean moist air. Dizzard oakwood, May 1986*

W11. *Oak – downy birch – wood-sorrel woodland.* Upland Britain on free-draining acidic soils. Oakwoods with birch, usually high forest derived from neglected coppice, and usually rather grassy.

W12. *Beech – dog's mercury woodland.* Southern England and Wales. Beechwoods on base-rich soils. Some of the 'hanging' beechwoods in the Cotswolds and Chilterns are this type.

W14. *Beech – bramble woodland.* Southern England, especially on clay plateau soils in the Chilterns, North and South Downs and New Forest. Tall beech high forest with deep shade.

W15. *Beech – wavy hair-grass woodland.* Local in southern England, mainly the Weald, New Forest and Chiltern plateau. Beech high forest on poor soils, often with oak.

W16. *Birch – oak – wavy hair-grass woodland.* Widespread but patchy on marginal land, mostly in England. Mixed oak-birch woods on poor soils in the drier parts of Britain, often dominated by bracken or bilberry.

W17. *Oak – birch – Dicranum moss woodland.* Upland fringes of the West and North. Mixed oak-birch woods on acid soils, often rocky woods full of Atlantic mosses and liverworts.

C. NATIVE CONIFEROUS WOODS

W18. *Scots pine – Hylocomium moss woodland.* A dull way of referring to the Caledonian pinewoods. Also includes well-established Scots pine plantations with natural vegetation. Only western Norway has similar woods.

W13. *Yew woodland.* Mainly on the North and South Downs, with a few outliers elsewhere. Spectacular woods which people come to England to see.

W19. *Juniper – wood-sorrel woodland.* Mainly in the east-central Scottish Highlands, but with outliers in uplands elsewhere. High-level juniper scrub, with or without birch.

D. MOUNTAIN SCRUB

W20. *Downy willow – greater woodrush scrub.* Mountain ledges in Scotland. Mixtures of rare willows only a few feet square!

3

THE WILDWOOD

A word with a fine resonance, 'Wildwood'. It combines the historical reality of a great forest that once covered the land with story-book memories of dark woods inhabited by unicorns, witches and wolves, places at once secret, savage and fearful. The idea of woodland as a beast-haunted wilderness runs deep in our culture. When our forebears left the woods they ceased to be savages and became farmers, whose place thereafter was in the safer, manmade fields. The wood turned into a wasteland, an obstacle to human progress – it was a reminder of our barbarous origins and threatened to engulf us once again. The few people who lived in woods became beast-like themselves: outlaws, murderers and highway robbers. Part of the fearfulness of woods is that people get lost in them: the knights of Arthurian legend were always losing their way, as were most of the cast of *As You Like It* in Shakespeare's Arden, that 'desert inaccessible under the shade of melancholy boughs'. Never mind that the woods of Shakespeare's time, or possibly even King Arthur's, were no more 'savage' and not much bigger than those of 1945; human attitudes to nature have rarely been constrained by reality.

But what was the Wildwood really like? To T. H. White it was almost impenetrable;

> . . . an enormous barrier of eternal trees, the dead ones fallen against the live and held to them by ivy, the living struggling up in competition with each other toward the sun which gave them life, the floor boggy through lack of drainage, or tindery from old wood so that you might suddenly tumble through a decayed tree trunk into an ants' nest, or laced with brambles and bindweed and honeysuckle and convolvulus and teazles . . . until you would be torn in pieces in three yards.

Scientists twenty years ago were confident that the Wildwood was a place of great oaks, growing so close together that a squirrel could leap from coast to coast without once touching the ground, and that much of it survived in a state of nature until the Saxons came along with their heavy ploughs and converted most of it to farmland. This notion of a monotonous oak forest covering hill and dale was not conjured out of the air. Most of the big trees preserved in peat bogs are indeed oaks, and oak pollen is abundant in peat core samples throughout the country. The pioneer ecologists thought more in terms of the present than the past, and, since oak is undeniably the dominant native tree today, so, they argued, it was in yesteryear. On the other hand the idea that the Saxons, very late arrivals in woodland history, were the first masters of axe and

It was all down, down, down, gradually – ruin, and levelling and disappearance. Then it was all up, up, up, gradually, as seeds grew to saplings, and saplings to forest trees, and bramble and fern came creeping in to help. Leaf-mould rose and obliterated, streams in their winter freshets brought sand and soil to clog and to cover . . . animals arrived, liked the look of the place, took up their quarters, settled down, spread, and flourished . . . The Wild Wood is pretty well populated by now; with all the usual lot, good, bad and indifferent.

Kenneth Grahame,
'The Wild Wood', Chapter III
in *The Wind in the Willows*

THE WILDWOOD

plough never had much to recommend it; but their laws, annals and literature have survived, while those of Roman and pre-Roman Britain have not. The nature of the sources has a powerful influence on how we imagine the past.

The more recent findings of archaeology and palynology (the study of pollen) offer better clues to the formation and destruction of the Wildwood, but, although they provide some of the answers to the 'where and when' questions, they are of little help in recreating what the living Wildwood actually looked like. There is much that we do not know, and it is fatally easy to mould what evidence there is to fit the latest scientific fads and fashions. Perhaps then, it is better to begin with the question 'When?' for authorities are so far still in broad agreement as to when the Wildwood covered the land and how it developed. One thing is certain: it did not rise from the newly bared earth fully formed. If the climate is warm enough for trees, bare ground soon turns into woodland unless prevented from doing so by large herds of animals or human beings with heavy machinery. But different trees have different climatic tolerances and some are better colonisers of open ground than others. By about 12000BC Britain had at last shed its mantle of ice, but it was still a cold sub-Arctic land, perhaps like parts of Lapland or the Shetlands today. Among the pools, bogs, heath and tufts of hardy grasses were deeper pockets of soil which supported a scrubby growth of tough northern trees – birches, willows and sallows, aspens and juniper. Around them, intelligent and artistic men in skins hunted reindeer and elk, and slew the last mammoths and the other great browsing and grazing beasts of prehistory. The extinction of these beasts probably helped to pave the way to the establishment of the forest trees that followed.

As the climate grew milder, in fits and starts at first, the original trees spread from their refuges, and, joined later by Scots pine and hazel, colonised much of Britain to form an open pioneer forest. Then, as temperate conditions returned, bigger, shadier trees returned to the North, reaching Britain across the land-bridge with the European mainland. First alder and oak, then lime, ash and elm, and, more slowly, holly, beech, maple and hornbeam spread from the South until the rising seas washing over the land-bridges ended the formative years of the Wildwood. The first trees to arrive had the advantage over those that followed, for while oak, lime and elm could compete successfully with birch and hazel, the later arrivals, like beech, found a shady broadleaved forest already in place and they had to wait for other trees to die to find a space. The early success of oak might be due to the jay, which has a convenient habit of burying acorns for later enjoyment and then forgetting where it has put them. (Acorns left lying on the surface are vulnerable to persistent droughts or frosts, to say nothing of foraging boars or mice.) Beech on the other hand lagged behind for many centuries and became common only in the Bronze Age, when it was able to move into clearings created by man.

In the fully formed Wildwood of about six thousand years ago, there were scarcely more than a dozen common trees but probably at least seventy, and possibly as many as a hundred, types of woodland vegetation. Much of this probably survives in modified form. There are reasons for believing that present-day ground vegetation in ancient woods may be descended from that of prehistoric times, although we may have lost some of it along the way, such as calcareous pinewoods, floodplain woodland and sub-alpine scrub. Preserved tree pollen in bogs and lakes suggests that the Wildwood covered most of Britain except for the northern extremities (see map below): there were alderwoods in boggy hollows and by lakes, mixed elm and hazel woods in Wales and south-west England, oakwoods around the upland fringes, and limewoods throughout lowland England. There were probably hornbeam-woods and beechwoods, too, though we know nothing about them. The Scottish Wildwood seems to have been limited to birch, pine and hazel until late in the day when, in the rainy Atlantic period, oak, lime, elm and finally ash struggled north to colonise the lowland forests. But none of these woodland 'provinces' were uniform. Within them were different communities of trees, punctured by rock outcrops, rivers, lakes and fens, which increased in complexity from north to south, and from west to east. Little is known, unfortunately, about what grew beneath the trees, for most woodland flowers produce only small amounts of pollen and even that decays easily. One unusually well-preserved sample from a Norfolk lake suggests they were the same as today – bluebells, dog's mercury, stitchwort and other familiar woodland flowers.

While it is possible to draw a rough map of Britain's vegetation six thousand years ago we can only guess at its physical appearance. No one in history, unfortunately, was far-sighted enough to preserve a fragment of virgin forest for future study (it is hard enough persuading the 'powers that be' to preserve a few scraps of unmanaged forest even now). We are therefore forced to look instead at surviving areas of virgin broadleaved forest in places like Poland and Czechoslovakia, which may not resemble British conditions very closely. On visiting Bialowieza in the former country, one finds soaring long-lived trees growing close together, with straight branchless trunks reaching up into narrow crowns. Most of them are mature, for saplings can get away only in the sudden burst of light after a tree topples over. Growth on the rich moist forest soils is fast and the young trees shoot straight up to the sky, reaching their full height before a tenth of their life-span has passed. Dead timber is everywhere, from standing stumps and half-fallen trunks, their vast root-plates torn from the earth by long-forgotten gales, to mossy logs in every state of decay. Much of the forest is swamp and the rest secluded in leafy gloom shot through by filtered shafts of light. There are a few places in Britain which have the same atmosphere – Mark Ash Wood in the New Forest for example, or Wistman's Wood on Dartmoor – which makes them useful for film and television, but their aura of primeval decay is a product of relatively recent history, not the remote past.

Was our own Wildwood all like Bialowieza? Probably not. The height of the canopy must have varied from low scrub on naturally thin soils in places like Upper Teesdale (where existing juniper woods have a pedigree of nine thousand years) to stands over 100ft (30m) tall in parts of the South East. A continuous dense forest is hard to reconcile with the abundance of hazel throughout the pollen record, for hazel is a low

THE WILDWOOD

Woodland vegetation c4000BC, before man became a settler. These 'woodland provinces' are named after the dominating trees, but were much more varied than their names imply

43

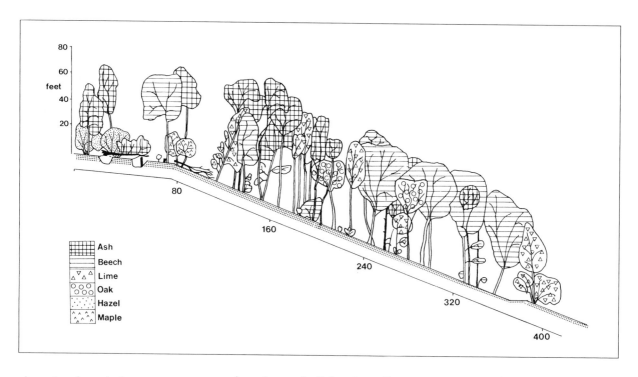

Legend:
Ash
Beech
Lime
Oak
Hazel
Maple

A section through the upper part of Lady Park Wood in the Wye Valley. Little disturbed since about 1890, the wood has become mixed high forest dominated by beech, ash, small-leaved lime and both native oaks, with a sparse understorey and much dead wood. This may be the closest approximation to virgin forest in Britain (based on unpublished research by G. F. Peterken)

tree that demands light; it will not regenerate when heavily shaded. Much of our present woodland wildlife depends on a plentiful supply of sunlight, and four-fifths of our native flowering plants grow *outside* woods today. Were all the butterflies and most of our flowers confined to glades, cliffs and other 'holes' in the continuous forest? Apparently they were, but there are emerging hints that large parts of Britain were only lightly forested from the very beginning. Recent studies of pollen and other preserved remains at Willow Garth in the Yorkshire wolds indicate that the forest canopy there was already discontinuous nine thousand years ago. In a recent paper in that august journal, *Nature*, the authors adduce evidence to suggest that some areas of chalk grassland were never forested at all.

Old ideas die hard. I was brought up to believe in something called 'climax forest', which, having evolved, would exist indefinitely in a 'steady state'. It only ceased to be steady after people had chopped it down. Since then, the NCC's Man of the Woods George Peterken, has travelled far abroad, looking at ancient woodland in places as different as Sweden, the United States and Crete, and witnessed the considerable impact of fire, wind, flood and insect damage on natural woodland. He now believes it is closer to the truth to imagine our northerly Wildwood suffering an endless series of catastrophes and traumas which prevented that ecologist's dream, 'the climax', from ever becoming reality. 'It is conceivable,' he writes, 'that "climax forest" is a concept only, never existing in practice due to catastrophes or because of the long time-lag in adjustment of vegetation cover to an ever-changing environment.'

One thing is certain: the ever-changing Wildwood was a more complex and interesting place than we can visualise. It was greater than the sum of its parts. Let it remain in our imaginations as a place of wonder, the awesome splendour of unharnessed Nature. Perhaps the fairy stories are not, after all, so very far off the mark.

The 'elm decline'

The most dramatic and mysterious recorded event in the history of the Wildwood took place simultaneously across the whole of north-west Europe about six thousand years ago. In peat deposits dating from before that time, elm pollen is abundant; but then, with startling suddenness, the level plummets. The 'elm decline', as the phenomenon is known, coincides with the rise of weeds like stinging nettles and plantains and with the first signs of permanent human settlement, and archaeologists were quick to link the two events. In Switzerland they excavated some contemporary wooden constructions, interpreted as cattle stalls, which contained the remains of quantities of elm leaves, presumably gathered as fodder. At that time hay was in short supply, so boughs of nutritious trees like elm and lime were lopped to feed the first farm animals in winter. The reason for the elm decline, it seemed, was the rise of the farmer and stockbreeder; the elms did not disappear, but their branches were lopped regularly and so ceased to produce flowers and pollen.

This theory was widely accepted until the 1970s, when we became helpless witnesses to another elm decline, this time from disease. To our generation, Dutch elm disease seems a more straightforward explanation of why elms disappear than Neolithic cattle fodder (elms outnumbered the early farmers by many thousands to one, and the latter had other occupations than lopping boughs). Neolithic farmers might have unwittingly unleashed an early and virulent form of Dutch elm disease by creating a more open landscape in which the bark-beetles that transmit the disease could increase to plague numbers. If so, the pioneer farmers probably cheered them on. The sudden death of one of the commonest trees created clearings without much effort by the farmer, and it also, by releasing stored nutrients, increased the fertility of the soil.

The elm decline, then, presents us with a conundrum of cause and effect: did early farmers cause the elm decline, or did they merely benefit from it? The truth, which may never be known, was probably more complicated, with changing climate and competition from other trees also playing a part. What matters is that the elm decline was real, and not a figment of science, and that its consequences were long-lasting, for never again in history has elm played such a dominant role in British woodland.

The lime mystery

The other tree that was common in the Wildwood but is not so common now is the small-leaved lime. At one time a traveller could walk from Kent to Lincolnshire and then turn west to the Welsh border and walk south to Dorset and be surrounded by lime trees most of the way. How do we know this? Until recently we didn't. The main evidence for reconstructing prehistoric woods is from pollen preserved in peat deposits. However some plants produce more pollen than others and pollen is preserved only in wet places; so the raw results of pollen analysis can be misleading. Oak and birch are wind-pollinated, and

produce far more pollen than hawthorn or rowan which are more reliably pollinated by insects. Alder pollen is preserved in abundance because that tree grows on wet ground. Lime is at a double disadvantage here because not only does it avoid excessively wet ground, but it is also insect-pollinated and so produces only relatively small amounts of pollen, most of which seems to fall nearby. When due allowance is made for the disparities of pollen production, however, lime turns out to be the commonest tree in the majority of pollen samples taken in eastern England.

There is another strand of evidence to support this conclusion. A tiny bark-beetle, *Ernoporus,* is today a rare insect of lime twigs and branches in a few ancient woods in the Midlands, yet in post-glacial deposits it is a common and widespread fossil. Since it is not known to have any other food-plant, the obvious deduction is that lime itself was once both widespread and common.

To judge from undisturbed woods in other countries, like France and Poland, the Wildwood limes were towering, majestic trees forming a canopy 100ft (30m) or more above the ground. No present-day British limes are like this, for they have all been coppiced or pollarded for fodder and fibre. But lime is a persistent survivor, withstanding all kinds of mistreatment except heavy grazing. Why then have most of the original limewoods been replaced by other trees? The pollen record suggests that, unlike elm, lime declined very gradually, but that it too was the victim of human interference. Presumably deliberate grubbing (digging up) of woods, expressed by the appearance of plantains, docks and bracken, accounted for most lime woodland. At Thorne Waste in Yorkshire, lime had become scarce by about 1200BC, recovered later, and then declined again, this time permanently, in 370BC. At some sites it disappeared much earlier, while Epping Forest, exceptionally, was still dominated by lime when the first Saxon settlers arrived in Essex.

But we do not need to invoke lime-slaying woodmen of the past to explain the tree's poor showing today. The clue lies in its own biology. Lime likes warm weather. Cool, wet conditions inhibit the growth of its pollen tubes while the short warm season in Britain prevents most of its fruits from ripening before they are shed. Consequently it hardly sets seed at all in the northernmost parts of its range, like Cumbria and the Peak District, except in hot summers like 1976 and 1984, and, even then, few seedlings manage to survive. The decline of the lime began about five thousand years ago, when the climate became permanently cooler and wetter, and it suffered proportionately more than most trees from its sensitivity to grazing. Limes and wood-pastures do not mix. Today native limes are good pointers to ancient woodland, so that the gradual disappearance of ancient woodland explains the lime's continuing long decline. It has become measurably less frequent in northern England during our own century.

The past in miniature

Peat deposits preserve not only pollen and wood but also parts of certain animals, especially snail shells and the hard parts of beetles. The study of such animal fossils has come into its own recently, for, from what is known about the likes and dislikes of their living descendants, they can provide evidence of past environments in areas like the southern chalk where little pollen has been preserved. They also provide useful corroboration of other evidence and give some 'fine-tuning' to the reconstruction of former landscapes. For example, it is to beetles, which respond more rapidly to environmental changes than trees, that we owe our knowledge of a remarkably rapid improvement in the climate some thirteen thousand years ago. Fossils also provide information about the nature of prehistoric forest, and with their help we can tell which trees were present and in roughly what proportion, their size and density, the amount of dead wood present, sometimes the type of soil, and whether there were open glades, streams, marshes or lakes.

Fossil snails are particularly useful pointers to forest clearance. They prove that the surrounding landscape was already open by the time Avebury and Stonehenge were built (we already suspected this from the prominent siting of Neolithic barrows on the skyline), but that two thousand years earlier still – about six thousand years ago – most of the southern chalk was dense forest. The soil profiles of some chalk sites show a sequence of snail fossils, beginning with those of damp woodland, through species of open ground and then back to woodland again, which suggests that the first forest clearings were only temporary ones. Only later, probably with the advent of iron tools and a larger population, did woodland clearance become widespread and permanent.

One of the most spectacular insect fossils ever found in Britain is a black longhorn beetle, *Cerambyx cerdo,* one of the largest insects in Europe, and exactly the sort of thing one might expect to lurk inside a primeval forest. *Cerambyx* bores holes in living oaks and, because of its monstrous bulk, only big trees are suitable. Occasionally fossils and holes have been dug up together, as at Ramsey in Cambridgeshire in 1976, where a large piece of Bronze Age fen-oak bore numerous holes the size of Havana cigars, made by the beetle, and even the beast itself, freshly emerged from its pupa inside the trunk. But the astonishing thing about this particular oak was its size. No less than 340 tree-rings were counted, but the trunk was still sound and measured an estimated 70ft (20m) from its base to the lowest bough and was a yard (or metre) thick 20ft (6m) above the ground. There are no living oaks quite like this in Britain, although similar specimens still occur in densely stocked high forest in France. In Europe, *Cerambyx,* now as then, needs well-grown oaks, and, since it can ruin valuable timber, continental foresters wish it the same fate that long ago overtook it in Britain.

Woodland soils

Ancient woods generally mark the poorest or heaviest soil, or the steepest land, in the parish. They lie, to borrow a phrase of Oliver Rackham's, not so much on land that is good for trees but on land that is no good for anything else. Those places that have been *continuously* covered by trees throughout history, and there are more of them than

WOODLAND HERITAGE

THE WILDWOOD

was once thought, were preserved from the ploughing, draining, liming and fertilising that has churned up and changed for ever the soil outside the wood. Primary woodland soils are nature's own, enriched by leaf mould, aerated by earthworms and sheltered from extremes of the weather by the canopy. Most ancient broadleaved woods have deep, brown earth soils, their precise chemistry depending on the nature of the underlying rocks or drift and the amount of water standing on top.

Ancient woodland soils, then, are of more than passing scientific interest. They are not, of course, completely undisturbed, for over the millennia carts have gouged deep ruts in them; pits, ponds and ditches have punctured the surface; earthworks have been piled on top; and, more fundamentally, most of the primeval tall forest has been transformed into coppices. Even so, primary ancient woodland soils still retain a greater degree of naturalness than any others. One sign of this is the surprising variation in woodland soil within quite a small area. Bedford Purlieus, for example, at less than a square mile in extent contains most of the major natural soil types known in East Anglia. Undisturbed soils tend to have a layered structure. In the Lincolnshire limewoods a surface of light acidic soil overlies a separate and contrasting zone of mottled alkaline or neutral clay. A single ploughing, or a heavy-handed modern forestry operation, would strip away the delicate upper layer, together with its historic meaning, for ever.

Soils give clues to the woodland past. Soils of open ground eventually start to show signs of leaching, when some of the contents of the upper layer are dissolved by soil acids and carried down to deeper layers. The absence of leaching in some medieval deer-parks is considered a sign that woodland has always been present. The typically thin soils of downland woods, on the other hand, lost their original depth and fertility during their previous incarnation as open grassland. The original soil was much deeper and less alkaline, and a probable example survives at West Dean Woods at Chilgrove (West Sussex) whose deep, reddish, acidic clay is quite different to more recent woods in the area.

Soil conservation is one solid scientific reason for preserving ancient woods, but soil people and tree people have yet to co-ordinate their efforts. A survey organised in 1981 showed that nearly half of the woods valued highly by soil scientists for their undisturbed profiles had not received any official protection.

The end of the Wildwood

The period between 5500BC and 3000BC is known as the Atlantic, a time of climatic upheaval after the long summer of the previous millennium. At its beginning Britain became an island and the climate grew rainier, although the summers remained warm. The virgin earth still lay untilled and humans were wanderers, living off the fruits of the land without physical toil, obedient to nature's rhythms and cycles: the Roman Varro's imagined Golden Age. As its end, much former forest in the highest and wettest areas had become waterlogged and there was a new kind of human being, settlers from southern Europe who, together with their imported crops and domestic animals, had already made a good start on taming and reducing the Wildwood. Some of the oldest artefacts of the landscape were by then in place: coppices and pollarded trees, enclosed fields and meadows, farmsteads, permanent trackways and, probably, hedges. It used to be thought that the Atlantic's other great contribution to the landscape, the bogs and moors, was the consequence of the deteriorating climate, conjuring up images of once majestic trees toppling ignominiously over into the rising peat . . . Such scenes did happen on occasion, for example in the Fens, but more often when you dig into a peat bog you find not a forest at the bottom but a field. People, not rain, had destroyed the Wildwood.

Tackling primeval forest with stone tools was no mean undertaking. It is relatively easy in parts of the world where woods obligingly blaze when lit, or in the Tropics where a single felling (with a chain-saw) puts paid to the tree. But in wet, temperate Britain forest fires in natural woodland are virtually unknown, except in pinewoods, and most native trees react to being chopped down by joyously regenerating from the stump. Once he had finished hacking through a tree with his stone axehead, the farmer was left with a useless trunk, and he still had to uproot the stump to prevent further growth. There are, perhaps, two great mysteries about the Neolithic or New Stone Age. The first is how, in the face of the above-mentioned difficulties, our forebears nevertheless managed to clear the Wildwood. The second is why they thought it worthwhile. They must have been evangelists from distant countries, burning with new ideas about human progress and destiny. We shall not see their like again.

We can at least gain an idea of how they went about it by looking at the places which pollen analysis tells us were cleared first. The earliest manmade open landscapes were mainly on light soils, especially sands and gravels and steep chalk escarpments, which were probably the easiest to clear and were the best suited to stone scratch-ploughs. The original hazelwood at Iping Common in Surrey was replaced by the present open heath at least six thousand years ago, almost certainly by deliberate clearance, and is one of the oldest known open landscapes in southern England. Iping Common was probably cleared to improve the pasture, but there are plenty of characteristic small, square Neolithic arable fields on the chalk, especially in Wiltshire. Certain early clearance sites, like the Breckland and the Cumberland coast, became the first industrial centres – for the mass-production of flints and stone tools. Woodland was not, however, a useless obstruction. The first farmers needed the forest for fodder, wood, hazelnuts and other products, as graze and browse for their livestock and, probably, to renew the fertility of these hungry, free-draining soils after a few years under crops. The pollen record shows that many early clearings were quickly abandoned and left to scrub over again, sometimes for a long time suggesting that, with permanent settlement, war and plague had arrived.

The clearance of the Wildwood probably grew more widespread and efficient as the technology of axes and ploughs improved. During the Neolithic and the succeeding age of bronze, European culture seems to have been more genuinely international than at any time since, and agricultural advances were common to places as far apart as Wales and

MORRONE BIRKWOOD: A GLIMPSE OF EDEN

Braemar used to hold the record for the coldest place in Britain. Its winters are long and snowy, its summers short and uncertain. Those who converge on the village in early September to watch the Braemar Games may need anoraks and precautionary drams of malt to sustain their enjoyment. The games arena is overlooked by a rounded green hill, Morrone, whose northern flanks support an attractive open birchwood broken by glades of heather and sedges and watered by mountain rills. No ordinary parish wood this: it is as high and exposed as any wood in Britain. None of the trees are taller than 30ft (9m) and nearly all are typical crooked little Highland 'lollipops'. Only Arctic species are present: downy birch, aspen, juniper, rowan and alder. Even Scots pine, which fills the glens hereabouts, is absent.

A walk through Morrone Birkwood in late May, with snow still lying on the distant tops, is an exhilarating experience. The newly green birches exhale that zestful lemony tang of Highland birkwoods, fritillaries chase one another over the juniper bushes, and alpine herbs flower by the rills and in the glades. Most of the trees are old and past their prime – they are probably among the oldest surviving birches, for the limited growing season and the very slow growth rate has prolonged their life to 120 years or more.

Core samples taken from peat deposits within the wood suggest that something very similar existed here in early post-glacial times, for birch, juniper and alder pollen, plus that of some of the alpine herbs, were all abundant here about eight thousand years ago. We do not know whether there has been a birchwood on the north slopes of Morrone continuously since that time, but it seems possible. At 2,000ft (600m) in the central Highlands there is no record of oak, ash, elm or other forest trees ever having displaced the original birches. Our wood may well be that very rare thing, a primary ancient birchwood. Dr Derek Ratcliffe tells me that Morrone Birkwood reminds him strongly of natural woods in the mountainous Dovrefjell district of Norway, at 62′ in latitude.

I suggest that much of the base-rich soil on mountain slopes in the central Highlands was originally covered by woods similar to Morrone Birkwood. Such woods do not have fixed boundaries, for birch cannot regenerate under the shade of its fellows. Regeneration here has probably always been erratic, hindered by grazing deer, as today, and by complete defoliations by moth caterpillars. The latter are a characteristic occurrence in natural arctic woodland, and last happened here in 1968. At times, Morrone might have been more open than now (the twenty-first century will be such a time, assuming the wood is spared); at others it was probably denser and extended further up the hillside. Its history, if largely unknown, has certainly not been static, but it has been such as to have perpetuated an archaic feature of British woodland – mountain plants and trees side by side – and provided a present-day window on the distant past.

Morrone Birkwood, near Braemar in Deeside. On the last day in May snow lies on the Cairngorms and the downy birches are newly in leaf. Below is a yard-high understorey of juniper, somewhat the worse for wear from grazing and old age.

EVENTS IN THE WOODLAND CALENDAR FROM LATE ICE AGE TO EARLY SAXON TIMES.

Date (approx)	Human culture	Manmade landscape features	The Wildwood
12000BC	Hunter-gathering on open ground		Retreating ice Open forest of birch and pine
10000			Open forest of birch, aspen, juniper and pine
9000		Hut platforms Woodland greens	
8000	Hunter-gathering under Wildwood		Rapid warming of climate Forest of pine and hazel Birch retreating to north; elm, lime and oak colonising in south
7000			Dense forest of elm, lime, oak, hazel Pine declines
6000			Beech, ash, maple and hornbeam establish
5000			Wildwood fully formed. Britain becomes an island
		Heaths	
4000		Wooden halls	
			Winters get colder Elm decline. Hazel, ash and alder increase
3000	Small-scale peasant farming under secondary woodland	Long-distance tracks Arable fields Coppices ? Pollarded trees	First woodland clearances for agriculture
2000		Downs, ? Hedges	Substantial area (? a third) under grass, heath or arable
		Open landscapes Villages	Slow decline of lime
		Hill-forts	Rainfall increases, summers get
1000		Managed woods Lynchets	colder. Acid-rain from volcanic eruption
			Growth of peat bogs
500			Hornbeam and beech increase
	Peasant farming in open fields	Barns	
0		Crannogs (artificial lake-islands)	Large-scale woodland clearances
	Intensive farming	Gardens, Orchards Plantations, Vineyards, Towns, Slag-heaps	Industrial coppices
AD500	Peasant farming in open fields	Churches	Secondary woodland on abandoned farms

Greece. The Bronze Age farmers cleared a great deal of woodland – just how much is debatable – or converted it to managed woods and wood-pasture, but their ploughs still splintered when they hit stony ground or got stuck when they met clay. With the increase in food supply came an increase in population, eventually producing the first major crisis in history at about 1200BC when demand finally outstripped supply. This was the time of the siege of Troy and the wanderings of the Mediterranean 'sea-people', of mythical heroes, of battles and the fall of forgotten empires. In Britain large and strongly defended hill-forts were built all over the country. To make matters worse, the climate took another downturn and some of the marginal land at the upland fringes became unworkable. Recent evidence suggests that a volcanic eruption in Iceland in about 1150BC caused a series of poor summers and freezing winters in northern Scotland, and an early manifestation of acid rain. Oak trees stopped growing and land abandonment on a large scale took place within a single generation. Out of turmoil and disaster came the crucial discoveries of smelting and working iron.

Iron ploughs are infinitely better than stone ones (though it is thought that stone axes remained hard to beat until the invention of the chain-saw). They not only cut more deeply into the sod but also turn it, and they score cleanly through clay soils that defeated the Neolithic farmer. By the end of the Iron Age, which we can arbitrarily place on the day that Julius Caesar invaded Britain, farmers could plough almost any but the wettest and stoniest soils. This was the time of the most extensive clearances of all. Wood was needed to smelt iron ore, which made cheap, strong ploughs, which paved the way to greater prosperity and yet more babies, who grew up demanding more and more land and a better standard of living than their parents. At the same time methods improved for increasing agricultural production and storing the produce. The result was that Wildwood on poor, wet soils as far apart as west Wales, Somerset and Yorkshire was cleared for the first time, and thick layers of sediment in downland valleys and along the Severn testify to the intensity of the agricultural boom around 500BC. Floodplains that had once been densely wooded became water-meadows, and the steep downland soils, stripped of their natural cover of trees, became lastingly thin and raw.

By Roman times, three-quarters or possibly even more of the Wildwood had gone, and much that remained was used as wood-pasture for cattle and pigs, or managed for timber and fuelwood. The growth of woodmanship, by now well advanced, is the theme of Chapter 5, and here we merely note that the landscape has already become familiar. Julius Caesar found a land 'thickly studded with homesteads' with fewer woods than Gaul. When General Agricola marched into Scotland a century later, he found already largely treeless northern pastures, with scattered scrubby woods of hazel and alder in hollows and by burns. The natives were already learning to live without oak. Only in the remote interior, among trackless glens and mountainsides, were there still substantial remnants of the legendary Wildwood of Caledonia.

WOODLAND HERITAGE

THE WILDWOOD

4
ANCIENT WOODS
IN THEIR PRIME

If we could return to the Middle Ages to visit a 'typical' wood on a lowland manor, what would we find? Contemporary descriptions are rare but there are numerous woodland hunting scenes illustrated in manuscripts and tapestries, most of them Flemish rather than English, which seem to provide an authentic picture of medieval woodland scenery. If we can manage to tear our eyes away from the unfortunate animal being 'worried' by hounds in the foreground, these pictures are often remarkably informative, even down to the exact species of toadstool and underwood shrub. Although their perspective was shaky and their human figures were wooden, medieval artists seem to have had an excellent knowledge of actual woods.

Let us assume that our time-machine has landed in a small wood in a well-populated and sparsely wooded district. We are in a valuable property, managed mainly for its underwood, which is divided up into coppices, each of which is cut over every dozen or so years, leaving about twelve slender standard trees per acre. Since there are few deer, and no grey squirrels, the regrowth on the cut stools is vigorous. The wood also contains permanent glades, cut for hay in July and used afterwards for grazing cattle. We might be surprised at the prevailing tidiness and good order: brambles and other weeds are kept under control and, because every bit of living and dead wood is used, even the leaves, bonfires are unnecessary. None of the trees or shrubs is planted except, perhaps, for the standard oaks. We look in vain for broad, straight rides, for they were a much later fashion, possibly linked with the rise of the sporting gun or 'fowling piece'. Instead we find a network of winding rutted tracks, perhaps filled with stone in the stickiest places to support heavy oxen and horse-drawn wood-carts and haywains. We see cabins and shelters, saw-pits, and small excavations for stone or clay. And depending on the season there will be plenty of people about their business, making wattle hurdles, gathering greenery, picking hazelnuts and crabs, coppicing underwood, binding faggots, cording timber and, an important use of woods according to medieval manuscript pictures, canoodling in the bushes. Essentially it is a familiar scene, not a lost Arcadia or a Hollywood fantasy. The flowers, butterflies, songbirds and toadstools are the same species as now, but there are more of them. We might make the same observation about the villagers.

In the Middle Ages, as long before, most people lived in small, more or less self-supporting communities. The basic unit of land was the manor, which is broadly the same as the parish, and most manors contained at

54

least one wood. The best land was either enclosed as individual fields or farmed communally in the well-known open-field system. There was permanent grassland in the meadows in the valley bottoms, which were cut for hay, and on the village green. Beyond the fields was poorer land, left unfenced and unploughed, and used as common grazing. The common included some, or most, of the woodland, where cattle were put out to graze and pigs turned loose in the winter, dead wood was gathered and turf cut. The lord often had his own private wood, reserved for his hunting and as a useful source of income from rents and sales.

The medievals knew their soils and their local woods generally lay on ground which was too wet, too infertile or too steep to be worth clearing for agriculture. You can often see this on soil maps today: the present boundary of Duncliffe Wood in Dorset, for example, matches almost exactly an island of infertile greensand. In the lowlands, woods often lay on the higher ground near or on the parish boundary, and appeared, as seen from the village, as a green line along the horizon, as in parts of Rockingham Forest today. Medieval woods were important places, providing brushwood for fuel; coppice poles for wattles, tool handles and spokes; and timber for building; as well as pasture for farm animals. They might also contain clay, lime or stone, winter fodder, fern for animal bedding, sedge for thatching, nuts and berries, the honey of wild

The mossy bank of a mysterious holloway. Behind is a rare example of English oak coppice with grotesquely shaped stools and an understorey of holly. Swanton Novers Woods, Norfolk. April 1988

Left: *An ancient park boundary, probably built just inside an existing wood, leaving a skirting or 'freeboard' of woodland for fencing material. The park was later managed as sessile oak coppice. High Wood, Charborough, Dorset, May 1986*

55

bees and the nests of hawks. Lowland woods, especially coppices, had boundaries that were fixed and (for some obscure reason) usually sinuous, marked by a bank and ditch and reinforced with a hedge or wall. Accounts studied by Oliver Rackham suggest that the earthworks were sometimes built by contractors, financed by the sales from underwood growing along the line of the excavations.

The majority of people in the medieval village were freemen with a personal stake in the running of the communal wood. They owned rights in the wood, such as the right to take living and dead wood and turf, and the right to graze a certain number of livestock at certain times of year. The degree of manorial control varied, but a typical situation was that the commoners owned the underwood and grazings, and the lord the timber trees and the soil, and this form of tenure prevented one party from imposing its interests over the other's. Commoners were allowed quotas of wood for different tasks and the taking was supervised by a woodward. *Housebote* was timber for repairing buildings, *ploughbote* wood for farm equipment, *haybote* wood for fencing, and so on. Fallen dead wood could be gathered freely for firewood, and dead branches on living trees could be removed with a blunt hook or crook — hence the familiar expression. Additional wood could be harvested from the lord's own wood on payment of a wood-penny, or in kind; in Scotland bolls of meal ('boll' is the name of a measure) were a popular currency, while at Shotover Forest near Oxford admittance to the king's woods could be arranged in exchange for a 'cokshote' of hens and eggs.

The medieval villager was a jack-of-all-trades. He may have been illiterate and ignorant of most things outside his immediate experience, but he knew his own patch and could perform a wider range of tasks than most countrymen could claim today. He is traditionally depicted as a hard worker puffing and straining behind his plough from dawn till dusk but, unless human nature has changed since, this is most unlikely. Most people work hard only when there is an incentive to do so; and unless there were good markets nearby a medieval commoner produced only enough for his own needs, plus a tenth share each for the lord and the priest. The hours might have been long, at least in certain seasons, but he took his time. In his idle moments, he drank prodigious quantities of ale, told smutty stories in the manner of Chaucer and, like the pioneers on the American frontier centuries later, whittled wood. He owned a collection of edged tools and made his own buckets and dishes, baskets and besoms, sabots and creels. Unlike the American pioneers, however, he could not build his own log cabin, because Britain has no suitable straight coniferous trees. Most wild trees were, and are, too crooked to make large planks and beams. Except in stone areas, ordinary houses had to be framed with bits of small oaks, and the spaces between filled with wattles made from the more plentiful underwood, daubed with local ingredients like clay and cow dung, and then plastered. It might sound squalid but, for the better-off at least, medieval houses were comfortable, warm and well ventilated — and bigger than today's housing-estate doll's houses. A good-sized farmhouse could require several hundred small oaks. And medieval carpentry has never been bettered, as many an old tithe barn can testify.

The medievals found a use for all kinds of wood, but some trees were valued more than others. Oak was the favourite structural timber and, after felling, the trunks and branches were hewn or riven into beams, shingles and lathes; medieval woodwrights avoided the saw if they could. Ordinary coppice woods contained few or no big oaks, since the standards were normally felled after three rotations – about sixty years. Even these small trees were limited in number since too many of them would shade and suppress the valuable underwood. A manor might possess a row of mature trees in the hedgerow or on the lord's desmesne, but the really big straight oak timbers needed for the roof beams of great halls and cathedrals had to come from the king's own woods or from overseas. Big timber trees were a valuable source of royal patronage, literally beyond price since mere money could not buy them.

The equivalent of the modern forester in the Middle Ages was the woodwright, who had an eye for the right tree to provide ridge beams, crucks, pillars, stanchions, sills, ledges, lintels, door-posts or side-posts. Ships needed an equally varied array of bits, including knees and futtocks. To cut all these shapes and sizes the woodwright needed a sizeable tool-kit. His most treasured possession was his sturdy felling axe with its heavy forged iron blade and long ash handle – a piece of technology now almost extinct and invariably made of inferior pressed iron. Smaller axes and bills were used for cleaning the trunk, lopping the branches and for dressing planks; as one writer put it, 'large trees were not so much felled as dismembered'. Five men could be employed for twenty days on a single tree, stripping bark and cutting branches, and a big oak (woodmen dreaded big oaks) could occupy the sawyers for months. Once the trunk was stripped it was drawn by horses to the work-place and then trimmed, split with wedges and worked with an adze or sawn into planks. The timber was dressed with smaller hand-saws, draw knives, shaves and hammers and, depending on its ultimate use, it would then be attacked with augurs and chisels for boring, notching, hollowing, mortising and carving.

So far we have looked at medieval woods from the point of view of the village freeman, who made a living from them. An equally important use of woods in the Middle Ages was for hunting and the supply of meat. To see how woods were organised for hunting, we have to look at them from the opposite end of the social pyramid. Hunting was first and foremost the king's business, and from the Norman Conquest until Magna Carta he imposed his will on an increasingly large area of his subjects' land. What the limits to his authority were in practice, and what impact it had on the shaping of today's woods, is the subject of the second half of this chapter.

The king's own forests

One of the most widely quoted passages from the Anglo-Saxon Chronicle is a piece of doggerel, written the year after the Domesday Book was compiled, lamenting the 'evil' deeds of William the Conqueror. Among the latter was the establishment of the first Royal Forests:

WOODLAND HERITAGE

ANCIENT WOODS
IN THEIR PRIME

He set apart a vast deer preserve and imposed laws concerning it:
Whoever slew a hart or hind
Was to be blinded
He forbade the killing of boars
Even as the killing of harts
For he loved the stags as dearly
As though he had been their father.
Hares, also, he decreed should go unmolested.
The rich complained and the poor lamented.
But he was too relentless to care . . .

This is of course a Saxon point of view – 'They would say that wouldn't they' – the truth of which we must address later. But observe that this passage, which might refer specifically to the establishment of the New Forest, is about animals, not trees. In our own century, a forest has come to mean little more than a big wood, perhaps with connotations of uniform coniferous composition. To King William it was a place for hunting wild animals, a meaning that still survives in the almost treeless

'deer forests' of the Scottish Highlands. The notion of setting aside large tracts of land for hunting was introduced to England by the Norman kings, who in turn probably copied it from the native French. The idea was soon imported to Scotland and Wales by kings and Marcher Lords respectively. William actually established fewer Royal Forests than some of his successors, and the system was at its height not in his time but in the second half of the twelfth century, when between a third and a fifth of England was under Forest Law – surely the most wide-ranging, and certainly the least popular, conservation measure in our history.

The traditional image of a Royal Forest is of a thickly wooded wilderness in which the Normans and Plantagenets galloped about in pursuit of deer and wild boar, while Robin Hood and his merrie men plotted mischief beneath the greenwood tree. There is plenty of contemporary warrant for this quintessential medieval scene. A twelfth-century document describes the Forests as:

> . . . the sanctuaries of kings and their chief delight. Thither they repaired to hunt, their cares laid aside the while, in order to refresh themselves by a short respite. There renouncing the arduous but natural turmoil of the court, they breathe the pure air of freedom for a little space; whence it is that they who transgress the laws of the forest are subject to the royal jurisdiction.

Medieval woodland boundary with outside ditch at Lobbett's Barrow, Dorset, showing a typically sinuous outline to the wood. May 1986

A woodland pond. This one is used by crested newts and more than a dozen species of dragonfly. Castor Hanglands, Cambridgeshire. May 1989

WOODLAND HERITAGE

ANCIENT WOODS
IN THEIR PRIME

We should however beware of one-sided interpretations like this. No doubt that is how the king regarded the Forests, but his subjects continued to own rights within them. And even the most fanatical kingly hunter scarcely needed a third of the entire realm as his retreat, even if he spent his whole reign in the pursuit of deer. In fact, with a few possible exceptions like the New Forest, most Forests rarely saw a royal visitor at all. Richard the Lionheart, under whom the system was at its zenith, visited England only twice, and then briefly, as king. The preoccupation of Norman Forest Law with deer and trees has led to the fallacy that the Forests contained little else. In fact the England revealed by the Domesday Book was a populous land with farms and villages covering a third of the land, compared with only about a sixth under trees – and much less than a sixth two hundred years later. Very little, if any, virgin woodland remained, and most woods were managed fairly intensively for grazings and underwood. The woods within Royal Forests were no exception.

Woodland historians are therefore careful to distinguish between the *legal Forest*, an area of land subject to the king's own Forest Law to protect the hunting, and the often much smaller *physical forest* within it where the wild deer lived. It is probable that all the earliest Forests contained a substantial core of woodland or waste, since one of their original purposes was to supply venison for the king's huge travelling household. But successive kings saw opportunities for asserting themselves and raising revenue by placing more and more land under Forest Law, whether there were woods present or not. At the height of the system whole counties, like Huntingdon and Essex, were made Forests, even though only a small fraction of them was woodland. The largest areas of waste within the Royal Forests were probably the New Forest and Sherwood Forest, which both amounted to several tens of thousands of acres. Sherwood was so big that it was held in common by the whole county of Nottinghamshire. Neither Sherwood nor the New Forest was a solid block of woodland, however, but rather a mosaic of unenclosed woods, open pasture, heath and bog, as the New Forest remains today. After 1215, when King John was obliged by his barons to release vast tracts of Forest land, the remaining Royal Forests became places where the king owned manors and estates or, at least, where his favourites did. Counties with a lot of royal manors, like Hampshire, Wiltshire and Somerset, were the most thickly beset with Forests. But Kent and the Weald, which were exceptionally well-wooded, had few or no Forests because the king owned little land there.

Forest Law decreed that the king owned all the deer, not just on his own land but also on that belonging to other people. This meant that taking deer without royal permission, or damaging their habitat by felling or grubbing up the trees, or enclosing woodland for clearance, was an offence, tried in Forest courts. However, other people continued to exercise their common rights within the Forests, including grazing and the collection of fuelwood, and Forest Law only limited them in so far as they interfered with the hunting. Fawning time, for example, was known as the fence month, when the number of grazing animals was restricted. Where the king owned the land, the task of his officials was to maintain a healthy stock of deer, timber and underwood, and to

The Royal Forests of England and Scotland in AD1300. Only those mentioned in this book are named. Both countries, and Wales, also had numerous private Forests and Chases. The legal boundaries of the Forests, especially in the uplands and in Scotland, are often uncertain

collect revenue from grazing and pannage (the practice of out-pasturing swine in the woods in autumn), from the sale of woodland products, and from fines awarded by the Forest courts. Some Forests contained quarries or were exploited for clay or lime and the Forest of Dean harboured one of the major iron-smelting industries of the Middle Ages. Dean, it seems, was one of the more intensively used Forests, but the system seems to have been fairly leisurely in practice: we need not suppose that the Forest bureaucracy was particularly efficient. Oliver Rackham has calculated that from all the Forests put together – about half a million acres (200,000ha) in 1300 – the king received less than a thousand deer, a few hundred big timber oaks and some thousands of acres of underwood annually. This hardly justified the enormous cost of maintaining an army of paid officials.

By the mid-thirteenth century, from which time date the earliest surviving day-to-day accounts, the system seems to have been remarkably easy-going, by twentieth-century standards, conducted on 'a nod and a wink'. Fines for collecting living wood or grazing stock illegally were seldom punitive and often amounted to little more than rent. Even after whole woods were felled and cleared without licence, offenders were not generally compelled to return the land to its original condition provided that they agreed to pay rent in cash or produce. Much no doubt depended on the venality of the Forest officials. In north-east Scotland, the king's foresters were themselves frequently fined for applying the 'blind eye' principle a little too blatantly. As for the famous Savage Penalties, the gougings of eyes and loppings of testicles decreed by the Norman kings and known to every schoolboy, the letter of the law may have been mistaken for the practice. Cash was always more useful than eyeballs and testicles. Hardened offenders like Robin Hood were generally imprisoned or outlawed.

The great contribution of the Royal Forests to posterity is that they slowed down the rate of woodland clearance at a time of rising population and land hunger. They did not prevent woods being cleared for agricultural purposes, but did manage to limit economic growth. Woodland regeneration may have been damaged by deer as much as by peasants: stray deer ate crops, underwood and saplings, and further damage was done by keepers seeking browsewood to feed their animals. It is impossible to know how much more ancient woodland would have disappeared had it not been for the Forests, but in some counties, like Buckinghamshire, Oxfordshire and Northamptonshire, most of the larger ancient woods that survive to the present day are on land which was Forest in the Middle Ages.

The administration of the Forests has been studied most closely in the century from 1250 to 1350, especially during the long reign of Henry III (1216–72), the rather uninspiring 'nondescript king' of *1066 And All That*. By Henry's time, government was no longer an endless procession of waggons and armed men pillaging their way around the country; it was established permanently in towns like Winchester and London. This reign was, by and large, a time of peace and growing prosperity, of rising population and of building projects everywhere. The wealthier parishes added aisles and spires to their churches and extended their halls, while Henry, who was fond of comfort, insisted on private

WOODLAND HERITAGE

ANCIENT WOODS
IN THEIR PRIME

ANCIENT WOODS
IN THEIR PRIME

bedchambers and panelled interiors. All this demanded increased production both from cultivated land and from woodland. An element of woodmanship was therefore needed in the dwindling Forests, and some at least were organised for commercial production, with coppice compartments and open grazing 'launds'. King Henry himself used up quantities of wood and timber from his estates, and liked to potter about supervising the work, rather like an eighteenth-century squire. His instructions to the Sheriff of Northampton to make improvements at royal hunting lodges in Rockingham Forest are typical: 'You are to build a new kitchen in my manor at Kingscliffe and repair the old one. Also to wainscot the king's chapel as far as the lower beam next to the altar: to make a mantelpiece and a privy chamber in the wardrobe ...' And so the list went on, itemising the mending of gates and paling fences, dredging fishponds, planting hedges and all the other everyday tasks on a medieval manor.

Oxfordshire
Ancient Woodland Total 1989

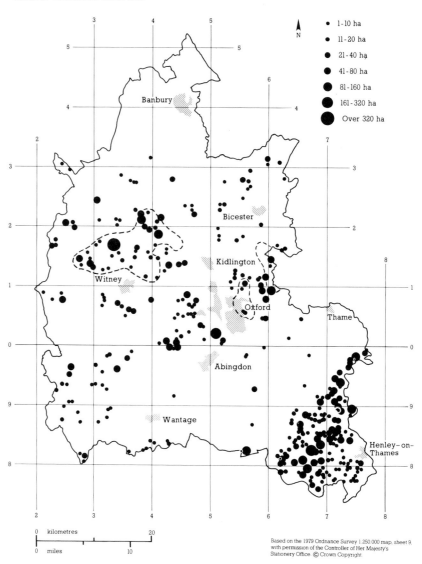

Ancient woodland in Oxfordshire, with the boundaries of the medieval Royal forests superimposed (details from the NCC ancient woodland inventory

Wychwood in Oxfordshire was a well-wooded Forest, partly owned by the king. Brushwood and poles for charcoal-making were harvested regularly from its many coppices, which were managed in the usual way by rotational fencing and cutting every twenty years or so. The Wychwood accounts hint at a gradual whittling away of the Forest woods and a difficulty in finding enough sound timber for royal building projects. A great gale in 1222, similar to the one in 1987, blew down many trees, and Henry ordered their valuation in situ before permitting their removal. The monks of nearby Eynsham Abbey were allowed to enclose part of the Forest for their own use and, in need of ready money, they sold some of the woods for agricultural clearance. Henry became so alarmed at the extent of agricultural encroachment that he regained the custody of the remaining woodland and, in 1257, suspended grants of timber in Royal Forests altogether.

Even here, however, where the Forest was part of the Crown estate, the king's authority was kept in check by the commoners. The majority of the woods in Wychwood were common pasture, subject to rights held by many villages which often lay several miles away. Villages and their commons were connected by a network of hedged lanes as intricate as the veins on a leaf, and many of them survive little-changed. The only really big timber trees were in the king's own woods, while the enclosed deer-parks at Cornbury and Woodstock were full of mighty pollards. The Forest gradually shrank during the Middle Ages as newly enclosed fields (assarts) nibbled away at the woodland, and the proportion of open fields to woods gradually increased, but within one person's lifetime the impression was probably one of stability, the Forest system preventing a wholesale destruction of woodland.

The Royal Forests in decline

The zenith of the Royal Forest system in Britain was short-lived and happened a long time ago. In 1215 the king was forced to disafforest all land belonging to someone else, but even before that date local associations of knights, freeholders and religious houses had bought their way out of forest regulations. In 1204, for example, the men of Devon paid 5,000 marks to free their county from Forest, except for Dartmoor and Exmoor. In the later Middle Ages more and more woodland in Forests owned by the Crown was sold or given away. At Wychwood, for example, licence was given fairly freely to neighbouring landowners to enclose large chunks of woodland as parks and smaller parcels of land for clearance and cultivation. The woods of Minster Lovell were detached en bloc in 1442 as a free chase – a separate 'mini-Forest' – for the Lovell family.

In Northern England, Wales and the Scottish Borders, Cistercian abbeys acquired extensive lands during the Middle Ages. Although they did manage some woods – indeed they were among the leading experts of their day – the Cistercians were more interested in managing sheep and more renowned for clearing woods than perpetuating them. Gerald of Wales mentions with sorrow a particularly fine wood full of tall, straight, branch-free oaks with small compact crowns (this is, incidentally, one of the few descriptions of woodland we have from the Middle Ages) which the monks chopped down and turned into a wheat field. The Cistercians were often given licence to graze their animals in whatever remained of the woods in the Scottish and Welsh Royal Forests (where Forest Law may not have amounted to much in any case), and, by cropping the young saplings and coppice shoots, they effectively prevented further regeneration. Ettrick Forest in Selkirk still contained extensive woodland in the early Middle Ages, but had been reduced to a few fragments by the seventeenth century. It was much the same story in north-east Scotland, where the five Cistercian houses were all founded in well-wooded districts. The king's writ ran but loosely in the wilder parts of Scotland, and woods in the Royal Forests became plundered of their timber and filled with grazing animals like everywhere else. Even so, it is surprising that the Scots did not do more to protect their woods considering how reliant they were on wood and timber. Perhaps they valued farmland more. Or possibly the endemic feuding of Scottish society meant that walls and fences were always being knocked down in tit-for-tat raids.

We will not follow the post-medieval history of the Forests in any detail. That book has already been written by N. D. G. James in his *A History of English Forestry.* By the mid-thirteenth century, the original purpose of the Forests as game reserves had given way to an increased emphasis on timber and wood production. Statutes were passed in 1482 and 1543 to safeguard coppice from grazing animals and to ensure that some trees were left standing when an area was felled. Crown woods were in general managed less intensively than private woods, and in time became valued more for their timber than their underwood. From the seventeenth century onwards, oak was widely planted, with varying degrees of success, and the worth of a Crown wood came to be judged in shipwright's terms: the navy wanted big branchy oaks with short trunks and numerous 'crooks' and 'knees' for shaping into a ship's rounded hull. By these standards at least, many Forests rated poorly. Wychwood was the subject of a scathing report by the Crown Commissioners at the outbreak of war with France in 1792. Not only did it possess few 'good Navy trees'; its fences were down and the coppices were full of freely roaming deer, cattle and swine, while the local poor were helping themselves to firewood. The woods of another Oxfordshire Forest, Shotover, had been disafforested 130 years earlier, after their stocks of underwood and timber were looted during the siege of Oxford at the end of the Civil War. Commoners were compensated with gifts of land and the remainder of the forest was leased to agricultural improvers who promptly grubbed up most of the remaining woodland.

Once the Forests had been disafforested and sold to private owners, parts, or sometimes even most, of the old woods were almost always immediately cleared. The Enclosure Acts gave landowners licence to do more or less what they liked, and that proved a fatal blow to many of the surviving woods. Hainault Forest in Essex was cut down to make way for third-rate agricultural land in 1851. The greater part of Wychwood followed a few years later when a thousand acres (400ha) of woodland were converted into a chessboard of neat square fields within sixteen months of its enclosure. Two-thirds of Bedford Purlieus in Rockingham Forest went the same way at about the same time. Epping Forest was narrowly saved from the same fate after a popular outcry forced through an Act transferring the landowning rights to the City of London and requiring its Conservators to 'protect the timber and other trees, pollards, shrubs, underwood, heather, gorse, turf and herbage growing on the Forest'.

In the 1920s, the Forestry Commission took over responsibility for Crown woods, and was required to put them to profitable use. Many of them had already been converted to broadleaved or mixed plantations before the Commission acquired them, and most of the others followed as wartime fellings gave an added impetus to plant up as much woodland as possible with profitable trees. The 1950s and 1960s saw the greatest loss of ancient and natural woodland in our history (see Chapter 10). Henry III would have difficulty recognising most of his Forests today. He would wonder where the unfamiliar coniferous trees came from and what their purpose was. He would worry about the neglect or absence of the underwood. Writs would fly. On the other hand he might be pleased about the number of deer sheltered by the dark boughs. If he looked more closely, with a woodman's eye for detail, he would begin to notice other familiar things. In some places, especially in the rides and around the edge, the ground flora would not have changed much; fewer primroses and violets maybe, and more dog's mercury, but at least not the alien transformation that has overtaken the canopy. Where underwood exists, that too would be recognisable, although there is more pure hazel or chestnut and fewer of the mixed coppices that Henry knew. From the few corners, here and there, where black hairstreak butterflies flit above old sloe bushes and nightingales sing in the dense young coppice, he would at least know that he was in the same country (though he might be puzzled by the call of collared doves!).

Where, if anywhere, would King Henry feel at home? Probably not at Wychwood, except among the ancient pollards of Woodstock, now part of the grounds of Blenheim Palace. He would search in vain for the original coppice compartments, with their earthen banks and hedges, the wooded pastureland and the open deer launds. The surviving core of Wychwood is now a shady place, a dense high forest of oak and ash and – oh dear! – Turkey oak and sycamore, except for the broad, straight, close-mown rides that slice through it like green canyons. But he might find some solace in the clear springs and fishponds in the middle of the wood, the natural limestone grassland glades and the overgrown quarries inhabited by the Roman snail. In nearby Shotover Forest, by contrast, Brasenose Wood still has an authentic thirteenth-century appearance: the underwood is cut on rotation, leaving a sprinkling of young standards, and the clearings are full of butterflies and wild flowers with neat piles of brushwood and log stacks.

But Brasenose is a very small wood. For a real medieval experience, it is hard to beat the New Forest which, minus its many enclosures, is the unique survivor of the commonland system. The Forest of Dean, the only other place which retains some vestige of its medieval administration, has long since been transformed into a huge oak plantation, and visitors presume it has always been like that. But most of

WOODLAND HERITAGE

ANCIENT WOODS
IN THEIR PRIME

Right: *A recently cleared coppice glade at Brasenose Wood, Oxfordshire. This is a real medieval woodland scene, although there are more standard oaks than was usual then and some spindly aspens have been spared for their nature conservation value. May 1984*

Above: *A different part of the same wood, coppiced about three years before and now forming a dense underwood of hazel and aspen beneath the oaks. This stage is particularly rich in wildlife. May 1984*

the features of medieval Forests still survive in compact form at Hatfield Forest in Essex, the subject of a recent monograph by Oliver Rackham. Here in the space of little more than a square mile one can find the coppices and pollards, warrens and pastures, ponds, streams and fens of an ancient medieval Forest, not 30 miles from the centre of London. Hatfield survived because it is so small. Instead of suffering the fate of nearby Hainault Forest in 1851, it was purchased in its entirety by a single owner who preserved it as a deer-park. There is probably not another square mile in Europe that has so rich an association of culture, landscape and wildlife, 'the only place', writes Rackham, 'where one can step back into the Middle Ages to see, with only a small effort of imagination, what a Forest looked like in use'.

But before leaving the Middle Ages, we should look at one other aspect of land management that has had a major influence on today's woods and their wildlife: the deer-parks.

Backdoor wilderness

Forests and chases were for the privileged few at the top of the social scale, but hundreds of lesser gentry possessed their own parks. These were not originally the grand vistas of avenues, lakes and planted trees of the era of Capability Brown, but rather miniature wildernesses, designed for the sport of kings 'on a layman's budget'. Like the Forests, medieval parks provided hunting, fresh venison and social dalliance against a backcloth of natural woodland and pollarded trees. They were most commonly stocked with fallow deer, an import from the Middle East which needed supplementary feeding in winter but, being only semi-wild, was well suited to the park conditions: the animals were always on display for their proud owner. The deer were confined by earthworks topped with cleft oak palings or a stone wall. Most parks were quite small, usually less than 200 acres (80ha), but they were very numerous and their total area was considerable. They were usually oval in shape since fencing was expensive and circular shapes ensured the largest area within the shortest boundary. The great age for park building was between 1200 and 1350, when the lord of the manor had little difficulty obtaining royal licence to enclose portions of Forest and could call on his feudal tenants to do all the necessary fencing and digging for nothing. After 1350, social changes and the sudden decline in population through plague and famine brought an end to cheap feudal labour, and, although some newly deserted land was enclosed as large open parks, few others were built in the later Middle Ages.

Most parks were carved out of *existing* woodland and waste, and so park woodland is a lot older than the park boundary, and in some cases probably thousands of years older and directly descended from the Wildwood. The earliest known park, Ongar Great Park, dates from late Saxon times, but essentially parks were, like the Forests, a Norman import, part of the Frenchification of old England (later on, they Frenchified Wales and lowland Scotland too). Before 1200, parks were playthings for those at the very top of the social scale, but increasingly they became status symbols for the lesser nobility and gentry, rather like a large yacht or private swimming pool today. In their heyday there were at least 1,800 parks in England, plus a smaller number in Scotland and Wales, scattered throughout the country at roughly one park to every 15 square miles (39km²), though denser in well-wooded counties like Herefordshire, Dorset, Worcestershire and Staffordshire. A few were very grand affairs. The royal park at Woodstock, one of the earliest, was, it seems, a most agreeable place. Henry I built a 9 mile stone wall around it and filled its woods and lawns with fountains, fishponds, gardens and a private zoo, probably in imitation of the Arabian water gardens so admired by the first crusaders. Most parks, though, were much more modest and were there for use, not mere decoration. Apart from venison, they provided pasturage, wood, quarried stone, peat,

ANCIENT WOODS
IN THEIR PRIME

Staverton Park, Suffolk. The enclosed fields within the park pale have alternated between arable and heath for at least the past two hundred years (details derived from G. F. Peterken, 1969)

pannage for swine, fishponds, stud farms, and warrens for that rare and delicate medieval creature, ~~the~~ rabbit. Some parks, especially large ones like Sutton Park near modern Birmingham, were divided into wood-pasture and coppice by inner compartments. But for all that, it is doubtful whether medieval parks ever made much money for their owners, since they were labour-intensive and expensive to maintain in good repair. Social prestige was much more important than money.

Many parks have long since fallen into ruin; some turned into woods called Park Wood or Out Wood; more have been ploughed, but are still discernible from surviving earthworks and curving field boundaries and hedgerows. Few retain all their original features, but they sometimes do still contain the most important one of all – their old pollarded trees, so vital to that sizeable element of our wildlife which needs aged bark and dead wood. Not a few insects and lichens owe their survival to medieval parks, for these Arcadian vistas of deer, cattle and sheep grazing placidly between grand old trees are among the oldest managed landscapes in Britain.

An example of medieval parkland at its most awe-inspiring is Staverton Park in the coastal Sandlings region of Suffolk, one of the places which has merited the close attention of the NCC's George Peterken, who is a secret Romantic. Staverton is a sylvan place of squat oak pollards with small crowns and straight-sided trunks like the legs of extinct elephants, set among glades carpeted with heather and grass and bordered with bracken. There are weirdly twisted trees like snakes or organ pipes, living sculptures resembling rock formations in underground caves with tufts of fern and even younger trees sprouting in their mighty clefts. There is also a jungle of monstrous hollies known as the Thicks. This extraordinary place is the product of time and stability. Its history is in fact unexceptional, although it used to be a valuable source of poles and wattle sticks in this predominantly treeless area, and also provided grazing for sheep, and sales from cut herbage and bracken, timber and bark. Staverton Park was in existence in the 1260s and a map of 1600 shows much the same scattering of oaks as we see today. There is an account of a cheerful monkish picnic there, five hundred years ago, when fun and games (*joco et ludo*) took place beneath the spreading boughs. Although some of the original park has since been ploughed, it remains essentially a medieval landscape with its pollard trees, its boundary bank with an external ditch, the sheep and the natural glades on acid windblown sand. Only the hollies, which provide much of Staverton Park's apparently timeless atmosphere, are, despite appearances, comparatively new. They all grew up after 1600, and might have originated from berries dropped by birds. Unlike the surrounding open heaths of the Suffolk Sandlings, the soils of Staverton Park are not leached, and retain their natural woodland profile. This is good evidence that the place has never been without trees, and the further evidence of drought-sensitive Atlantic lichens on the pollard underhangs confirms our suspicions that it is primary forest. It is now, very properly, a Site of Special Scientific Interest, unique in its prodigious growth of giant oaks, hollies, birches, rowans and hawthorns, 'showing the extreme forms adopted by these species after long and vigorous growth'.

5
WOODMANSHIP

The first woodmen

From the earliest times, man showed an understanding of the properties of different types of wood. The oldest wooden artefact in the world is a spear-shaft made of yew, found at Clacton in Essex, and made about forty thousand years ago, perhaps to throw at some passing mastodont. It would be hard to better the choice of wood. Since the Ice Age, the earliest evidence of man's use of wood comes from Star Carr in the Vale of Pickering, which was excavated between 1949 and 1953. Long ago this district was largely birch forest and swamp around a now vanished lake. A party of hunter-gatherers had built a platform among the reeds of birch brushwood, stones and clay for use as a base for hunting operations in the surrounding forest. Among the artefacts dug up by archaeologists ten thousand years later were a long thin paddle of birch, the earliest known navigational aid, and mysterious tightly rolled sheets of birch bark. These might have been floor-mats, roof covers, floats for fishnets, stores of resin for mounting arrow heads or tinder for starting fires – or, indeed, all of them. Just as the Highlanders did (until quite recently), these ancient tribes showed great inventiveness in adapting birch trees to their particular needs.

More recent surveys of Mesolithic camps in the southern Pennines suggest that woods were deliberately cut over to create open greens, full of tempting young shoots of alder, birch, rowan and hazel to attract game and provide a harvest of nuts and berries. Several excavated camps also reveal unnatural quantities of ivy pollen, probably from mounds of green ivy gathered as fodder to attract animals after the autumn leaf fall. This is all the more plausible when we reflect that, so far as we know, these people depended entirely on large wild animals, especially red deer, for meat and skins, and that swift-footed beasts in forest are difficult enough to shoot with rifles, let alone stone spears and arrows, unless they are first enticed into the open or rounded up by dogs. The results of these archaeological digs suggest that human hunter-gatherers had a greater impact on the Wildwood than was thought possible only a few years ago. There is evidence that in parts of Britain, especially around the upland fringes and the coast, some of the original woodland had already been replaced by a more open landscape long before the first farmers arrived. The abrupt fall in tree pollen and the corresponding rise of grassland and weeds is a sure sign of man, not nature. So too is the increase in seeds of fat-hen, nettles and chickweed, which were not then

It was not on Tower Hill that the axe made its most important contribution to English history.
Keith Thomas,
Man and the Natural World

69

A coppice clearing at Swanton Novers, Norfolk, showing a season's growth on the unusual high-cut lime stools of this wood. April 1989

A giant ash stool about six feet in diameter, a testament to centuries of regular cutting. Lobbett's Barrow, Dorset. May 1986

Inset: *The stark architecture of neglected small-leaved lime coppice, last cut about forty years ago. Here the stools are almost level with the ground. Easton Hornstocks, Northamptonshire. May 1989*

mere nuisances, as today, but the ingredients of a kind of porridge, nutritious enough if not particularly tasty. Tollund Man, that poor garrotted corpse dug out of the peat of Denmark some years ago, had eaten such a snack shortly before his untimely demise.

There were also changes taking place in the composition of woodland trees. The pollen record reveals a widespread sharp decline in birch and a corresponding rise in hazel around ten thousand years ago. Hazel is virtually fireproof and thrives on cutting, and so would have flourished under a slash-and-burn routine, which the Mesolithic peoples very probably employed. Hazel is moreover a useful tree, providing excellent browsing and delicious nuts, the charred remains of which are a common feature of Mesolithic camps. By contrast, birch and Scots pine are the most inflammable of our native trees, and on light soils they could have been set ablaze and the resulting open heath maintained by regular burning. At the moment, however, we do not really know whether these observed changes in wild woods were due to man or whether they arose principally from 'natural' climatic and biological causes.

The earliest evidence that man had acquired carpentry skills comes from the Somerset Levels. In the permanently wet peat of the Levels, which preserves wood from rotting, several wooden trackways have been discovered, the oldest of which dates from about 4000BC. This prehistoric duckboarding is made up of poles and rods of uniform size cut mainly from ash, hazel and oak. Straight pieces of young wood are hard to find in unmanaged woodland, and they indicate that the people of

WOODMANSHIP

Somerset were by then cutting underwood to produce a crop of suitable poles every twenty years or so. A modern coppice, managed on a long rotation, would produce exactly the sort of wood used to construct these trackways. The preserved wood includes well-crafted hazel wattles, all carefully trimmed and split with stone axes. Nor was this skill confined to Somerset. Recent excavations from the same remote period at Eskmeals in Cumbria also reveal an unexpected local knowledge of wood management and a capacity for skilled carpentry. The traditional crafts and customs of our native woods evidently have a six-thousand-year history.

Excavations at Flag Fen near Peterborough are providing one of the most fascinating glimpses so far into man's use of timber and woodland in the distant past. In autumn 1982, Dr Francis Pryor was commissioned by English Heritage to conduct a 'rescue dig' to look for evidence of the past beneath the surface of the fen, before the site was drained and built over. He was searching the side of a freshly cleaned ditch one foggy morning in November 1982 when he stumbled on a protruding log. Knowing that there were no living trees in the vicinity, he decided to start digging. Three weeks later, a mass of logs and planks had been uncovered along 80yd (73m) of the ditch, some of them bearing axe marks and pegged mortice-holes. A hasty radio-carbon test revealed that these timbers were some three thousand years old and belonged to a Late Bronze Age habitation on the edge of the Fens. Just how important a discovery this was did not become clear for some time, but boreholes dug into the surrounding fields indicated that the timbers extended over at least 2–3 acres (0.8–1.2ha). Some of the more recent finds have been startling: bronze and iron swords deliberately snapped in half, a pair of iron shears in their box, not unlike the ones in your shed, an impaled dog, a willow ladle, a human skeleton, apparently tossed, coffinless, into the swamp . . . And, above all, the vast collection of timbers of all shapes and sizes protruding from the muddy peat, some mere brushwood poles, others fashioned into posts, planks and beams.

This tangle of timber was once the platform of an artificial island, supporting seven wooden buildings and connected with the land by a long wooden causeway. To build it the local community had to find, cut and transport at least four million pieces of timber. It seems to have been constructed at a time of rising sea-level, when shallow waters were beginning to flood land that had once produced crops. The sea continued to rise in later centuries and eventually the island and its causeway were swamped by the tide and so lost to view that the Romans built a road straight over them without suspecting their existence. But the water and mud which entombed the site also preserved it, so that not only timbers but small seeds, twigs and insects, even sand sprinkled on wet floor surfaces, have survived the passage of centuries intact.

Archaeologists learn a great deal about man's use of timber, and, by extension, the early management of woods, from sites like Flag Fen. The smaller brushwood at the site is mainly willow, alder, poplar, ash and yew, which probably grew close by, around the edge of the Fens. Large ash trunks were laid as foundations, but most of the building timber was carefully worked oak, apparently from fast-grown trees about fifty years old, not, you will notice, virgin forest giants. Both the quantity and straightness of the oak pieces suggest strongly that they came from managed woodland, not primeval jungle. The builders of Flag Fen, like their successors, wanted small timbers for posts and supports: they had no use for thick trunks. They must have had an organised supply system since oak does not like wet ground and it probably came from further inland. Pollen evidence indicates that oak, along with elm, lime and hazel, then grew on the drier ground west of Peterborough, where Thorpe Wood lies today. Whatever the reasons were for constructing this elaborate and expensive edifice in the Fens, and the evidence so far suggests a sacrificial temple, wood in this quantity indicates organised production and transportation, social rights and obligations extending over a large area, and the knowledge and skill to build on an ambitious scale – in short, civilisation. If only these people had been able to write, our view of the accomplishments of prehistory might have been a great deal more respectful.

WOODLAND HERITAGE

WOODMANSHIP

The first industries

Until fairly recently, historians tended to assume that, because few documents survive from Roman Britain, the Romans must have made little impact on the native lives and landscapes, apart from their roads, walls and forts. But the sheer density of granaries, villas, potteries, ironworks and other hives of activity that have yielded to aerial photographs and the archaeologist's spade has forced a drastic upward estimate of the population and industrial potential of Roman Britain. It now appears that by the third century AD woodland covered no more than 15 per cent or so of the lowlands, and that much of that was intensively managed for timber and fuelwood. Even before the Roman conquest, we have Caesar's own word for it that south-east England was well populated. One commentator has gone so far as to suggest that 'large areas of the then British countryside must have looked not unlike the landscape of the seventeenth century on the eve of the Industrial Revolution'. The Britain of Queen Anne would not have been too unfamiliar to Queen Boadicea.

The Romans brought two innovations to a land which already possessed a high degree of native woodmanship. The first was better-quality forged-iron tools, including billhooks, which enabled the woodman to cut more and faster. The other was an unprecedented organised market and a national system of transporation for wood and timber. Romans lived in towns, which devoured fuel and timber for buildings, heated baths etc, and greatly expanded the native industries, especially the iron-smelters and potteries that depended on charcoal from local woods. The Ordnance Survey map of Roman Britain reveals that the densest industrial centres were in well-wooded districts like the Wye Valley, the edge of the Fens near Peterborough and the Weald. This set the pattern for the centuries which followed, and it was only with the replacement of charcoal with coke that the ironworks moved out of the woods to the open coalfields.

Industrial production on the Roman scale required enormous quantities of fuelwood. Unfortunately we have no direct knowledge of

A tangle of prehistoric timbers excavated at Flag Fen, Peterborough. The uprights are oak support posts and the planks once formed a platform for a prehistoric temple

Roman woodmanship in Britain, but it has been possible to gauge the scale of exploitation in some places. It took about 84 tons of wood to make a ton of iron. At Bardown, in the Sussex Weald, studies of ancient slag-heaps indicate that 32-37 acres (13–15ha) of woodland must have been cut over annually to feed the local blast-furnace. Since there were similar furnaces dotted all over the Weald, a rough calculation indicates an annual yield from some 23,000 acres (9,300ha) of woodland. If one adds the additional demand for land and wood from the work-force, this implies that much of the woodland in the Weald was managed for commercial production in the second century AD. But it did not destroy the woods, for in Saxon times this same area became the great *Andredeswald*, one of the biggest, wildest woods in all England, and it remains the most densely wooded part of England to this day. One lasting change the Romans did make in this area was to introduce sweet chestnut from southern Europe, which provided more usable coppice-wood per acre than native trees. Some of today's chestnut woods probably originate from those times: they are the oldest plantations in Britain.

Charcoal-burning

Probably most of us learn about charcoal-making, once the biggest single use of ancient woods in the North and West, from children's books like *Brendon Chase* and *Swallows and Amazons*. Charcoal provides the steady intense heat needed to smelt iron ore, and its production is an ancient art as old as the use of iron itself. The industries were based not only on, but *in* woods, since it was cheaper to bring the iron ore to the charcoal than the charcoal to the ore. It is a widely stated myth that charcoal-burning destroyed woods to feed the ravenous appetites of the blast-furnaces. Careful investigation of the evidence, especially (in Scotland) by J. M. Lindsay, suggests that the reverse is true, that many oakwoods in Wales, the Lake District and the Scottish Highlands were preserved *because* they were properly and profitably managed for wood production. It was the unfenced woods, used unsuitably to shelter cattle and sheep, that were, and are, dwindling.

As we have noted, charcoal-burning was big business in Roman times, and it continued on a large scale, after a possible pause in the Dark Ages, into medieval England and Wales. The forges of the Forest of Dean provided fifty thousand horseshoes for Richard the Lionheart's crusade. Machen Forest in Gwent produced 9,969 loads of charcoal in a single year, 1316, and the burners still had enough time left over to conduct a local war. But the real heyday of the industry was between 1550 and about 1750, when in Scotland and elsewhere iron-masters bought or leased large woods in remote places, removed the locals together with their livestock, and managed the wood intensively on a short coppice rotation. Most of the accounts of the charcoal-burner's way of life date from the end of this period, but there is every reason for believing that, like the woods themselves, it had not changed much over the centuries.

Charcoal is made by burning wood in controlled conditions with limited amounts of air. Most trees and shrubs can so be used, but

A charcoal hearth in Johnny's Wood, Borrowdale, Cumbria

coppiced oak, cut over every fifteen to twenty years, was the best. Charcoal from alder and juniper was preferred for making gunpowder because of the fine-grained powder produced. The coppice poles were felled by the woodmen, chopped up into standard lengths known as billets and tied into bundles. The charcoal-burners or 'colliers' then stacked the billets closely around a strong stake, the 'motty pin', in a clearing close by, to form a conical or domed mound some 20–40ft (6–12m) across and about 10ft (3m) high. Sometimes the burning took place inside a pit or, latterly, in steel kilns. On steep slopes, the mounds were made on specially levelled platforms called *hearths,* which are still a feature of many western woods. The completed mound was then covered with turves, surrounded by hurdles in the case of windy sites, and fired.

The burning could last for anything between twenty-four hours and a fortnight, and was regulated by vent-holes in the mound. During this phase the woods fumed with rising columns of smoke, which, from their distant vantage point, travellers of romantic sensibility found most edifying. Inside the wood, however, the smoke-blackened colliers were living squalid rough lives in wigwams made of poles, brushwood and turves, sometimes with their whole families. In summer, noted a visitor in 1800, the whole lot of them ran around naked 'and seemed not ashamed'. After the wood had burned through (signalled by a change in the smoke from grey and plentiful to blue and thin), the colliers opened the reeking mound, raked out the charcoal and, after leaving it to cool, shovelled it into sacks. In the mid-nineteenth century it sold for around ten shillings a ton.

During the late eighteenth century, coke from coal began to replace charcoal for smelters and glassworks, and, although charcoal was still needed, it could now be obtained as a by-product from the dry distillation of wood to make methylated spirit. This meant that, while the cordwood continued to be cut from ancient woods, the charcoal-burners in their wigwams gradually vanished from the woodland scene.

A charcoal mound ready for use, Dalavich Wood, Argyll. This must be a demonstration model, for the turf has begun to sprout!

Bizarre ruins deep in the woods. An eighteenth century tile kiln at Ebernoe Common, Sussex

Arthur Ransome remembered burners in Lake District woods at the beginning of the century, but in most woods today they are but a memory enshrined in names like Collier Wood and a thin layer of soot in the soil.

Tanbark

In one of those publications which were probably unremarkable at the time, but have since become important sources for the historian, Andrew Gilchrist, a Stonehaven forester, wrote a detailed account of the art of skinning an oak, shortly before that traditional practice disappeared. Oak bark is richer in tannic acid than that of other native trees, and this property once made it indispensable for tanning, the process of curing hides into leather by softening them in liquid in which bark has previously been soaked. Bark had been used for tanning for hundreds of years (was not William the Conqueror the grandson of a tanner?), but only as a relatively minor woodland by-product. The real surge in demand was from about 1780, reaching a peak during the Napoleonic wars, when high prices were paid for bark: Wellington's soldiers were shod and draped in leather. Coupled with the then fashionable zeal for improvement, bark production was an obvious incentive for owners to convert their scrubby, untidy woods into commercially organised coppices. After 1815, prices fell, and the demand for tanbark gradually declined until in the middle years of the century it collapsed; by then leather merchants could purchase imported tanning agents more cheaply than homegrown ones. The heyday of tanbarking was over by the 1870s, although small bark-stripping enterprises continue here and there to this day. While it lasted, the tanning industry gave a new lease of life to many former charcoal woods, and it perpetuated their management as coppices. Since it was still oak and little else that was wanted, however, oak was promoted in these woods at the expense of other native hardwoods, and the bark trade re-emphasised the myth that oak is the dominant tree of British woodland.

The best tanbark comes from young oaks, and to ensure the greatest possible yield woods were cut over every twenty years or so. Bark-stripping was a communal task, sometimes involving the whole family, and took place in the spring when the rising sap made it relatively easy to detach the bark from the boles. The cutter ring-barked the boles with a handbill close to the ground and again at about a yard in height before felling them with an axe and dressing the stools with his adze to prevent water from collecting on the stump and rotting it. The peelers, often women, then got to work with handbills and peeling irons, first beating the bark with mallets to ease the stripping process. The skill lay in removing as large a piece of bark as possible. There is a good description of the peelers at work in Thomas Hardy's novel, *The Woodlanders*, which refers to the 'curious sound . . . during the barking season, not unlike the quacking of ducks, with the tear of the ripping tool as it ploughed its way along the sticky parting between trunk and rind'. Following behind the cutters and peelers, another party, sometimes of children, gathered up the brushwood. The fresh bark was bound in bundles and brought to the shelter of the drying range, usually in an airy place within the wood, stacked neatly and left for two or three weeks. After scraping off any moss or lichen, the weathered bark was then carted off to storage sheds, or chopped up into squares there and then and put into sacks ready for the tanner.

Maintaining woods for oak tanbark was quite labour-intensive. Fences and walls had to be kept in good repair to exclude cattle and sheep, which could cause years of damage in a few hours. Drains had to be kept clean to raise the soil temperature and provide a larger feeding area for the roots. The oak stools had to be thinned two or three times to remove ill-grown shoots and ensure that the remaining two or three stems were sufficiently vigorous. Owners could offset some of their costs by selling barked wood and thinnings for spokes, crates, pitwood and fuel.

Many surviving oakwoods throughout Wales and in Argyll, Dumbarton, Stirling, Perth and Aberdeenshire were managed in this way. After the trade petered out in the 1880s, there was a short-lived revival during World War I, when imports were restricted by German U-boats. In some woods the coppice stools are still there, but in many more they have been killed by the shade, and many of the present-day oaks are maidens, planted in the vain expectation that ships would always be made of wood. Fortunately uneconomic woods are not always felled, since, in Andrew Gilchrist's words, 'oak is grown for ornament and shelter, as well as profit'.

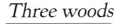

Three woods

To conclude this chapter, I have selected three examples of woods, each of outstanding interest for wildlife, which owe their present-day appearance to intensive exploitation in the past – though this may not be apparent at first sight. Two of them, Methven Wood and Glen Tanar, both in Scotland, stand for many other upland woods that have survived a pasture phase, then a commercial phase and latterly a phase of near-neglect. With our third wood, the Mens in Sussex, this unstable history is manifest in an extreme form, for the Mens is one of the wildest places in Britain today. All three show how important it is to know about the past in order to make sense of the present.

Methven Wood (Perthshire):
A SCOTTISH OAK COPPICE

Today well-preserved Scottish oak coppices are few and far between. The majority are in Perth, Stirling and Argyll but there is a scattering of others elsewhere. Methven Wood is one of the best, a compact 130 acre (52ha) oakwood perched 50ft (15m) above the River Almond. Like most ancient woods, it has its individual beauties and its mysteries – a vast ash stool in a drift of snowdrops, cliff-hanging alders, a big double-ditched bank which leads, apparently, nowhere. The wood is dominated by multiple stems of oaks rising from stools 6ft (1.8m) and more across. There is a straggly understorey of hazel and pole ash gasping for light,

Pages 78-9
Methven Wood, Perthshire. An overgrown Scottish oak coppice, now managed largely for the benefit of nature. September 1987

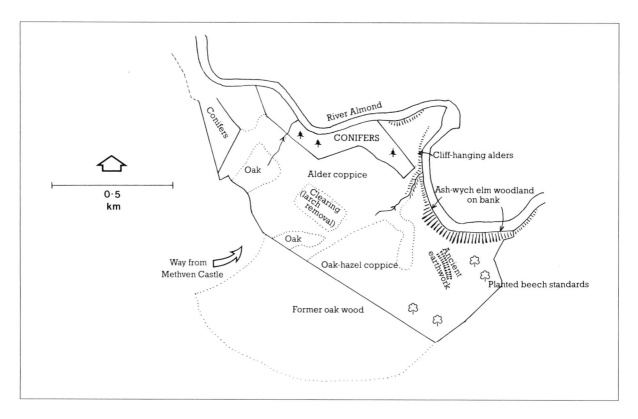

Methven Wood, Almondbank, Perthshire

thorns grey with feather lichens and exotic inclusions of spruces and pines, including a line of huge, shaggy Douglas firs.

As for most Scottish woods, the documentary records for Methven Wood go back only two hundred years or so, but we can be reasonably certain that it is ancient. Robert the Bruce camped hereabouts in 1306 and was chased out of the wood by the Earl of Pembroke leaving his cooking pots behind. The lairds of Methven were keen leading improvers three hundred years ago, gamely planting oak and other trees on bare moorland. In 1800, when demand for oak was at its peak, and bark and timber fetched high prices, Methven Wood was twice its present size and was divided into eighteen divisions, each cut over about once every twenty-five years. Some oaks were left as standards and sold as timber. The owner 'caused all the places deficient of oak shoots to be planted up with young oak plants as the yearly cutting advances'. Both species of oak seem to have been planted, although, as usual in Scotland, it is hard to tell the difference. Until the markets collapsed in the mid-nineteenth century, Methven Wood generated a good income from tanbark, spoke-wood and timber, whose combined sales totalled £3,310 between 1818 and 1841. Birch was cut in winter for fuel which was given to the poor. The wood must have been cut over at least twice, and today it is impossible to tell which oaks were planted and which are indigenous.

Methven Wood owes its survival to its beauty. In the late nineteenth century it ceased to be a working wood and became an amenity for the owners of Methven Castle, who laid out carriage drives, access roads and bridges between the castle and the wood and 'beautified' it with planted spruce, pine and beech. Later, half the wood was sold off, felled and planted with conifers. When these all fell down in a gale a few years ago, that part was cleared and put to grass, leaving an unnaturally straight southern boundary to what remains. Methven Wood is now a Site of Special Scientific Interest and, under the terms of a management agreement with the NCC, some of its exotic trees are being removed and natural regeneration encouraged by fencing.

Glen Tanar:

A WORKING PINE FOREST

'Saw an inch and rive a span / is the mark of a good Glen Tanar man' was a saying in the days when the pines of Glen Tanar provided work for a whole village of woodmen living in the depths of the forest. Glen Tanar is the most easterly of all the ancient Caledonian pinewoods, and one of the closest to a substantial timber market, in this case Aberdeen. Being so far east means that Glen Tanar receives less rain than the other native pinewoods. It has no forest bogs or natural lakes and not many trees other than the dense ranks of Scots pine which line its slopes. Exceptionally, there is even vigorous natural regeneration taking place on some of the stubbled pudding-basin hills between the tributary glens, the reverse of the situation in the picturesque but moribund pinewoods along the west coast. Glen Tanar is healthy in forestry terms, and the majority of its trees are comparatively young.

Although Glen Tanar is a native ancient wood it is no more a natural wilderness than any other British wood, although its size and dramatic scenery can certainly make it seem so. The glen has been inhabited for at least three thousand years, and the wood has been subject to commercial exploitation for at least the past three hundred. Between 1744 and 1865 most of the forest was cut over at least once, the trunks being converted into planks on the spot or floated by agile workmen down the River Dee to the shipyards of Aberdeen. Naturalists who visited the glen at this time returned disappointed and, probably, fuming. One of them, William MacGillivray, searched in vain for the majestic old 'Methuselahs' he had expected, noting only 'hundreds of stems not a foot in diameter' and lamenting the destruction of much of the forest. Apart from the trees, he grumbled, there was nothing interesting in Glen Tanar, 'the hills not being of great elevation, nor the streams of much beauty'.

In 1809, no fewer than eight thousand pines were advertised for sale, and purchasers were invited to take their pick from the forest. Even a wood as big as Glen Tanar could not have sustained felling on that scale, and it was fortunate for its survival that a wealthy English banker bought the estate in 1865 and turned it into a deer forest. The locals were turfed out of their homes and in their place the forest was filled with red deer. There was little subsequent natural regeneration, but at least some of the surviving trees now had a chance to reach middle age. Then, in 1920, part of the wood caught fire, a natural hazard of pinewoods, and thousands of trees burned down before rain eventually put out the blaze. The most recent natural disaster was the 1953 Great Gale, although the natural woodland lost fewer trees than nearby plantations.

Inside a native pinewood in Abernethy in Speyside. Scored and plated trunks, blue-green hummocks of blaeberry, and a many-textured underlayer of juniper and birch

Fortunately time is a great healer and ancient woods are resilient places. Glen Tanar could easily have been lost through mismanagement in the first half of the nineteenth century, as was the neighbouring Forest of Birse. It was threatened again by Canadian lumberjacks during World War II, but the laird managed to divert them to plantations nearby. Today Glen Tanar estate is restocking the wood using primarily methods of natural regeneration broadly compatible with its beauty and conservation value. The native pinewood is probably larger now than at any time in the past century and a half, and it is still one of the best places in all Scotland to look for crossbills, capercaillies, red squirrels, wildcats and birds of prey. It is still a place of solitude and great beauty, of the aroma of pine, the sound of running water and bird-song, and the exhilarating crispness of the clean hill air. Visitors repeating William MacGillivray's walk nearly 150 years ago will probably be a good deal more impressed with Glen Tanar than he was.

The Mens and the Cut (West Sussex):

WILDERNESS REVISITED

The Mens and the Cut: an individual name for an extraordinary place. Even that normally dry, restrained publication, the NCC's *Nature*

Conservation Review (1977), piles on the superlatives, commenting on its richness no fewer than four times:

> the lichen flora . . . is certainly among the richest for woodland in the south-east . . . the fungal flora . . . is one of the richest in Britain, and may even be the richest . . . entomologically, this site is regarded as extremely rich with many extremely rare beetles and thriving populations of most of the woodland butterflies.

WOODMANSHIP

The Mens fits like an irregular piece of jigsaw puzzle into the landscape of the Sussex Weald. It straddles an area of level ground but of complicated geology, around the headwaters of the River Arun, where acid sands join the Wealden clay, itself cut across by bands of limestone and sandstone. On the face of it, the Mens looks as close to a state of nature as anywhere in lowland Britain. There is no cultivated land within its bounds; probably there never has been. Instead we find a tremendous diversity of woodland plants and animals, trees in all shapes and sizes and an abundance of dead standing wood, all features associated with virgin forest. Surely, here is a wood that history passed by.

All of which goes to show how misleading appearances alone can be. The Mens has a thousand-year documented record of human use, beginning with a Saxon charter revealing that it was then wood-pasture with grazing rights, like much of the rest of the Weald. 'Mens' is probably derived from the Saxon word *gemaene* meaning a common. Throughout the Middle Ages, the Mens was less wooded than it is today, but the only surviving hints of its original use are a few old pollard trees and islands of grass and scrub among the trees. In Tudor times, coppice wood from the Mens supplied charcoal for nearby blast-furnaces and glassworks. These past uses have all influenced the present-day ecology of the wood. Ruth Tittensor, who has investigated the history of this place in considerable detail, suggests that air pollution from Tudor smelters might have eliminated certain sensitive species of lichen which have been unable to recolonise the site.

A hundred years ago parts of the common were enclosed illegally by the then lord of the manor, a timber merchant. The fences were removed after a successful High Court action brought by the commoners, but since 1882 cutting and grazing have virtually ceased. Most of the woodland we see today is actually the product of the past hundred years in which the ancient pattern of scrub, pollards and grass was gradually submerged beneath the present one of dense oaks, beeches, falling trees and rotting wood.

The 'naturalness' of the Mens is therefore an illusion: it is really a common gone wild. Nevertheless, despite the various episodes in its history, it is a truly ancient place. The structure and variety of the soils indicate that they have never been tilled, and there were probably always some trees and woods present. It is this essential *continuity* which, despite a complex and unstable history, has handed down to us virtually intact one of the richest floras and faunas in Britain. The Mens is now safe in the hands of the Sussex Naturalists Trust. It has become an experiment in non-management: here man has for once taken a step back from his apparent control of nature. He has become a mere observer, waiting patiently to see what will happen next.

Is there not room in our crowded island for a few more places like this?

6

FLOWERS OF THE FOREST

Introduction: coping with shade

From the moment you set foot inside a wood the climate changes abruptly. The wind drops, the humidity rises, and, although the tree-tops may bend and shiver, far below all is still and you can breathe the sweet smells of decomposition and hear faint rustles in the undergrowth. At midday in the summer it will feel cooler than the open land outside; in the winter, warmer (you rarely find frost deep inside a wood). The light is of course subdued, still comparatively bright beneath the gentle dappling of mature ash, but dark as a cave under overgrown coppice by late afternoon in summer. As photographers know, the woodland floor receives most light when the sun is veiled by thin cloud, since the sun's rays are then diffused and can filter through the canopy from many angles. But in bright sunshine at midday the floor becomes a chaotic pattern of deep shadow and pools and flecks of light, confusing the eye and shrouding detail – and defying the photographer's best efforts. Woodland soil and ground vegetation also receive less direct rainfall than open land, since most raindrops are captured by the leafy canopy and evaporate, or trickle down the trunks to be taken up by mosses and other epiphytes before reaching the ground. On the other hand the enormous rate of transpiration from woodland foliage keeps the air moist and humid, and dense woods, or those on badly drained soil, are often squelchy underfoot even on dry days.

Given the internal climate of a wood, it is paradoxical that nearly all woodland flowering plants need warmth and sunlight. Few of them flower well in permanent shade and what they need from the wood is rather a degree of protection from heavy grazing, drought and other hazards. Woodland flowers can be classified according to the different ways in which they overcome the problems of shade into 'shade-evaders', 'shade-avoiders', and 'shade resisters'. The shade-evaders include many of the best-loved woodland flowers, the bluebells, primroses, wood anemones, lesser celandines and others which contribute their colours to the beautiful patchwork of woodland floors in April and May. These all flower and manufacture most of their food while the trees are still bare and at least a third of the light of spring can reach the woodland floor. They are particularly well attuned to coppice cycles, which alternate regular periods of light and shade in which these plants can flower in profusion for a few years without being overwhelmed by aggressive colonisers like thistles or willowherbs.

Coppice seems to benefit most woodland flowers, and some which were once thought to prefer shade have since been revealed in their true colours as light-demanders. One example is the rare yellow sedge, *Carex flava*, which grows only in Roudsea Wood nature reserve in the Lake District, along a narrow zone where a limestone pavement runs into a peat bog. This plant was supposed to be a shade species – why else did it grow in a wood? – so trees were planted on top of it. Luckily its further progress was monitored by the reserve warden, who noticed that *Carex flava* was reacting with a conspicuous lack of enthusiasm, increasing only in another part of the wood that had lately been thinned. What it needed in fact was not dappled shade but dappled *light*. Which all goes to show the advantage of field observation over merely reading books.

The species mentioned thus far are all long-lived plants which survive vegetatively under shade, producing flowers whenever enough light returns. Others grow up from buried seed, stimulated by the sudden access of light after coppicing or felling. These are chiefly species with short life-spans which produce large amounts of seed, such as foxglove and various species of spurges, rushes and St John's-worts. They behave rather like garden weeds, shooting up from buried seed on bare ground in rides and glades, or in places which have recently grown boggier. Their seeds can lie dormant in the soil for a long time, which might account for the occasional sudden appearance from nowhere of spurges and other plants. The record so far seems to be 125 years, held by the wood spurge.

A much smaller number of flowering plants grow more vigorously under shade and decline initially after coppicing. They are typically plants with broad flat leaves which grow in dense carpets, smothering other vegetation. Heading the list of these *shade-resisters* is dog's mercury, which is commonest in older coppice, especially on chalk and limestone. It is probably more common in ancient woodland today than in the Middle Ages, since it is sensitive to trampling and comes into its own in neglected woods. Other plants typical of shady woods include ramsons, herb paris, dewberry, enchanter's nightshade and wood woundwort. The latter pair are more common in secondary woods, and in ancient ones tend to occupy disturbed places like the sides of paths. Certain flowers, like primrose and oxlip, combine both shade-evading and shade-resisting tactics, growing most vigorously after coppicing but persisting for a long time under shade, although permanent deep shade would probably eliminate them in the end.

In deep, lasting shade, under old hornbeam pollards, for example, or high forest beech on rich soils, few wild flowers can survive, and the floor is dominated by fallen leaves with struggling tufts of grasses and moss cushions here and there. But a few species manage to grow successfully in the gloom by deriving their substance in unorthodox ways, thus avoiding the need for sunlight. Woodland orchids rely for help on a fungus living within their swollen roots, and among those characteristic of ancient woodland are the greater butterfly orchid, early purple orchid, fly orchid and several species of helleborine. The most extreme practitioners of this art, bird's-nest orchid and ghost orchid, and the unrelated yellow bird's-nest, lack chlorophyll and feed like toadstools on the deep layer of humus and leaf mould in shaded woods.

Toothwort is an interesting variation on this theme. Like the bird's-nest orchid it lacks all greenery, but it obtains food supplies not by imitating fungi but by tapping the roots of woodland trees, especially elm, maple and hazel. Stressed trees, such as recently coppiced stools, are particularly vulnerable to attacks of toothwort. Jonathan Spencer tells me that he has often found its bunched, bone-white flowers by paths where pounding human feet or deer hooves have damaged the tree roots. Although it does not need much light to grow, toothwort is pollinated by bumble-bees and, perhaps in order to attract them when they are at their busiest, it flowers in the spring, often in open woodland.

Shade-avoiders are woodland plants which are not adapted to shade at all, and grow only in the permanent open spaces within a wood, along the rides, in natural clearings or around the edge. They have been called 'circumboscal' – meaning around, but not in, woods – and they frequently outnumber the shade plants. In Bedford Purlieus, for example, no fewer than 288 species out of a magnificent total of 462 grow in grassland, marsh or disturbed ground within the wood; a further 24 grow in ponds. Thus, in intensively farmed districts, ancient woods may form a refuge for grassland and marshland flowers as well as woodland ones. The advance of agriculture has in effect turned certain grassland flowers like betony and devil's-bit scabious into woodland ones.

The less common wild flowers of a wood are often found on the boundary between two contrasting habitats: between pondwater and dry land for instance, or between a grassy ride and the trees behind. And a few of them seem to specialise in growing *near* woods, rather than actually inside them. The best-documented is the rare crested cow-wheat, a singular plant with pagoda-like stacks of spiky multicoloured flowers. Although I have seen it just inside Monk's Wood in Cambridgeshire, in the boundary ditch in fact, it more often grows in hedgerows where woods *used* to be, along with woodland 'relics' like bluebells and dog's mercury.

Flowers that grow around the wood's periphery or in its open spaces have suffered greater losses than those adapted to shade. There are probably few ancient woods in the Midlands and East Anglia that retain a broad border of herb-rich grassland and scrub; more often the waving wheat ripples right up the woodbank. There are also fewer permanent spaces in woods than there were before 1950. Forestry grants compel owners to fill them in with trees, while in neglected woods they scrub over naturally: either way the open spaces are lost. Spaces too wet for trees get drained. The result is illustrated most dramatically by the decline of flowers like the saw-wort, which has gone from all but one of its former woodland stations in Cambridgeshire after neighbouring farmers ploughed up the grassy wood borders on which it grew. The removal of these sheltered flower-rich places also means that many insects, especially butterflies, bees and solitary wasps, lose one of their principal habitats. Perhaps it is no accident that the reddish buff, a species of moth unlucky enough to need saw-wort at mealtimes, has become one of Britain's rarest insects.

FLOWERS OF THE FOREST

I know a bank whereon the wild thyme blows,
Where oxlips and the nodding violet grows,
Quite over-canopied with luscious woodbine,
With sweet musk-roses, and with eglantine.

A Midsummer Night's Dream
II.i.242-245

Flowers as historical signposts

One of the most obvious differences between ancient and secondary woodland is in the composition of the ground flora. A small wood in my own parish, called Wothorpe Grove, contains both kinds. The edge of the wood has an earth bank and just inside it the flowers and shrubs are typical of ancient limestone woods in Northamptonshire. The biggest trees – three giant cherries and a line of beeches along the bank – were probably planted for timber, but there are several native limes and a large wych elm stool inherited from the Middle Ages. The underwood contains a large proportion of Britain's native shrubs, some of which, like spindle and Midland hawthorn, are confined to ancient woodland in this part of England. The flowers too are numerous. None are rare, although a few, like wood goldilocks, often turn up in interesting woodland, but on returning to them each year I find them in the same places, not scrambling over each other for light and space but inhabiting their own particular niche as if tended by an invisible gardener. There is a lot to see within this five-hundred-yard stretch of wood, especially when one adds all the mosses, toadstools and – a local speciality – slime moulds. I would expect to find much the same scene, if the wood is spared, fifty years hence, and would not be greatly surprised if Thomas Cecil, who built the now ruinous Wothorpe Towers above the wood four hundred years ago, would recognise it at once.

Walking further into the wood, however, we meet change. The ground is suddenly heaved into hummocks and boggy dells – the inside of the wood is in fact an old quarry which tumbled down again into woodland after it was abandoned, probably in the nineteenth century. Thomas Cecil might have got his building stone from here. And in this part of the wood we find not stability but riot. There are brambles galore and carpets and banks of ivy spilling down from crooked ash trees. There are more nettles there now than two years ago and in places the luxuriant herbage is topped by a froth of cow parsley and hogweed. At first sight this is a wilder place than the nearby ancient wood, but its constituent plants are those of hedgerows, wasteland and rubbish dumps, not woodland. It is in fact typical vegetation of disturbed ground, although in this case the disturbance is not recent.

What emerges from places like Wothorpe Grove is that new woods do not acquire woodland flowers overnight. Plantations on farmland are quickly taken over by aggressive plants bounding in from the hedgerow and revelling in the nitrate-laden soil. We do not really know how long it takes for a recently planted farm wood to become carpeted with primroses and wood anemones, but for those surrounded by arable fields in the east of England the answer may very well be that they never do. Even after the passage of two or three hundred years it is usually possible to tell the difference between ancient woods and recent ones. The inside of Wothorpe Grove may eventually stabilise and acquire more woodland species, since the younger part lies next to the old without an intervening gap, but once the soils have become disturbed they take a very long time to revert to their original condition. The sites of long-abandoned settlements in woods are betrayed by patches of elders and nettles, since wherever humans spend much time the soil accumulates high doses of phosphate from bonfire ash, bones and rubbish.

But even if conditions are perfect, many woodland flowers cannot spread quickly because that is not their nature. Flowers like wood anemone and lily-of-the-valley are poor colonisers, producing relatively little fertile seed. An extreme example, the coralwort, rarely if ever ripens seed in Britain, relying instead on small bulbils which develop in the leaf axils beneath the spray of lilac flowers. It is restricted to moist soils in some of the Chiltern beechwoods and along the banks of woodland streams in the Weald, and its isolated colonies are probably all long-standing ones. Poor powers of spread did not matter in the least during that long, tranquil era when most of Britain was one big wood and all a plant needed to do to survive was cling like a limpet to its own patch of soil. In modern conditions though, opportunism is proving a better survival tactic than mere persistence. Elders and nettles are increasing, while the fate of wood anemone and coralwort is closely linked to that of ancient woodland, and that can only mean decline since ancientness is, by definition, a fixed asset.

In most districts of Britain, but especially in the South and East, it is possible to compile lists of flowering plants and ferns which are found in ancient woods but rarely in hedges or recent secondary woodland. One of the most thorough surveys of this kind was undertaken in central Lincolnshire by my more famous colleague George Peterken during the 1970s. It produced the results shown on these two pages.

About 174 species of flowers and ferns occur regularly in Lincolnshire woodland, of which 62 are more common in ancient woods than secondary ones. Some of the latter rarely colonise recent woodland, and if you find pendulous sedge, sweet woodruff, yellow pimpernel, cow-wheat, bird's-nest orchid or herb paris in mid-Lincolnshire you are almost certainly standing in an ancient wood. Such plants are therefore useful to a woodland historian who will keep an eye out for them. They help to endow a wood with meaning, being important clues in the detective game of discovering the past. A glance at Peterken's lists will show that there is nothing rare or exotic about most of them – they include old friends like wood-sorrel, lily-of-the-valley and columbine.

In Lincolnshire the polarisation between ancient woodland plants and 'weeds' of wayside and hedgerow is particularly pronounced. Most woods in the county are isolated from one another by intensive farmland, and in this relatively dry area it is only in woodland that plants are assured of permanently moist soil and cool, humid air. In western counties more of them grow outside woods. Some of the earliest evidence of this 'East–West divide' was adduced by one of the founding fathers of British plant ecology, Prof Ronald Good, who spent much of the Second World War tramping along Dorset lanes looking for primroses. He found them wherever his feet met damp clays and loams, but not when the soil switched to chalk or sand. In the west of the county primroses were common in hedges as well as woods, but in the east they were found mainly in woodland. The primrose, then, needs moist deep soils rather than woodland *per se*, but in eastern England the one often depends on the other.

Since the geography of Britain is so varied, it is dangerous to

Fast-colonising species present in both ancient and recent secondary woods

Cuckoo-pint
Slender false-brome
Enchanter's nightshade
Broad buckler-fern
Male fern
Narrow buckler-fern
Broad-leaved willowherb
Giant fescue
Herb Robert
Wood avens
Ground ivy
Ivy
Twayblade
Honeysuckle
Three-veined sandwort
Rough meadow-grass
Dewberry
Bramble
Wild raspberry
Blood-vein dock
Sanicle
Wood woundwort
Black bryony
Red campion
Sweet violet
Stinging nettle
Hairy brome

Shade-tolerant species frequent in secondary woods but scarce in ancient woods except on tracks, disturbed ground etc

Ground elder
Hedge garlic
Cow parsley
Greater burdock
Lesser burdock
False oat-grass
White bryony
Rosebay willowherb
Creeping thistle
Spear thistle
Cock's-foot
Common hemp-nettle
Goosegrass (Cleavers)
Hogweed
White dead-nettle
Nipplewort
Common forget-me-not
Annual meadow-grass
Wild strawberry
Creeping cinquefoil
Broad-leaved dock
Woody nightshade
Chickweed
Dandelion
Hedge parsley
Ivy-leaved speedwell
Field pansy

Pendulous sedge, Carex pendula. *The fawn brushes are male flowers, the pendant rat's tails, female. Later in the year the former will wither and the latter grow even longer. Bedford Purlieus, Northamptonshire. May 1989*

Wood spurge, Euphorbia amygdaloides. *Bedford Purlieus, May 1989*

Toothwort, Lathraea squamaria. *A leafless parasite, deathly pink flower-clusters, like a set of dentures for a horse. Sturt Copse, Oxfordshire. April 1985*

generalise too freely about 'ancient woodland indicator species'. Lists of plants associated with ancient woodland can be very useful but they need to be based on local knowledge, and it should be borne in mind that widespread plants grow more vigorously in some districts, and in certain soils, than others. Bluebell woods usually prove ancient in Norfolk and Warwickshire but not, oddly enough, in Cambridgeshire, and certainly not along the western seaboard where bluebells carpet hillsides and sea-cliffs. The wood spurge is a reliable indicator of ancient woodland in East Anglia and on the acidic Oxford clay, but it is widespread in secondary woodland on chalk and limestone in southern England.

In places where native woodland is unusually thick on the ground, like the Sussex Weald, the North Downs or the Cotswolds plateau, one would be hard put to find any tree, flower or fern which ecologists, lovers of order and nature's hidden patterns, could seize on as an infallible sign of ancient woodland. Old stools of small-leaved lime possibly, or the hay-scented buckler fern, of which more hereafter, but, in the south of England at least, both are too rare to be of much use. Nevertheless, although the presence or absence of individual 'ancient woodland plants' is not always significant, the *total number* of species supported by a given wood definitely is. The table shown here lists the plants which NCC surveyors use in evaluating woodland for conservation purposes. They do not claim that any of them are confined to ancient, natural woods, but woods containing a suite of twenty or more of them are nearly always interesting places with a past. If these

Woodland plants in southern England which are 'most strongly associated with ancient woodland and are typical components of botanically rich ancient woodland communities'. This list, prepared by Drs Richard Hornby and Francis Rose, is used by the NCC in woodland survey and evaluation. It omits rare species found only in a small number of woods.

* These species are only counted if they occur well within the wood and are not obviously planted.
SE: Kent, Surrey, Sussex, London and Hertfordshire
S: Hampshire, Wiltshire, Buckinghamshire, Berkshire and Oxfordshire
SW: Cornwall, Devon, Somerset, Avon and Dorset

Trees and shrubs

	SW	S	SE
Alder buckthorn	x	x	x
Aspen	x	x	x
Crab apple*	x	x	x
Field briar	x	x	x
Field maple*	x	x	x
Guelder rose*	x	x	x
Holly	x	x	x
Hornbeam*		x	x
Midland hawthorn		x	x
Red currant*	x	x	x
Sessile oak*	x	x	x
Small-leaved lime*	x	x	x
Whitebeam (all species)	x		
Wild cherry	x	x	x
Wild service tree	x	x	x
Wych elm	x	x	x

Flowers

	SW	S	SE
Allseed		x	
Barren strawberry	x	x	x
Bastard balm	x		
Beautiful St John's-wort	x	x	x
Betony	x	x	x
Bilberry	x	x	x
Bird's-nest orchid	x	x	x
Bitter vetch	x	x	x
Black bryony	x	x	x
Bluebell	x	x	x
Broad-leaved helleborine	x	x	x
Bush vetch	x	x	x
Butcher's broom	x	x	x
Chaffweed		x	
Climbing corydalis	x	x	
Columbine*	x	x	x
Cornish moneywort	x		
Cow-wheat	x	x	x
Early dog-violet	x	x	x
Early purple orchid	x	x	x
Golden-rod	x	x	x
Greater burnet-saxifrage			x
Greater butterfly orchid	x	x	x
Green hellebore	x	x	x
Herb paris	x	x	x
Ivy-leaved bellflower	x		x
Lady orchid			x
Large bitter-cress		x	x
Lesser skullcap			x
Lily-of-the-valley*	x	x	x
Marsh violet	x	x	x
Meadow saffron	x	x	
Monkshood	x		
Moschatel	x	x	x
Narrow-leaved everlasting pea	x	x	x
Narrow-leaved lungwort	x	x	
Narrow-lipped helleborine		x	
Nettle-leaved bellflower	x	x	x
Opposite-leaved golden saxifrage	x	x	x
Orpine	x	x	x
Pignut	x	x	x
Primrose*	x	x	x
Ramsons	x	x	x
Sanicle	x	x	x
Saw-wort		x	x
Solomon's seal	x	x	x
Small teasel	x	x	x
Spurge laurel	x	x	x
Stinking iris	x	x	x
Sweet woodruff	x	x	x
Sword-leaved helleborine			x
Three-veined sandwort	x	x	x
Toothwort	x	x	x
Tutsan	x	x	x
Violet helleborine		x	x
Water avens	x	x	
Wild daffodil*	x	x	x
Wood anemone	x	x	x
Wood goldilocks	x	x	x
Wood-sorrel	x	x	x
Wood speedwell	x	x	x
Wood spurge	x	x	x
Wood vetch	x	x	x
Yellow archangel	x	x	x
Yellow pimpernel	x	x	x

Grasses, sedges and rushes

	SW	S	SE
Bearded couch	x	x	x
Creeping soft-grass	x	x	x
Giant fescue	x	x	x
Greater wood-rush	x	x	x
Hairy brome	x	x	x
Hairy wood-rush	x	x	x
Pale sedge	x	x	x
Pendulous sedge*	x	x	x
Remote sedge	x	x	x
Smooth-stalked sedge	x	x	x
Southern wood-rush	x	x	x
Thin-spiked wood-sedge	x	x	x
Wood barley		x	
Wood club-rush	x	x	x
Wood meadow-grass	x	x	x
Wood melick	x	x	x
Wood millet	x	x	x
Wood-sedge	x	x	x
Wood small-reed	x	x	x

Ferns and fern allies

	SW	S	SE
Beech fern	x		
Golden-scaled buckler-fern	x	x	x
Hard fern	x	x	x
Hard shield-fern	x	x	x
Hart's-tongue fern*	x	x	x
Hay-scented buckler-fern	x		x
Narrow buckler-fern	x	x	x
Polypody (all species)	x	x	x
Soft shield-fern	x	x	x
Sweet mountain fern	x	x	x
Tunbridge filmy-fern	x		
Wood horsetail	x	x	x

species make a good showing in a small isolated wood we can be reasonably confident that the wood is ancient. Large woods, like Wytham Wood near Oxford, are often more complicated – mixtures of ancient woodland and secondary woodland, and planted and natural woodland. Some of the secondary woodland at Wytham is almost as flower-rich as the older parts for there are few intervals of open ground to form ecological barriers. But Charles Gibson, who, unusually for an Englishman, lives in the middle of the wood, nevertheless detects certain differences. In particular, ramsons, herb paris, nettle-leaved bellflower, toothwort, violet helleborine and a few other species, most of which, incidentally, are shade-tolerant, seem to be the 'hard-line' ancient woodland indicators at Wytham, stubbornly refusing to move far from their aboriginal homes.

The richest woods for flowering plants in Britain are all ancient woods. They may contain upwards of 250 species, including at least half of those listed in the table. What kind of woods are they? In East Anglia, the best woods of all tend to be ash-maple-hazel woods on boulder clay which have been cut over as coppice until recently. The well-known Bradfield Woods in Suffolk have been managed uninterruptedly in this way for at least seven hundred years. Possibly Bradfield was always rather exceptional because of its variety of natural soil types but, because of its unique record of continuous management, it has also lost fewer species than the others (though even Bradfield has lost four). In the South, most of the richest woods are larger than 100ha (250 acres), but one exceptionally diverse place, Sydlings Copse in Oxfordshire, occupies a mere 2ha (5 acres). In Kent, the richest woods lie on the dip slopes of the North Downs and contain a mixture of lime-rich soils and acidic plateau clays. The western half of the Weald is another area of exceptional ancient woods, especially where there are local limestone outcrops, as at the Mens and Ebernoe Common. The single richest wooded area in the South, and possibly in the whole country, is the Wealden Edge Hangers in Hampshire, a string of hanging woods extending along 12 miles of a steep chalk scarp. One might have expected woods on chalk or limestone to be richer in species than those on acidic soils but, surprisingly, this has not been borne out by experience, probably because chalk woods tend to be rather dry and uniform, whereas acid-clay woods often contain non-woodland habitats like flushes, marshes, ponds and rides.

WOODLAND HERITAGE

FLOWERS OF THE
FOREST

The race is not to the swift,
nor the battle to the strong . . .

Ancient woodland flowers often grow in patches, which implies that they spread vegetatively rather than by seed. Such indications as we have suggest that woodland vegetation is remarkably stable and can change little even after centuries. When a new area of woodland grows up on neglected ground nearby, the rate at which plants can colonise it varies from species to species. The speed of advance of different plants has actually been measured at Hayley Wood in Cambridgeshire and Short Wood in Northamptonshire. At the former, oxlip is creeping at a

Oxlips in managed coppice,
Knapwell Wood,
Cambridgeshire. April 1971

Wood melick, Melica uniflora.
An attractive grass, often found
on raised wood-banks, as here.
Brasenose Wood, Oxfordshire,
May 1985

snail's pace – about a yard (or metre) per year – into an adjacent triangle of secondary woodland. But dog's mercury is moving in faster, and bluebell faster still. Sanicle, normally one of the slower spreaders, has managed to colonise the edge of the path through the 'Hayley Wood triangle', probably because its hooked fruits stick to the trousers of botanists measuring the advance of oxlips and bluebells. At Short Wood in Rockingham Forest, dog's mercury has spread 25yd (23m) down a hedge planted on the north side of the wood in the late eighteenth century, at an average speed of roughly 6in (15cm) per year; but it has progressed about 100yd (90m) along a hedge on the south side which has been in existence since at least 1635.

The remarkable persistence of woodland ancient plants means that they can survive along the 'ghost boundary' of former woods in hedges. At 'Judith's Hedge' near Monk's Wood in Cambridgeshire, a patch of dog's mercury has persisted long after the original wood was cleared, but has barely begun to spread into the adjacent hedgerows, planted 150 years ago. These few very modest plants are therefore historical artefacts, as significant as antique coins or fragments of pottery. And like pottery, their value lies not in themselves but in the association of that particular plant in that particular place.

A sense of place

A walk through any ancient wood reveals how the flora changes from place to place in a kaleidoscope whose facets are governed by soil, shade and water (but not usually the species of tree). Well-drained but still

FLOWERS OF THE
FOREST

moist soil may carry a carpet of bluebells or yellow splashes of wild daffodil, while boggy ground by a stream is likely to be a place of sedges and towering marsh thistles. Deep soil may be heavily shaded by well-grown trees harbouring a smelly expanse of wild garlic. Steep north-facing banks are especially favoured by mosses and ferns. I do not propose to go into any detail about natural woodland vegetation, which has already been given a thorough airing in numerous books, but rather to concentrate on the life strategies of individual species, and in particular three well-known flowers typical of ancient woodland: bluebell, wood-sorrel and dog's mercury (or boggart). Enough is known about these to suggest why they grow where they do, and in particular why they are tied to ancient woodland in some districts but not others. Let them stand in the place of many other woodland flowers which have not yet received the same attention but which are likely to share some of their characteristics.

LAKES ON DRY LAND: THE CASE OF THE BLUEBELL

Gerard Manley Hopkins got it right: 'brakes wash wet like lakes'. No woodland scene has the power to move the heart more than a bluebell wood in May. The massed flowers seem to shimmer like a lake, reflecting and scattering the light so that the separate plants dissolve in the wash of blue. This is one of the sights of nature which plant-lovers come to Britain to see, for it is only in our moist climate, and in a few other places along the Atlantic seaboard of Europe, that bluebells grow in profusion. Yet, despite its abundance, the bluebell is quite a demanding plant. Its deep roots become waterlogged if the water level is too high, but since its fleshy, sappy leaves have poor powers of water conduction it cannot grow on very dry soils either. In damp woods, therefore, bluebells cling to raised banks and mounds or, as at Bedford Purlieus in Northamptonshire, to pockets of well-drained soil. On very dry soils, by contrast, one seeks the bluebell in hollows and other places which are never dry for long. But, providing that the water content is right, the bluebell is reasonably accommodating. It is perhaps most common on moderately acid, sandy loams, often growing with bracken, creeping soft-grass and wood anemone, but it can be found in clay woods and chalky hangers and under all kinds of trees from birch to hornbeam.

Botanists living in the eastern half of Britain have long associated bluebells with old, undisturbed woods. In 1925 Sir Hugh Beevor wrote of his own county, Norfolk, that 'Our original woods may, I believe, be readily identified, because every wood containing the wild hyacinth I take to be such. Outside the wood, bluebells rarely appear in the hedgerows, if so, they proclaim a woodland that has disappeared.' The truth of this assertion was later demonstrated for another county, Warwickshire, when a resident schoolmaster, G. H. Knight, found on investigation that the bluebell was virtually restricted to woods known or reasonably suspected to be ancient, and was seemingly unable to colonise new sites. Knight deduced an explanation in terms of the bluebell's limited powers of dispersal, its lack of seed dormancy and the lack of suitable conditions for germination outside its isolated woodland sites. Exceptionally among woodland plants, bluebells regenerate almost entirely by seed. These are comparatively large, spilling from holes in the dry papery seed-packets like coal from a scuttle, and most of them probably land within a few inches of the parent plant, unless propelled a little further by a human boot or some other large animal brushing past.

Bluebells are 'shade-evaders', blossoming in the spring, especially after recent thinning or coppicing. Their main pollinators are bumble-bees and they may therefore depend on the periodic availability of sunlit bee-loud glades. Knight suggests that many bluebell carpets are a survival from the aboriginal forest. If so, the bluebell vistas we enjoy each spring may be unfathomably old, waxing and waning according to the vicissitudes of light, climate and woodmanship, but essentially changing little. Such stability calls for remarkable powers of persistence, and here the bluebell scores highly. The shoots of all woodland plants need to be tough enough to push through the surface litter each year, and in the bluebell's case there is added power in numbers, for its massed, robust leaves simply push any competitors aside and shade them out. Like many woodland plants, bluebells are poisonous, containing glycosides similar to those found in the foxglove, and are therefore avoided by native woodland animals, although horses and cattle are apparently stupid enough to sample them, given the chance. They also stand up remarkably well to picking, doubtless a centuries-old practice. Experiments at Kew forty years ago demonstrated that the bulbs were not appreciably weakened by picking or pulling the flower stalk, and that a large patch of bluebells could withstand indefinite moderate picking without harm. They are, however, sensitive to trampling, and all the rolling about in them we did as children did them no good at all. Bluebells can survive even the complete destruction of their woodland home, persisting under hedgebanks and bracken as echoes of the lost trees.

THE WOOD-SORREL

With its fresh-green, sharp-tasting shamrock leaves and crisp white spring flowers, the wood-sorrel is among the best-known woodland plants. It seldom occurs in large masses like the bluebell or the oxlip, but it is widespread in woods over a wide range of soils throughout Britain. In the East Midlands and East Anglia it is regarded as a good ancient-woodland indicator, but not further north or west where it also occurs in shaded, non-woodland habitats like under bracken, on mountain ledges and in limestone grykes, and may even colonise conifer plantations. So the felling and replanting of ancient woods which can eliminate this species in Lincolnshire may have no appreciable effect on it in Shropshire or Northumberland. Probably the main reason for its greater scarcity and restriction to woodland in the East is that this shallow-rooted plant needs constant moisture and is therefore vulnerable to drought. It is also uncomfortable in the predominantly lime-rich eastern soils. In Priors Coppice in Rutland it is restricted to pockets of humus on rotting stumps and undisturbed piles of leaves raised above the level of the surrounding soil.

On the other hand wood-sorrel is potentially a good colonist. Its sticky seeds are produced in quantity and are discharged explosively from the capsule. If they stick to a passing mouse or pheasant, they may be transported considerable distances. Seedlings are common, and, like

WOODLAND HERITAGE

FLOWERS OF THE FOREST

Pages 98-9
A bluebell wood in late April.
Thorpe Wood, Peterborough.
(Inset) The boggart-flower
carpeting hazel coppice at
Bedford Purlieus,
Northamptonshire. May 1989

97

FLOWERS OF THE
FOREST

the woodland violets, the wood-sorrel has a 'fail-safe' mechanism against bad springs, producing closed, self-pollinated flowers later in the summer. It is also rather unusual among ancient woodland plants in that its seeds are persistent and can survive for a long time dormant in the soil. It is relatively shade-tolerant and in upland Britain can grow in dense plantations so long as the fall of litter is not too heavy. In other respects the wood-sorrel is a typical woodland plant, being slow-growing, flowering early in the year, often forming patches of identical genetic composition known as clones. And, by producing quantities of oxalic acid, it has built-in protection against herbivorous animals, though to us humans the acid imparts a sharp refreshing taste. We can perhaps regard its life strategy as a sensible blend of opportunism and tenacity.

THE BOGGART-FLOWER

The boggart, better known as dog's mercury, lacks colour apart from a gloomy green and has not inspired many artists and poets. Country people thought it was put there as food for adders and other unpopular animals. But botanists like the dog's mercury because a good stand of it on the prevailing acidic soils of the North and West means a high lime content, and therefore an interesting wood, and in non-limestone soils elsewhere it hints that the wood is ancient. Dog's mercury flowers and sets seed early in the season but, unlike most spring flowers, it is tolerant of shade and its leaves persist throughout the summer. In many woods it becomes the most abundant plant once the canopy leaves have expanded. It is commonest on chalk and limestone, not because it particularly likes a lot of calcium but because it dislikes the aluminium ions produced in waterlogged conditions, and therefore needs well-drained soil.

For such a common plant, its means of regeneration are remarkably poor. The rather heavy seeds do not have any obvious means of dispersal, although they are said to contain oils which make them attractive to ants. Neither do they persist long in the soil. Seedlings of dog's mercury are an acknowledged rarity. Instead, it gets around by pushing out rhizomes just beneath the soil surface, linking the plants together in a dense bottle-green army and enabling it to spread along hedgerows and other shady places. It should, on this basis, be a slow coloniser. George Peterken, who has a taste for nature's minor mysteries, tested this idea by tracking down all the colonies of dog's mercury he could find in central Lincolnshire. His task was made simpler by the fact that virtually all of these lay in woods or hedgerows. From his knowledge of woodland history in this area, George deduced that 119 out of the 154 dog's mercury sites were living relics of ancient times. The rest had probably been established in recent centuries, mainly in places close to the relic sites. Most dense stands of dog's mercury in central Lincolnshire must be at least several hundred years old and some may be directly descended from the primeval forest.

Here, then, is another example of poor colonising ability but remarkable persistence: the dog's mercury in central Lincolnshire belongs to the surviving scraps of uncultivated land and its future depends on the preservation of the existing pattern of ancient woods

Plants of old and young woodland	
Old woodland species (eg wood anemone, herb paris, oxlip)	*Recent woodland species (eg ivy, rosebay willowherb, bramble)*
Need a stable environment	Are opportunists and quick to colonise disturbed areas
Are confined to woods over much of Britain	Are also found in hedgebanks, field corners and waste ground
Are poor colonists	Are efficient colonists
Produce few seeds	Produce many seeds
Have large seeds which fall near the parent plant	Have small light seeds, often tranported by wind, or berries
Are slow-growing	Are fast-growing
Are long-lived	Are often biennials or annuals
Have no persistent seed-bank	Can lie dormant as buried seed
Are adapted to shade	Are indifferent to shade
Often grow in localised patches	Are common and widespread
Are often poisonous	
Thrive under traditional coppicing regimes	Thrive on disturbance and modern forestry methods
Are declining	Are increasing

and hedges. However what has been proven in one area does not necessarily apply to others. George found that dog's mercury was a rather more efficient coloniser only 50 miles away in Rockingham Forest, perhaps because here more original woodland remains. And on limestone in the Peak District and on the chalk in southern England it can be almost as abundant in recent woods as in ancient ones. Evidently the factors which make dog's mercury a good ancient-woodland indicator in parts of the country but not in others are complex, but depend to some extent on the nature of the soil and the amount of surviving ancient woodland.

Rarities

Rare flowers add to a wood's individuality and finding one is always a highlight of a woodland ramble. Not that one necessarily has to look very hard, for some of them can be quite abundant within a limited area. The massed blooms of oxlips in ancient woods on the East Anglian boulder clay have long been a source of wonder and delight. The Mendips ashwoods are distinguished by the blue gromwell, whose star-shaped flowers, the colour of a Mediterranean dusk, can appear in profusion after felling has taken place. Wet woodland banks in the

West Country are often strung with the delicate stems and tiny coin-shaped leaves of Cornish moneywort, and visitors to certain woods on the Kentish chalk in late May may find a gaggle of gossiping lady orchids, the size and shape of potted hyacinths.

Rarer, in actual numbers, than most of these are plants like the green hound's-tongue and that other fine orchid, the sword-leaved helleborine, which, to look at their distribution in the *Atlas of the British Flora*, seem to be quite widespread. But their colonies are few and far between, and usually small. The rarest plants of all are both few in number and restricted in range. Perhaps the prize for the rarest woodland flower in Britain could be shared between the ghost orchid (seen less than a dozen times between its discovery in 1842 and the early 1950s, although it has since appeared almost annually in one place), the wood calamint (confined to a few hundred yards of wood-edge on chalk in the Isle of Wight) and the starved wood-sedge (two small and widely separated wood-edge colonies).

The special rarity of my own local wood, Bedford Purlieus, is the caper spurge which appears in varying quantity at the side of some of the rides, especially after thinning. I have never seen it elsewhere, except on rubbish-tips. It was evidently once cultivated in mistake for the edible caper (a bad mistake since our plant tastes very nasty indeed) and so is regarded by British botanists as a garden escape. But one would never deduce this from the Bedford Purlieus plants which certainly behave as if they were natives, though they do have an undeniably exotic look.

Spurges are interesting plants. Among them are several more woodland rarities, all of them rather erratic blooms which come and go according to light conditions, but grow most vigorously after coppicing or felling. The Irish spurge grows in fair quantity in a few damp woods

Yellow birds-nest, Monotropa hypopitys. *Clusters of tiny meerschaum pipes, alone among the dead leaves. Surrey*

on acid soils in the West Country, often by streams, but, as its name implies, is more at home in the mild climate and rain-soaked woods of south-west Ireland. Visiting botanists from the continent find this behaviour very odd since across the Channel it can grow commonly in quite dry places. The Tintern spurge is another very local plant, restricted to woods along either bank of the river Wye in Gloucestershire and Monmouthshire including, as its name implies, the very shadow of Tintern Abbey. It is an annual and a swift coloniser of coppice clearings, in William Condry's words, 'quick to come prancing out of the woods onto bare soil with all the brio of garden-weed spurges'. Around the abbey its attractive flowers colour woodland banks yellow in June. This is one of the areas of primary woodland and parts of the Wye Valley boast some of the least disturbed woods in Britain, although whether or not this has something to do with the curious distribution of the Tintern spurge is not known. Yet another rare spurge, the hairy spurge, used to grow in coppices on limestone near Bath, where it was first recorded in the reign of Queen Elizabeth I. Like the Tintern spurge, it used to spring up from buried seed in newly coppiced glades and would 'follow the woodman' around. I use the past tense because no one has set eyes on a hairy spurge in Britain for at least fifty years, and it seems to have become the first woodland flower to become extinct in Britain since records began. Coppicing ceased in the Bath area at the turn of the century, and thereafter the fortunes of the hairy spurge took a steep downward plunge. The best hope is that dormant seeds still

Crested cow-wheat
Melampyrum cristatum
'. . . flowers stacked as elaborately as a Christmas table decoration'
– Richard Mabey

FLOWERS OF THE FOREST

survive and that renewed cutting may coax them to germinate.

Why are some woodland plants rare and others common? In only a few instances does the answer seem reasonably clear. The lady's-slipper orchid, always restricted to open woods on the hard limestones of northern England, was so ruthlessly collected by gardeners and botanists that only a single plant now survives in the wild, surrounded by slug pellets and voluntary wardens. Other woodland plants which have suffered in this way locally are primrose, lily-of-the-valley, wild daffodil and royal fern. The yellow sedge, *Carex flava*, is unlikely to attract similar attention, but it evidently needs peculiar conditions, for its main colonies cling to a shelf of woodland on top of a block of limestone and bordered by a peat bog, whose acids have etched scallops and fissures into the hard stone. *Carex flava* likes its soil pH to be about 6.4 and one might hazard a guess that its particular requirements are not found very often.

The green hound's-tongue, on the other hand, grows in what seem at first sight to be ordinary patches of woodland and scrub; yet something must be amiss, for it has disappeared from nine out of ten of its historic localities. It has big heavy hooked seeds, called in Sweden 'monk's lice', which could easily be carried from place to place on fur or trousers. It is a light-demander and probably depended on regular coppicing in some of its sites. I have seen it in only one – a nettle patch among decaying elm stumps on a roadside bank in the Chilterns, not on the face of it a likely place to find a rarity. But on further investigation this place proved more special than it looked. The modern road follows a deep hollow way described in a tenth-century charter, and at the point where the hound's-tongue blooms it passes through what appears to be ancient woodland. Felling the elms may have provided the necessary light for the plant to grow vigorously for a time, but the presence of stinging nettles, possibly the result of the the sudden release of nutrients from the dying trees, is ominous.

Another rare biennial, the downy woundwort, is confined to the oolitic limestone of west Oxfordshire where it grows at the edge of copses, on scrubby banks and in ancient hedgerows derived from woodland. Most of its recorded sites in Oxfordshire lie within or close to the original boundary of the Royal Forest of Wychwood, and it survives in broad hedges where periodic thinning produces alternating conditions of light and shade similar to coppicing. The seeds of downy woundwort are comparatively large and heavy, but as several colonies border ancient tracks it is possible that they were transported in the mud on cartwheels and animals' hooves in the days when these lanes were heavily used. Downy woundwort and green hound's-tongue may be rare through a combination of restricted range, exacting requirements and no obvious means of dispersal at present.

The rather scarce herb paris is a good (but not quite infallible) indicator of ancient woodland in Britain, though its unusual spidery flowers and quatrefoil leaves are easily overlooked among the dense carpets of dog's mercury in which it usually grows. Each fertile plant produces just a single big black poisonous berry which does not seem designed to attract birds. In Britain herb paris is a slow coloniser, yet in the Pyrenees it grows in recent scrub by riversides and other pockets of rich moist soil, in the kind of places one finds the arum lily in Britain. It evidently has some means of seed dispersal abroad which is lacking in Britain. Possibly, as Jonathan Spencer speculates, one of its agents is the wild boar, which feeds like a vacuum cleaner on edible matter on and in the woodland floor, and travels great distances. Perhaps the British herb paris lost its main long-distance vector when the boar became extinct; certainly its distribution suggests that it was more common formerly.

Most native plants, except for those that live only on coasts and mountain-tops, presumably once grew in woodland. Among our rarest flowers are some that are probably original wood-edge species, but woodland clearance has left them stranded in the open. Two well-documented examples are crested cow-wheat and downy woundwort, and others may include lesser pear, starved wood-sedge, spiked rampion and limestone woundwort, which eke out their existence in a few southern hedges and scrubby banks. At the other end of Britain, certain mountain plants may have been original inhabitants of native birch and pinewoods or sub-alpine scrub, to judge from their behaviour overseas. The large and succulent blue sow-thistle grows in ungrazed scrub in Norway, but in Scotland it is confined to a few high rock ledges. But it is not at all well adapted to extreme mountain conditions – possibly it once grew lower down the hill but was grazed to oblivion before the botanical discovery of Scotland got under way. It now grows only where deer and sheep cannot get at it.

On the other hand, some rare woodland plants may be recent colonists, not prehistoric relics. The pretty little May lily brightens the flora of half a dozen woods in eastern England, at least three of which are, beyond question, ancient. But the other sites, which include a sycamore wood, a Sitka spruce plantation and a Scots pine wood, are not, and it is hard to see that they have anything in common apart from the lily. Our plant seems to like acidic soils that stay dry in winter, which may restrict it to woods near the East Coast. The May lily has been known in Britain since 1597, and was rather more widespread in the recent past than at present, but, desirable though it may be to claim it as a native, I doubt whether it is a genuine survivor from the ancient Wildwood. It produces edible berries and could equally well have been transported by migrant birds, which roost in large numbers in woods near the eastern seaboard. In one Norfolk wood it was evidently introduced at the same time as some exotic conifers. But, although the historical significance of the May lily in a British wood may be dubious, this does little in my view to diminish the thrill of finding it there. If passing thrushes care to drop a few more berries of exotic alpine herbs in our native woods that is all right by me.

Pinewood flowers

Nearly a hundred years ago the Scottish naturalist F. Buchanan White listed twinflower, coralroot orchid, creeping lady's-tresses, chickweed wintergreen, medium wintergreen and one-flowered wintergreen as plants which were confined to old native pinewoods. They are certainly characteristic, if normally rather scarce, features of the native pinewood

WOODLAND HERITAGE

FLOWERS OF THE
FOREST

Above: *Hay-scented buckler-fern*, Dryopteris aemula. *Soft, warm green, crisply feathered, once recognised, never forgotten. Look for it on steep wooded slopes in the west.* Coille Mhor Woods, Colonsay

Right: *Tunbridge filmy-fern.* Hymenophyllum tunbrigense. *Glistening, translucent fronds, each 'tipping over another in masses like the half-ruffled plumage of a bird' – C. N. Page.* Knapdale, Argyll. (Inset) *One-flowered wintergreen,* Moneses uniflora. *A better name is St Olaf's Candlesticks. A rare treat of northern pinewoods, like this one near Golspie, Sutherland*

Left: *Blue sow-thistle*, Cicerbita alpina. *Perhaps displaced by deer and sheep from its natural home in Highland woods to remote mountain ledges.* Lochnagar, Aberdeenshire

flora, but in the Scottish Highlands the distinction between plants of ancient woods and recent woods is much less marked than in the south and east of England. All of Buchanan White's species occur outside the Caledon pinewoods, sometimes in greater abundance. The coralroot orchid, for example, is locally common on acidic dunes between the Forth and the Moray Firth, and often appears mysteriously among wet moss in young birchwoods. In Angus I have seen it growing through damp clinker on a disused railway line. As for *Moneses*, the one-flowered wintergreen, the rarest of the group, its best sites seem to be in Scots pine *plantations*, not native pinewoods, although it is possible that some of them replaced earlier native woods. Certainly something limits its distribution in Scotland, but we do not yet know what it is. Twinflower, the favourite flower of Linnaeus, is another very local plant, usually growing in small tight patches like a heap of tiny coins. It needs sufficient light to produce its pretty pendant pair of bells and in some colonies it flowers with reluctance and seeds rarely. Twinflower can easily fall victim to attempts to increase timber production by screefing the ground, and well over half of its recorded colonies in Aberdeenshire have gone, including the Wood of Inglismaldie in the Mearns (incidentally not an ancient wood) where it was first discovered in Britain in 1795.

Indeed, the only vascular plant which is, so far as we know, confined to native pinewoods is a recently discovered variety of bracken, 'the northern bracken', *Pteridium aquilinum* subspecies *latiusculum*, which can be distinguished from the ordinary kind by its red scales, paler green fronds, earlier growth and non-aggressive habit. Of course even this may turn out to be more widespread. Its discoverer, Chris Page, believes that certain ferns and their allies which grow on what is now open hillside originated under woodland. The interrupted clubmoss, for example, occurs only occasionally in pinewoods, but more often among rocky heath above the tree-line where it sprawls over damp sheltered hollows among the heather or along the gravelly banks of streams. Elsewhere in the world this is a forest species and in Scotland it may have been left stranded on the hillside during the gradual downhill retreat of woodland. The same may be true of the 'hybrid alpine clubmoss', *Diphasiastrum* x *issleri*, and the beautiful, and in consequence, alas, very rare oblong woodsia.

Ferns and horsetails

A wood full of ferns and horsetails has an undeniably prehistoric look which is fully justified by the geological record. Coal is full of fossils which resemble living species remarkably closely. Today, as in the distant newt-haunted jungles of the Carboniferous, ferns and horsetails seek moist shady places, and woods are one of their main refuges. Ferns are edible and ill-equipped to survive invasion by herds of cattle; they thrive on fences. The best woods are in the North and West, for these are not only moister but physically better suited to ferns, providing more rocks, eroding banks, stream gullies and ravines. The conspicuous exception to all these generalisations is bracken, an important species in woodland on deep, well-drained soils, where it is less of a nuisance than on the open hillside and co-exists harmoniously with bluebells and wood anemones.

The majority of ferns and horsetails have fairly precise needs and are more sensitive than most flowers to extremes of drought, heat and grazing pressure. A relatively large proportion of them are also poor colonisers, and they thrive best in undisturbed stable conditions. In Hampshire, for example, only the oldest woods have wood horsetail, scaly male-fern or narrow buckler-fern. Chris Page, the author of a recent scholarly book on British fern ecology, believes that large colonies of oak fern, beech fern, wood horsetail or any of the three native species of filmy-fern probably always indicate places that have been undisturbed for centuries. It is no accident that the most fern-rich places of all are rocky ravines, for these not only provide a mosaic of rock and soil, moist seepages and sheltered banks, but also must be about the least disturbed places in our islands. The most interesting part of a ravine is right at the bottom, in the region of cool, moist, turbulent air around mossed stumps and tree roots, wet rocks and the tumbling watercourse. Here, where the air is permanently saturated with damp, ferns abound, and this is the main place to find the glistening, translucent fronds of Tunbridge filmy-fern and Wilson's filmy-fern, often embedded in pillows of moss. These are Atlantic species, extremely sensitive to drying and only common in places of high rainfall, but they occur more locally further east in pot-holes, deep stream gorges and, in the case of the Tunbridge filmy-fern, wooded sandstone gullies near the town of that name. The rarest filmy-fern of all, the Killarney fern, is so water-demanding that it prefers to grow by or behind waterfalls. Like many ferns, these species are slow-growing and the Killarney fern was almost wiped out during the Victorian fern craze.

The Atlantic woods of sessile oak and birch which line the rocky western coast are among the richest places for ferns in the whole of Europe. They provide in ideal measure the humid, shady, ungrazed conditions in which ferns thrive, and when one sees the elegant fronds tumbling down steep banks among mossed boulders and fallen logs one scarcely needs reminding that these are ancient woods. That exceptionally beautiful fern, the hay-scented buckler-fern, is sometimes among the commonest species in such places, but it is an extremely local and exacting plant. It seems to need permanently moist conditions with cool summers and warm winters (the winters of the west Scottish coast are as warm as those of the Mediterranean), and, being even more slow-growing than most other ferns, demands a long growing season. Its distribution suggests that it was a widespread species in the original forest, but it now occurs only in the least disturbed places of all. Chris Page believes that it may be a survivor not of post-glacial but of *pre-glacial* forests, for parts of the west Scottish coast were probably kept free of ice by the warm maritime currents throughout the succeeding ages of cold. Standing among its waist-high fronds at Mealdarroch in Argyll, or some other equally ferny wood in the area, it is not difficult to imagine primitive deer and three-toed horses browsing on hay-scented buckler-fern in the evergreen subtropical forest of west Scotland ten million years ago.

WOODLAND HERITAGE

FLOWERS OF THE FOREST

THE GIANT HORSETAIL
It is not only the hot countries of the world that harbour spectacular plants. The giant horsetail, *Equisetum telmateia*, is the world's largest deciduous-stemmed horsetail and no other living plant more perfectly evokes images of the coal forests of the Carboniferous. Its brittle, ivory-white stems with their whorls of fresh-green leaves are renewed each year, and, since on occasion they grow up to 8ft (2.5m) tall, this requires an enormous growth rate, comparable with bamboo. For that reason, the giant horsetail is found only in places liberally supplied with nutrients, notably where permanent seepages of mineral-rich water run across deep soft clay. It is a useful plant for geologists since it frequently marks the join between two strata. The natural habitat of the giant horsetail is open woodland, commonly under hazel or alder, but man has widened its range by transporting clay containing horsetail rhizomes to spread on roadside and railway banks, and as a result it is sometimes found some distance from woodland.

Pages 110-11
Like a dense forest of pine seedlings, the giant horsetail (Equisetum telmateia) *dominates this wet hillside near Evesham in Worcestershire*

7
PLANTS OF BARK AND SHADOW

This chapter is concerned with small 'primitive' plants that past writers have described with such unflattering epithets as 'the evil ferment of the earth', 'bastard excrescences', or, in the passage quoted above, 'queer little plants'. They are the mosses and liverworts (generally lumped together as bryophytes), the lichens and the fungi. It is hard to miss them in woods, at least at certain times of the year, but country people pay them scant attention. It is only recently that we have started to gather woodland toadstools to eat, and very few of us can tell one moss from another. The only ones to have received an English name are those like lungwort which have mystical properties. Mosses and liverworts are plants of moist, sheltered places, and western woods contain many more of them than those further east. Lichens, too, are commoner in the West, although this is partly the result of air pollution, since close examination of medieval timbers shows that East Anglian trees were then far more lichen-draped than today's bare trunks. Ancient woods and wood-pastures form the main refuge for many rare species in both groups, and an especially impressive list of species is considered a sign of lack of disturbance. In the lowlands, certain lichens are virtually confined to aged pollards in medieval deer-parks.

Bryophytes and lichens are free-living plants which make their own food by photosynthesis or absorb nutrients from all over the body of the plant. Most of them need a firm, long-lasting surface like bark or rock, and the more delicate species grow most vigorously in permanently moist places like ravines, stream banks or shaded fallen logs. The carpets of mosses one sees covering the rocks and bare floor of some well-shaded woods are made up of robust, relatively drought-resistant species. Many bryophytes and, particularly, lichens grow well only on trees, and then usually only on certain parts or at certain stages of growth. These species are termed epiphytes. Old hardwood trees with their thick trunks and fissured bark contain a kaleidoscope of micro-habitats in which these small plants can find a place. In open situations in a wood or park, the trunk of a tree receives varying amounts of light, and at different intensities, as the day progresses. Early morning sunshine from the east tends to be filtered by mist, whereas the southern and western sides of the trunk are more likely to receive the full heat of the sun's rays. These subtleties are important for lichens which are generally light-demanders but have varying degrees of tolerance to drought. It is not uncommon to find the south side dominated by tough feather lichens of the genus *Usnea* or some of the less succulent lobe-like (foliose) species.

Mosses, on the other hand, are shade-tolerant but very sensitive to drying, and so in the drier parts of Britain it is generally the north side of the trunk which is moss-grown. Then there is the rain factor. The side to the windward, usually the western or south-western side, receives most rain, but on mature bark raindrops trickle slowly groundwards in a maze of tracks, accentuating the differences in wetness and dryness, light and shade, hot and cold, which determine the patterns of growth of bryophytes and lichens.

The age and type of bark also decide what species are present. Young bark is relatively smooth and species-poor, although certain crustose lichens and cushion-forming mosses, like the species of *Ulota* and *Orthotrichum*, favour well-lit twigs and small branches. Large old trees, especially pollards, contain a much wider range of niches for epiphytes, such as dry bark recesses, standing dead bark-free wood and craggy underhangs and bosses. With age, the bark of trees like oak, ash and elm becomes more fissured and spongy in texture and, most importantly, less acidic. On well-lit old trees in unpolluted areas one might find up to forty species of lichens on a single tree (and, if you are proficient at naming them, it is certainly great fun counting). A succession of different moss and lichen communities has been described for bark of increasing age. In the case of the mosses, this sometimes forms a cycle, with the small pioneer species being succeeded by other, more weighty, mosses until the final heavy mossy pile topples off the branch and the cycle starts again. With lichens, however, the succession goes on through the lifetime of the tree, eventually reaching a definite 'climax' stage which characterises old forest and may last for many years until the natural death of the tree. The most spectacular old-forest lichen community is the *Lobarion*, named after the large *Lobaria* lichens that are sometimes the most spectacular growths among a colourful patchwork of lichens, some of them as big as a cabbage leaf or a dinner plate. Such vegetation probably clothed many of the better-lit trees of the Wildwood, but it is now restricted over most of Britain to ancient and undisturbed sites which have been wooded continuously for a long time.

Very old bark eventually becomes loose, dry and brittle, at which stage certain kinds of crustose lichens that require little moisture often move in. In the end the loose bark falls off and is attacked first by lichens which specialise in breaking down the lignin content of the wood; then, finally, when it is soft and rotten, fungi and slime moulds complete the decay process. Moist rotting logs are the home of a characteristic group of bryophytes. Many fungi also depend on dead wood, and a third or more of the larger species in a wood are likely to be found on rotting stumps, logs and branches, or on moribund trunks.

In the following sections we take a closer look at these 'queer little plants', concentrating on those which are characteristic of ancient woodland. As a group they are a key part of the woodland ecosystem, providing most of the epiphytes and decomposers visible to the naked eye, and they indicate subtle differences in habitat, as well as providing clues to the ecology and history of the wood. Many are also objects of fascination in their own right, ranging from the exquisite and ornamental to the sinister and grotesque. It is unfortunate that few of

WOODLAND HERITAGE

PLANTS OF BARK
AND SHADOW

Pages 114-15
Ideal habitat for many ferns, mosses, and liverworts; a shaded, rocky slope, sheltered by native trees. Rassal Ashwood, Wester Ross

113

I could not help laughing at this odd little man; for it was not the beautiful blossoms, such as you delight to paint, that drew forth these exclamations, but the queer little plants which he had rummaged for at the roots of the old trees, among the moss and the long grass. He sat upon a decayed trunk . . . making an oration over some greyish things, spotted with red, that grew upon it, which looked more like mould than plants . . . I gathered him a beautiful blossom of the lady's slipper, but he pushed it back when I presented it to him, saying 'Yes, yes;' tis very fine. I have seen that often before; but these lichens are splendid.

From the Canadian diaries of Susanna Ann Moodie (c1800), quoted in *The Vanishing Lichens* by David Richardson.

PLANTS OF BARK
AND SHADOW

them have been blessed with an English name and that they have the reputation of being difficult to identify. Many mosses, lichens and toadstools are in fact no harder to name than flowering plants, except that they are generally smaller and may therefore need the aid of a hand-lens. Their study presents a challenge, but those who embrace it often become 'hooked'.

Mosses and liverworts

In contrast to the preferences of many flowering plants, the majority of bryophyte-rich woods are on hard, acidic rocks. The best areas are in Devon and Cornwall, the valleys of the Wye and the Severn, the Lake District, west Wales, and north and west Scotland. In the south and east of England, most woods are relatively poor in mosses and liverworts, except where special conditions exist, like the cool, wet rocks lining the gill-woods of Kent and Sussex. Britain is world-famous for oceanic or 'Atlantic' bryophytes, which need the moist, mild climate of the western seaboard. Most of them inhabit damp, shady places, such as stream gorges and waterfalls, where evaporation is kept to a minimum. A few species are mainly, or entirely, epiphytic, such as the tight cushions of *Ulota calvescens* on hazel twigs, and the liverworts *Plagiochila punctata* and *Leptoscyphus cuneifolius*, mainly on birch, but it is doubtful whether any bryophyte is completely confined to woodland in Britain. Continual moisture and a low temperature range throughout the year are necessary for many species, but in some parts of the western Scottish coast these conditions can be found in mist-laden valleys and ravines without the prior need for tree cover. Nevertheless woodland is the main home of the Atlantic bryophytes and close study has revealed a surprising disparity between woods which are rich in these plants and apparently similar woods which are not. Most Lake District oakwoods, for example, are not particularly exciting as moss localities, and yet those in Borrowdale, by Derwent Water, are among the best in all England. The same is true in Wales, where a wooded ravine called Tyn y Groes is an outstanding site but the neighbouring woods, which also have streams and gullies, lack the less common species. Why?

Dr Derek Ratcliffe, the NCC's erstwhile head of science, investigated this question in the 1960s and deduced an explanation in terms of woodland history. Most oakwoods in the Lake District, west Wales and elsewhere have been cut over regularly for many centuries, and the natural dead wood and decaying old trees were usually removed as part of standard practice. The loss of the protective woodland canopy, either by clear-felling or by coppicing, exposes the bryophytes to the scorching of the sun, with the result, even in the humid West, that many mosses and nearly all the liverworts immediately curl up and die. The original flora takes a long time to recover and the rarer species, which often have very limited powers of colonisation, may never return. A few woods seem to have escaped intensive management, however, either because they were inaccessible, or because the trees were too bent and twisted to be worth harvesting, or by some other chance. Thus we have the strange, apparently random, distribution of bryophyte-rich woods today: Coed Crafnant in the Rhinogs of Merioneth, Tycanol Wood in Pembroke, Thornton Glen in Yorkshire, and so on, all probable primary woods in areas of high rainfall. A similar phenomenon has been observed in coniferous and temperate forests in continental Europe. Comparing the bryophytes of virgin and managed spruce forest in south-west Sweden, for example, workers found that the delicate liverworts of large fallen logs were extremely sensitive to disturbance and were virtually restricted to unmanaged stands.

Rare mosses and liverworts often lie hidden among clumps of hardier plants, and require patient searching. There are two in particular that, although nationally rare, occasionally turn up in fair quantity in special places, usually ancient woods. *Adelanthus decipiens* is a 'leafy liverwort' that forms delicate bottle-green tufts on rocks and stones in humid but sun-exposed places under native trees. Another good place to look for it is on the branches and roots of trees by waterfalls. The frequency with which this species is mentioned in botanical descriptions of top-quality Atlantic oakwoods cannot be coincidental. It is probably a survivor from the ancient forest and, being infertile in Britain, lacks the means to spread far. *Sematophyllum demissum* is a slender golden-green moss with a characteristic glossy sheen when dry. In Tyn y Groes it forms flattened patches and flakes on sloping rocky slabs that are flushed over by running water after rain. Like *Adelanthus*, it prospers in light shade, and nearly always grows under trees. This is a mysterious moss. There may be as much of it in Tyn y Groes as in the rest of Britain put together, and yet it is a fertile species, often peppered with tiny fruit-stalks in autumn, and therefore able, presumably, to produce ripe spores. By contrast, its close relative, *Sematophyllum micans*, is completely infertile, not only in Britain and Ireland but possibly worldwide; it seems to have forgotten about sex and reproduction – and yet it is a much commoner moss than the fructiferous *S. demissum*. It is a puzzle!

Most woods in the south and east of Britain contain a very limited number of mosses and liverwort species, and the richest sites tend to be those woods that contain numerous old trees and dead timber in sheltered, shaded places. Hayley Wood, a boulder-clay wood in Cambridgeshire, is one of the few eastern sites for a delicate purple-red liverwort, *Nowellia curvifolia*. This grows on fallen logs at a late stage in their decay after the bark and sapwood have rotted away. At Hayley it is limited to about twenty fallen oak trunks, but in suitable woods in the West it can be much more abundant, sometimes colouring entire logs a lurid purple. In the West it is fertile but further east it has no obvious means of reproducing itself other than by bits dropping off it. Perhaps it is unable to colonise recent woods, and is therefore stuck in a few isolated ancient woods like Hayley, where there are enough rotting logs to support it. The presence of *Nowellia* is one small reason, among a host of others, for believing Hayley Wood to be primary woodland, a direct, if much modified, descendant of the East Anglian Wildwood.

Most ancient woods have been less fortunate than Hayley Wood. The conversion of broadleaves to conifers severely reduces the original bryophyte flora, and even the species which grow on bare soil and rocks seem to find the cavernous shade and accumulation of acid needle-litter

Adelanthus decipiens. *A beautiful and distinctive 'leafy liverwort' confined to oceanic (Atlantic) woods. Inchiquin Valley, near Kenmore, Co. Kerry*

Ptilium cristacastrensis. *A troop of miniature ostrich feathers carpeting a native pinewood near Loch Treig, Inverness-shire. An easily recognised moss which prefers old woodland*

too much for them. Unfortunately this has happened on a large scale in important districts for bryophytes, such as Knapdale in Argyll. Air pollution and its deadly consequence, acid rain, is even more pervading since even nature reserves cannot escape its effects. Mosses which grow on exposed twigs, often at the top of trees, like *Ulota* and *Orthotrichum*, receive the worst effects of acidity, while those of sheltered underhangs and crevices may escape. The decline in lowland woods of robust mosses like *Antitrichia curtipendula*, which forms stringy mats on boulders and the branches of trees, and *Pterogonium gracile*, which produces cylindrical clusters of shoots on rocks and bark, has been attributed to a combination of sulphur dioxide pollution and the felling of old trees.

Lichens

Lichens are the union of two different plants growing in intimate partnership: a fungus which forms the bulk of the plant and the microscopic cells of green or orange algae buried within it and colouring the plant. By the agency of these algae the lichen obtains its food by photosynthesis in the same way as higher plants. They therefore prefer well-lit places and generally avoid the shady ravines and underhangs favoured by mosses and liverworts. Except in open, rocky woods, most forest lichens are epiphytes on trees and are most prolific at the wood-edge, at the top of the canopy or on isolated trees in parks and wood-pasture. The older the tree, the richer the lichen flora is likely to be, and most of the species which are believed to indicate ancient woodland are confined to the bark of mature trees.

The 1,400 or so British species of lichens fall broadly into three types, in all of which epiphytes are well represented. *Fruticose* lichens are either bushy in shape or form irregular strips and tassels attached at the base. A well-known woodland genus is *Usnea*, the beard lichens, which grow on twigs and branches and include strange forms resembling flowers or strings of sausages. *Foliose* lichens form lobes and rosettes, attached firmly to the surface by root-like threads. They include most of the prominent grey and orange lichens of tree-trunks, species of *Parmelia, Physcia* and *Xanthoria*, which form a patchwork on well-lit old trunks in unpolluted parts of Britain. *Crustose* lichens, as the name implies, lack lobes and resemble more the top of a cauliflower, all lumps and small cracks allowing the plant to expand after a wetting. The crustose species tend to be more drought-resistant than the others, and are particularly plentiful on very old dry bark.

At one time lichens grew thickly on trees all over Britain. Victorian naturalists took an interest in them and their records show that even a hundred years ago many species were much more common and widespread than they are today. The main cause of the decline is air pollution, with habitat loss for once taking a second (but still significant) place. Lichens are notoriously intolerant of impurities in the atmosphere and, in the most industrialised parts of Britain, few species have survived. The bark lichens include some of the most pollution-sensitive species, and they have been used as indicators of sulphur dioxide levels in the atmosphere. Trees at the edge of a wood, or which are exposed to

PLANTS OF BARK
AND SHADOW

Twenty important sites for
woodland lichens in lowland
Britain:

Boconnoc Park, Cornwall
Low Stile Wood, Cumbria
Arlington Park, Devon
Lustleigh Cleave and Bovey
    Valley, Devon
Cranborne Chase, Dorset
Melbury Park, Dorset
Mark Ash Wood in the New
    Forest, Hampshire
Brampton Bryan Park,
    Herefordshire
Wychwood, Oxfordshire
Horner Wood, Somerset
Barle Valley Woods, Somerset
Eridge Park, Sussex
Parham Park, Sussex
Longleat Park and Woods,
    Wiltshire
Glenlee and Garroch Woods,
    Galloway
Rossdhu Park, Dumbarton
Coedmore, Dyfed
Dynevor Park and Woods,
    Dyfed
Coed Crafnant, Gwynedd
Gregynog Park, Powys

the prevailing wind, are more susceptible to pollution than those in the centre, but in most parts of East Anglia and the Midlands the lichen flora of whole woods and parks has become greatly diminished. Epping Forest, for example, used to be famous for lichens of old beech and hornbeam pollards, but less than a third of the 118 species recorded here still survive. Gopsall Park in Leicestershire fared even worse and has lost all but twelve of its original flora of 106 species. Hayley Wood retains a slightly more substantial ghost of its former flora, with a few old forest indicator species surviving on the dry bark beneath the overhangs on old boundary pollards.

In only moderately polluted areas, lichens survive best in valley woods, such as along the Sussex ghylls, which lie at angles to the prevailing wind, or on mature trees with nutrient-rich bark, like ash, elm and maple, which can act as a buffer to harmful acidity. Lowland woods with no large old trees are seldom rich in lichens and most of the best sites are now in wood-pasture, parks and hedgerows. In the past some lichens, especially nutrient-demanding genera like *Xanthoria*, *Physcia* and *Ramalina*, enjoyed a good dusting from organic dust particles enriched by animal dung and urine. Modern levels of chemical fertilisers, however, are too rich a cocktail for these simple plants to cope with, and the loss of most mature elms in hedges has hastened their decline. Locally, drainage and groundwater abstraction have also adversely affected woodland lichens.

The result is that to see really rich, lichen-draped trees today one must visit woods along the Atlantic coast of Scotland, Wales, northern England and the West Country, or certain ancient wood-pastures in clean-air districts. Medieval deer-parks can be outstanding sites. Boconnoc Park in Cornwall is one of the best in Europe boasting 191 species of epiphytic lichens within less than 100ha (250 acres) of old wood-pasture. Melbury Park in Dorset, which is even richer, has 213 species and the New Forest is, as usual, richest of all, although even there the best areas are very localised. Further east, Eridge Park and the Mens in Sussex are outstanding sites. Within old parks even exotic trees can acquire an interesting lichen flora once they reach a sufficient age, especially sycamore, walnut and tulip tree (*Linodendron*).

In a recent publication, Dr Francis Rose listed seventy-seven species of lichen which he believes are faithful to old forest areas in the lowlands, and whose presence indicates a long continuity of suitable habitat conditions and an absence of major disruption. Some of the seventy-seven need an expert eye to sort them out; two of the best old-forest indicators, *Lecidia cinnabarina* and *Haematomma elatinum*, are similar-looking greyish crusts, differentiated mainly by the contrasting colours they display when splashed with caustic potash. *Thelotrema lepadinum* seems a more useful indicator to the lay person, since it is easily recognisable with its wrinkled, pearly surface and tiny spore-bearing cups which have been compared to 'craters on miniature volcanoes' or, alternatively, to 'small goose barnacles'. *Thelotrema* also has a useful habit of growing on both branches and trunks, on young trees as well as old, and on a wide range of trees, especially hazel, beech, holly and oak. It is a convenient indicator of ancientness in woods lacking aged trees.

The best-known bark lichens are the big lobate plants which characterise large old trees in moist environments. The largest are the four species of *Lobaria*, of which the lungwort, *Lobaria pulmonaria*, is perhaps the most famous of all lichens. It bears a superficial resemblance to lung tissue and, by the 'Doctrine of Signatures', was therefore held to treat disorders of the chest (in the same way that dog lichen was used to treat cases of rabies!). Lungwort is relatively drought-resistant, changing in dry weather from deep green to pale buff and losing in the process its characteristic cabbage-like succulence. In the right conditions it can smother whole trunks with its beautifully lobed 'lungs', like seaweed-covered driftwood. Great Wood near Keswick in the Lake District is said to be the finest *Lobarion* in Britain, with lungwort smothering every mature wych elm and oak in a continuous sheet as far as the tree-tops. In the north and west of Scotland it is fairly widespread and can colonise recent woodland; I have seen birch branches heavy with lungwort and in some places it also grows on mossy rocks. In areas of moderate air pollution, it is confined to base-rich bark on old ash, sycamore and elm. Its present-day distribution is in fact an artefact of air pollution, to which all *Lobaria* species and their allies are extremely susceptible. Far from being a true western, 'Atlantic' species, lungwort at one time occurred in all but six English counties, and may have been among the most prominent lichens in the Wildwood. It is now an old-forest relict not only in Britain but over most of Europe, and pollution has caused its virtual disappearance from the north European plain.

The *Lobaria* species are but the most prominent part of this wonderfully rich old-forest community of lichens, but there is space here to mention only a few of the other members. Species of *Sticta* resemble small versions of *Lobaria* but are distinguished by the presence of white pits on the undersurface and, for some of them, a decidedly fishy smell. *Pseudocyphellaria crocata* forms unmistakable dark-brown lobes dotted with golden yellow on mossy trunks. In similar places one can also find the chestnut and grey cusps and crisp curls of *Nephroma laevigatum*, looking like withered leaves on a mossy lawn, together with the big blue-grey rubbery discs of *Parmeliella plumbea*, often peppered at the centre by fertile cinnamon spots, and the more delicate, silver-margined lobes of *Pannaria rubiginosa*, lined beneath with blue felt and patterned all over with dark ascocarps shaped like jam tarts.

The lichen communities of broadleaved woods in Britain and temperate parts of Europe are thought to be very ancient, and may have originated several million years ago in the late Pliocene, before successive ice sheets obliterated the countryside and its forests. In some coastal woods in the West the lichens may well descend directly from that remote period, since they were kept warm and ice-free by maritime currents. Unfortunately lichens do not fossilise well, and so we have no direct means of telling what the Wildwood lichen flora was like. There are good reasons, however, for believing that the exceptionally rich flora of ancient wood-pasture is a faithful echo of it. Possibly sites like Boconnoc Park today possess even more lichens than their equivalent area in the original forest, since park trees are probably better lit and their bark is enriched over the centuries with organic dust. Francis Rose

however believes that the structure of ancient parks and wood-pasture is much closer to the conditions in which lichens originally grew than dense high forest. Together with the mosses and invertebrates of over-mature trees and dead wood, our old forest lichens are true living links with the prehistoric woodland past.

Fungi

Fungi are the most mysterious and unpredictable of all woodland plants. For most of the larger species, the fruit bodies appear only in the autumn, when, for a few weeks, the forest floor suddenly sprouts multicoloured toadstools and related forms shaped like balls, starfish, corals, clubs and tiny bird's nests complete with eggs. Some of them turn up in more or less the same place year after year but others are more ephemeral, appearing only occasionally, and apparently at random. Almost any ancient wood of any size has the potential to support several hundred species of toadstools and their allies, although seldom more than a small fraction of them will be visible on any single visit. To produce anything like a complete fungus flora of a wood therefore requires great dedication as well as expertise and will certainly take several years. When one adds the difficulty of naming even some of the large toadstools and bracket fungi, to say nothing of smaller moulds, parasites and disc fungi, it is perhaps not surprising that full lists of fungi are available for very few woods and that knowledge of fungal ecology in general is still in its infancy.

Lichens on hazel at Rassal Ashwood, Wester Ross. The large grey ovals are Parmeliella plumbea, *the olive-green lobes, lungwort,* Lobaria pulmonaria, *and the almost black flakes,* Leptogium burgessii

Pseudocyphellaria crocata, *an Atlantic lichen, thriving in the Highland mist and rain in the woods of Glen Nant, Argyll*

Habitats for larger fungi in woodland. The figures are not, of course, to scale and the examples named could be multiplied a hundredfold

Although they are invisible to us for most of the year, fungi play a vital role as the principal decomposers in woodland. Unlike green plants, they cannot manufacture their own food but obtain it from living or dead organisms. Some, such as most species of *Mycena* ('fairy bells'), *Marasmius* and *Collybia*, live on organic debris in the soil, including buried bits of wood and pine needles. In damp places where decay is slow, their white threads or mycelia can be found just beneath the surface leaves, matting the older, half-decayed leaves together. The leaf-litter layer has a different group of fungi to the mineral soil beneath, and this is different again to the zone around the living roots of trees and other plants. Many woodland fungi are restricted to the neighbourhood of particular trees, such as the famous fly agaric, *Amanita muscaria*, which grows beneath birch and, less commonly, pine; the greyish-buff milk-cap *Lactarius circellatus* near hornbeam; and the ochre caps of *Russula fellea* near beech. Such associations are far from accidental since these toadstools are actually attached beneath the ground to the tree

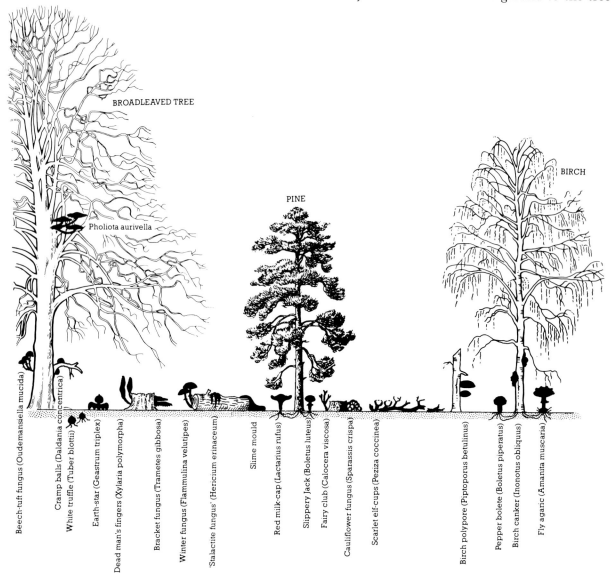

BROADLEAVED TREE

Pholiota aurivella

PINE

BIRCH

Beech-tuft fungus (Oudemansiella mucida)

Cramp balls (Daldania concentrica)

White truffle (Tuber blottii)

Earth-star (Geastrum triplex)

Dead man's fingers (Xylaria polymorpha)

Bracket fungus (Trametes gibbosa)

Winter fungus (Flammulina velutipes)

'Stalactite fungus' (Hericium erinaceum)

Slime mould

Red milk-cap (Lactarius rufus)

Slippery Jack (Boletus luteus)

Fairy club (Calocera viscosa)

Cauliflower fungus (Sparassis crispa)

Scarlet elf-cups (Peziza coccinea)

Birch polypore (Piptoporus betulinus)

Pepper bolete (Boletus piperatus)

Birch canker (Inonotus obliquus)

Fly agaric (Amanita muscaria)

roots by a dense tangle of fungal threads (mycorhizae) which surround and penetrate the living tissue of the tree. These 'mycorhizal' fungi derive some of their life-supporting substances from the tree, and in return help the latter to obtain water and nutrients from the soil, as well as protecting it from fungal parasites. This relationship seems to be particularly important on poor soils, but the roots of most healthy forest trees are probably infected to a greater or lesser extent by mycorhizal fungi.

PLANTS OF BARK
AND SHADOW

Fungi have the unique capacity among plants to feed on wood and are the main agents of timber decay. Their hyphal threads can penetrate solid stumps and logs in a way impossible for other plants, and proceed to break down the cellulose and, in some cases, also the tougher lignin content of the wood. A succession of species occurs on dead wood, beginning with small fungi feeding in the sapwood, followed by the true wood-rotting fungi, including most of the larger brackets, and finally fungi which finish off the damp wood-pulp and sawdust. Among the latter are the slime-moulds, strange blobs of wandering naked protoplasm of no fixed shape which digest all kinds of decaying plant remains in their way, including rotten fungi. Some dead-wood fungi are able to utilise a wide range of trees but others are limited to a single host. In native woods old beech and Scots pine stumps have a particularly rich fungus flora, including many rarities. Oak timber has a more restricted flora, possibly because of its high tannin content, but it includes two of the best-known brackets, 'the beefsteak fungus', *Fistulina hepatica*, which some people claim is edible (having once tried one I am not of their number), and the hoof-shaped *Daedalea quercina*, which is easily recognised by its maze-like pores. *Daedalea* can be useful when looking for traces of oak in 'coniferised' ancient woods, since it will grow on otherwise unrecognisable decayed stumps and logs. Relatively few bracket fungi attack healthy trees, and, although those few include some of the most serious pests of conifer plantations, they are much less significant in ancient woodland. Unlike in plantations, there is seldom any pressing need to remove dead wood from natural woods on grounds of forest hygiene.

The table indicates the relative importance of the principal forest trees for fungi. Mixed woods on rich soil are likely, in theory at least, to contain more species than woods dominated by a single type of tree or those on poorer soils, although the exceptionally interesting fungus flora of native Highland birch and pinewoods suggests that this is not always true. The diagram indicates something of the range of habitat niches for fungi in a mixed wood containing dead timber in various forms and states of decay. Not uncommonly some parts of a wood are richer in fungi than others. The eastern side of isolated woods on level ground is often better than the western, probably because the latter is windier and dries out more quickly. The northern sides of sloping woods are generally better places to look for fungi than the sunnier, and hence drier, southern aspect. In the Highlands, the great native pinewoods of the Spey and the Dee seem to have a richer fungus flora than their congeners further west, possibly because the former occupy more level ground with a deeper layer of humus.

Occasionally, however, one comes across a wood which is

THE IMPORTANCE OF FOREST TREES FOR LICHENS[1] AND FUNGI

Tree	Number of lichens recorded	Notes	Notes on fungi (asterisks indicate relative importance for agaric fungi)
Oak (both species)	326	Nearly a quarter of British lichen flora occurs on oak bark.	** Old oaks in wood-pasture are richer in rare fungi than most oakwoods.
Ash	265	Bark similar to oak, but more nutrient-rich. Lacks some of the lichens of old oak.	* Few dependent species.
Beech	213	Bark smooth and acidic. Rich lichen flora confined to old beech trees in, eg, New Forest.	*** Mature southern beechwoods are the single richest fungal habitat.
Elm (all species)	200	Bark nutrient-rich and moist. Elm has an important lichen flora, now threatened by Dutch elm disease.	** Some dead-wood species have benefitted from Dutch elm disease.
Hazel	162	Fairly good flora in uplands; coppiced hazel usually poor.	** Hazel-rich woods are often quite rich, but contain few rare species.
Sallows (Salix cinerea and S. capraea)	160	Quite rich in humid parts of upland Britain.	*
Birch (both species)	134	Smooth acidic bark, but old trees in upland Britain can be quite rich in lichens.	*** Especially mature Highland birchwoods.
Native Scots pine	133	Acidic bark, in general similar to birch, but some native pinewoods have a characteristic and important flora.	***Many species confined to native pinewoods.
Alder	116	Acidic bark with poor water retention; usually poor but locally quite rich in North and West.	** Alderwoods have a specialised fungus flora.
Maple	101	Nutrient-rich bark, but too few large standard trees to be of much significance.	*
Holly	96	Smooth bark; a limited but specialised lichen flora.	
Lime (all species)	83	Hard fibrous bark with poor water retention.	*
Hornbeam	44	Probably similar to beech, but natural range confined to polluted areas.	**A few characteristic species, shared with hazel.

[1]Based on Harding and Rose (1986)

phenomenally rich in rare fungi for reasons which are harder to explain. Gait Barrows in Lancashire is one of these. Here woodland surrounding a central island of massive limestone pavement ranges from tall scrub to mature coppice-with-standards and is at least partly ancient. Because limestone soils are free-draining and do not retain moisture for long, it is unusual to see large numbers of fungi there at any one time, but over a decade Len and Pat Livermore have found nearly a thousand species, of which four hundred are toadstools or brackets. If other limestone woods in the area had been studied with the same degree of thoroughness, Gait Barrows might perhaps seem less exceptional, but it is certainly one of Britain's premier fungus sites. The Livermores suggest that its importance owes something to its 'wilderness' quality, with fallen wood and undisturbed leaf litter, and also to the presence of scattered wild

Top right: Rozites caperata, *a native pinewood indicator species. Inveray, near Braemar*

Right: Phellodon tomentosus *clustered on a buried Scots pine stump, Inveray, near Braemar*

Below: Russula decolorans, *another native pinewood indicator. The specimen on the left is a different species of* Russula, *probably* R. vinosa *(yet another indicator species!)*

yew trees, the hosts of several rare species. It also lies within a zone where northern and southern fungus floras (much more distinctive than those of flowering plants) mix. A feature of Gait Barrows is that a small area can be very fruitful for a few years and then suddenly become barren, while a hitherto dull area elsewhere springs to life. The implication is that large woods may be better sites than small ones.

A second wood of special interest lies near Braemar in the eastern Highlands. This is a pinewood of some 50ha (120 acres) on level free-draining gravels beside the River Dee which separates it from the native pinewood of Glen Lui. This is a classic place to see some of the rarities associated with native pinewoods, such as *Russula decolorans*, whose orange caps look like lumps of toffee, and *Rozites caperata*, which has a flatter, buff-coloured cap and a ring around the stem, and incidentally tastes delicious. These and many others appear in spectacular numbers

in August and September, when the fleeting combination of warm sunshine and rain provide excellent conditions for fruiting. Heavy grazing may be the key to the interest of this small wood. It is unfenced and used by herds of red deer for much of the summer. By autumn the heather and blaeberry sward has been grazed almost flat, leaving perfect conditions for the growth of pinewood toadstools. Tall vegetation is less suitable – mycologists are not pleased at the fencing of nature reserves like Rassal Ashwood, in Ross and Cromarty, which has encouraged tree regeneration at the expense of their former standing as prime fungus sites. Deer and sheep maintain a short sward without poaching the upper layers of the soil or enriching it much with their droppings. Cattle, on the other hand, both churn up the soil and smother it in nitrate-laden cowpats, and a raid by cows seems to be as catastrophic for woodland fungi as it is for flowers and ferns.

Our third special site is Coed Afon Pumryd near Llanymawddy in Snowdonia. This small sessile oakwood is probably the richest site in Britain for slime-moulds, with sixty-one species present, including three for which this is the only Welsh locality. It lies in an area of high rainfall and lines the slopes of a ravine terminating in a spectacular 20m (65ft) waterfall. The woodland is probably ancient and contains a good mixture of other broadleaved trees, wet moss-covered rocks and plenty of decaying wood. The air is permanently damp, by contrast with most Welsh woods which are small and exposed to drying winds, and therefore unsuitable for the oceanic species of slime-moulds, liverworts and other delicate plants. Even so, it is hard to single out any particular factor at Coed Afon Pumryd that is not shared by other Snowdonian oakwoods. One suspects that the outstanding fungus flora of this wood may be due to a long history of non-intensive management in which logs and boulders were left undisturbed and the canopy was not frequently interrupted by industrial coppicing.

Flowering plants, bryophytes, ferns and lichens form distinctive communities of species, some of which have been given names by phytosociologists, and, with experience, these units of vegetation can readily be recognised in the field. It is uncertain whether fungi also behave like this, although broad types of woodland, such as yew-woods, native pinewoods and calcareous beechwoods certainly possess a characteristic fungus flora. Some toadstools and brackets seem confined to large mature trees. An experiment to test the relationship of fungi to growing birch trees at the University of Aberdeen indicated that a succession of toadstools appear as the young trees mature. In the first five years after planting, the main toadstools to appear were species of *Laccaria*, *Inocybe* and *Hebeloma*, small drab fungi often found on recently disturbed or open ground, and analogous with annual weeds like groundsel and chickweed. Only later did the characteristic fungi of more mature birch woodland appear, namely species of *Leccinium*, *Cortinarius* and *Russula*. Some common birchwood fungi, notably species of *Amanita* and *Tricholoma*, did not appear at all during the experiment and may occupy a still later stage in the succession.

It would be reasonable to suppose that, with their precise habitat requirements and sometimes slow growth rate, some toadstools are typical of ancient and natural woodland. And this is almost certainly right, although we are only just beginning to realise it. Field observations suggest that plantations accumulate fungi as they age, as we might expect, but that ancient woods are richer than even long-established plantations. Toadstools and other fungi produce vast numbers of spores, it is true, and are therefore potentially good colonists, but it is only in exceptionally favourable circumstances that these spores ever bear fruit. The majority of toadstools are in fact very local indeed, and perhaps require subtle soil conditions or a long continuity of mature tree roots. The large and spectacular milk-caps, *Lactarius representaneus* and *L. resimus*, for example, are seldom seen outside long-established and undisturbed Highland birchwoods. Some species probably need exceptionally large trees, like the beautiful *Hericium erinaceum* whose brittle coral-like spines are occasionally found growing from the broken limbs of dead or moribund beech. This species can appear annually for many years in a particular tree without spreading further, and the removal of that tree results in its loss from the area. P. D. Orton, who has studied the fungus flora of Scottish woodland for half a lifetime, listed twenty-four species of toadstools and their allies which he believes are confined to native northern birchwoods, and thirty which occur only in native Caledonian pine forests. Among the latter are *Russula decolorans*, *R. vinosa*, *Cortinarius caledoniensis*, *C. fervidus*, *Rozites caperatus*, *Pholiota graveolens* and *P. inopus*, of which Orton states that 'If any of these occur in a pine wood in the Highlands, then I should say that this was a fair indication that Caledonian pine was present, though this would not necessarily be true for other parts of Europe.'

Are woodland toadstools in decline like the once common field mushroom? It is impossible to give a definite answer since too little is known about the past and present distribution of even the most easily recognised toadstools to make any valid comparisons. But some species certainly seem to be much less common than they used to be. Among them is the 'scarlet elf cup', *Sarcoscypha coccinea*, which was once a familiar object of woodland walks in January, sprouting from moss-covered sticks, especially hazel. Its decline has been noticed because this fungus used to be sought and gathered by flower-arrangers, and was also popular with photographers and artists. On the European mainland, where people gather toadstools for food and hence pay more attention to them, severe declines have indeed been noted. In one state in West Germany, nearly half of the larger fungi are listed as endangered. This may be due not so much to habitat destruction as air pollution. In Holland a survey of that delectable toadstool, the chanterelle, showed that it had disappeared from many former sites, particularly in the most polluted parts of the country. It avoids strongly acidic soils, and chemical changes in the soil caused by acid rain have been suggested as the probable cause. If so, the effect is unlikely to be confined to the chanterelle. Air pollution has already wiped out most of Europe's old forest lichen flora and, if lichens are sensitive, so in all probability are fungi. If so, this has serious implications for woodland as a whole, since trees are weakened physiologically by the loss of their community of mycorhizal fungi. It is time environmental watchdogs began to take a closer interest in wild woodland toadstools.

WOODLAND HERITAGE

PLANTS OF BARK
AND SHADOW

8

WOLVES AND WOODPECKERS

. . . at one time these same
woods, which we now traverse
so securely, were infested to
such an extent with ferocious
animals, that a journey of any
length was, on this account,
affected with considerable
danger . . . In the oak woods . . .
the wild-boars lurked while
munching their store of acorns,
or wallowing, as is their wont,
in lacustrine mire . . . Many a
traveller then had cause to rue
the sudden and unexpected
rush of some grand old patriarch
of the 'sownder', who, with
gnashing tusks, charged out
upon the invader of his do-
main.

   J. E. Harting, *British Animals
Extinct Within Historic Times*

The last million years of Britain's prehistory have seen dramatic changes
as the climatic pendulum swayed to and fro, alternating scenes
reminiscent of Lapland with those resembling southern Europe, but
with periods of open grassland, like a waterlogged version of the Russian
steppes, interspersed. Throughout most of this period the landscape was
full of great beasts, so that it looked more like an African national park
than like anywhere in modern Europe. Numerous large bones dug out of
ancient sediments beneath Trafalgar Square enabled the *Illustrated
London News* to reconstruct scenes of 'London 100,000 years ago' with
hippos wallowing in the Thames and strange straight-tusked elephants
plodding through open maple and hornbeam forest, stalked by sabre-
toothed cats. This last warm period was succeeded by sixty-thousand
years of cold, when ice-caps advanced as far south as South Wales and
the Wash, and the remainder of Britain became frozen tundra and open
grassland. The sea-level fell by some 300ft (90m) and broad land-bridges
connected eastern England with France and the Low Countries, and
Northern Ireland with Galloway. This Ice Age was also dominated by
great beasts that lived in migratory herds, this time well-insulated ones
like the woolly mammoth, woolly rhinoceros, Irish elk, musk ox and
bison.

   Man was present for much of the time since, even during the Ice Age,
summer temperatures could rise to a fairly temperate 7°C (46°F). Man
almost certainly hunted the largest animals to extinction. Of the smaller
ones that have survived to the present day, the mountain hare is well
adapted to cold and would probably have been at home in southern
England during much of the Ice Age. Other animals which might have
been present for at least part of the time include red deer, most of the
voles and shrews, and the hardier carnivores like fox, stoat and polecat.
The twenty or so native Irish mammals must have colonised that
country before it was sundered by the rising sea, and this probably
happened before the land became densely forested.

   With the possible exception of the hares, all our surviving native land
mammals once lived in woods. Woodland animals are smaller on
average than those of the open plains and most live within fixed
territories. Those which arrived from the Continent in the wake of the
first forest trees probably included roe deer, badger, weasel, dormouse,
red squirrel and most of the bats. By the time Britain became an island it

was the home of twice as many mammals as Ireland, but only about a third of those found on the European mainland. Some of the latter would certainly have colonised Britain if the land-bridge had held longer, but they presumably arrived north too late to make the crossing.

Archaeological excavations of Mesolithic hunting camps built about 9,500 years ago indicate that by that time Britain had become densely wooded. At Star Carr, in the Vale of Pickering in north-east Yorkshire, bones and antlers from a variety of mammals were uncovered, including red deer and elk in abundance, wild boar, aurochs (a prehistoric wild ox), beaver, wolf, pine marten, badger, fox and hedgehog. A similar hunting camp of about the same date near Thatcham in Berkshire also contained many red-deer bones and among other remains uncovered were those of wild cat and horse. Woods of that time were clearly much richer in large and medium-sized mammals than any of the present day, and, as we saw in an earlier chapter, man seems to have modified the natural forest to attract grazing animals to open glades full of forage. Such glades might have become permanent, maintained by browsing animals like deer and wild cattle.

WOLVES AND
WOODPECKERS

Lost beasts of the Wildwood

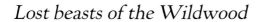

Once people began to build permanent settlements, introduce domestic livestock and till the land, native deer and other large mammals ceased to to be valuable and became a nuisance. Britons have a long record of unfriendliness towards wild mammals, and one wonders how much the animals' present-day shyness and nocturnal habits have to do with persecution, and whether there was once an Eden-like period when they were more prominent and active by day. Those put most at risk by farming and woodland clearance were large animals requiring extensive tracts of woodland, notably bear, elk, lynx, wolf, boar and beaver. None of them are, of course, present-day inhabitants of our woods, but in the distant past they were of great importance – botanists tend to underestimate the impact of animals on natural vegetation. The three last-mentioned beasts still lived in woodland at the time of the battle of Hastings; so let us linger here to consider their fate.

The beaver fascinated ancient writers, but they copied from each other so assiduously that it is difficult to know how much of medieval beaver lore is based on actual observation. So far as British beavers are concerned, the answer is probably very little. The most solid evidence of its past occurrence are the numerous bones dug out of peat in the Fens and elsewhere, which indicate that it was reasonably common and widespread in the Bronze Age. Continental beavers live in fertile floodplain woodland, such as the Rhone valley, with dense undergrowth and plenty of water. They must have lived in similar places in Britain, but our own broad lowland floodplains were cleared and drained long ago, certainly before the Middle Ages when beavers were apparently confined to Scotland and Wales. The main literary evidence for British beavers is in *The Journey through Wales,* a record of the journey made by Gerald of Wales in 1188. According to Gerald, beavers were very rare and confined to the Teifi in Ceredigion and an unnamed river in Scotland (a sixteenth century Scottish historian,

WOLVES AND
WOODPECKERS

Boece, claims it was the Aberdeenshire Dee). Unlike lowland England, the valleys of South Wales were then still well wooded and, from what we know of them, they might well have been capable of harbouring beavers.

Gerald described at length the habits of these semi-legendary animals, half-beast, half-fish, whose magic testicles and skins were capable of healing all manner of ills (they do in fact contain the main ingredient of aspirin) and whose tails could be eaten during Lent. Nowhere, though, does he claim to have actually seen one, and his account is evidently influenced by what he had read, for it is full of quotes from Pliny the Younger and St Bernard. The zoologist Brunsdon Yapp has questioned the assumption, based mainly on Gerald, that beavers survived into the Middle Ages, pointing to the rarity of beaver pictures in native medieval manuscripts and the absence of any other convincing evidence. He suggests that Gerald's local informants had meant otters, which still live by the Teifi and whose Latin name *fiber* could be confused with that of the beaver, *Castor fiber*. But, assuming that there really were Welsh beavers in 1188, their numbers would have dwindled in the large-scale felling of lowland Welsh woods in the later Middle Ages, and their valuable pelts (in Europe, worth seven times as much as a wolfskin) would have put a price on the heads of the remaining few. According to ancient writers the cunning beaver escaped the hunter by shedding its magic testicles at full speed, but, unfortunately, this was not enough.

The wild boar was common enough in the first two centuries after the Norman Conquest to be designated a beast of the chase, along with deer. A squat, dark and dangerous animal, it was the opposite of the graceful hart, fit to be hunted by heroes and eaten by kings. Boars inhabit large lowland woods dominated by oak or beech and most medieval boars probably lived in specially protected chases and Royal Forests, or later, introduced into enclosed parks. Oliver Rackham, who has researched the contemporary documentation, suggests that the last free-ranging wild boars dwelled in the Forests of Pickering and Dean in the thirteenth century. The last Dean boars ended up as Christmas dinner to Henry III and his friends, but their demise was probably linked to the increased exploitation of the Forest of Dean to fuel its expanding iron industry. Boars may have survived longer in woods in parts of Wales and Scotland, and certainly tall stories involving fierce boars are common in Scotland, but there is little hard evidence. Boars kept in parks outlived their wild compatriots by several centuries and the last of them seem to have perished in the Civil War, when the old park system fell into decline. Without the protection given to it in by the Normans and their successors the boar would not have survived long, since it roams far and wide and needs extensive areas of undisturbed forest. It is no doubt significant that all present-day woodland mammals can live in relatively small woods.

Wolves were Man the Hunter's main competitors for deer in the original forest; so the mutual enmity between wolves and humans has deep roots. European wolves hunt in packs within a home territory which nearly always contains some woodland cover, but usually also open ground including bare hillsides, and moors. Wolves were so common in Saxon times that the month of January, when wolf cubs were born and the pelts were at their thickest, was set aside for hunting them. King Edgar tried to curb their numbers by imposing an annual fine of three hundred wolf skins on his opposite number in Wales, one King Ludwall. Edward I also experienced trouble with Welsh wolves and introduced a bounty system, combined with the destruction of their woodland refuges, to get rid of them. By 1486, wolves were evidently becoming rare in England for the *Book of St Albans* mentions the introduction of a close season for wolf hunting, presumably in an attempt to preserve the last few. They apparently survived longest in forests in northern England, namely the Forests of the Peak and of Bowland, and in the Yorkshire wolds.

In wild and politically unstable Scotland the wolf continued to thrive for at least another century. A two-shilling bounty was introduced in 1427 to reduce the 'plague of wolves', later changed to as much as five shilllings or as little as sixpence, depending, presumably, on the degree of emergency. In 1563 Mary Queen of Scots and her party killed five wolves in a great drive in Atholl Forest – which does not suggest they were common by that time. In the Highlands fear of wolves seems to have been out of all proportion to the danger they really presented. Spittals (refuges) were built along remote roads, especially in well-wooded areas, and large areas of forest are said to have been felled or burned in places like Lochaber, Rannoch and Loch Sloi to expel the wolf. No one seems to have shown the slightest desire to protect it, once it had become rare, and, according to the Welsh traveller and naturalist, Thomas Pennant, the last known wolf in its former stronghold of Perthshire was killed in 1680, and the last few in Scotland had gone by the turn of the century. Man's irrational fear of wolves survives in fairy tales, red lupine eyes reflecting the campfire in the darkness beneath the boughs. The extinction of the wolf may in fact owe more to the expansion of sheep ranching in the Middle Ages than to any other factor, for the Cistercian abbeys, which owned vast acreages of hill land in the Borders and elsewhere, wanted, and got, more pasture-land and fewer woods and wolves. The extermination of this important predator has had serious long-term consequences in unfenced Highland woods, for, in the absence of a sensible substitute culling programme, there are now more deer than the shrinking natural woods can hold, and regeneration has all but ceased.

Big animals, small woods

To survive as a large mammal in crowded Britain requires wits and adaptability. Two, red deer and fox, survive because of their sporting value. The others, even the harmless badger, have all been treated as vermin and our forebears did their best to get rid of them. Wild cat, polecat and pine marten were all brought within a whisper of extinction by game interests, and if Britain did not happily contain large tracts of sparsely populated land they would not have survived. They may never return to their pre-nineteenth-century numbers. Deer, on the other hand, now prosper to a surprising degree. The roe deer was quite scarce in the Middle Ages, and there are probably more of them about now than at any time since the Wildwood. Red deer too initially lost popularity in favour of the more tractable fallow deer, and in the nineteenth century they were confined to the North and Exmoor. It is one of the ironies of natural history that this forest animal is now associated with moorland and glen. Modern conditions in lowland woods favour an expansion of deer numbers – so much so that, in addition to the two native deer, four introduced ones, fallow, muntjac, sika and Chinese water, are all expanding their range. These animals use woodland as a hiding place but generally feed in the open. The expansion of modern forestry may provide a partial explanation for the present-day abundance of deer, especially the small roe and muntjac which can move about in quite dense cover and like wide grassy rides and greens. But the obvious explanation is Oliver Rackham's: fewer people, and especially fewer people with guns, work in the fields and woods than ever before. It has become easier for deer to avoid us.

Today's managers of ancient woodland have to live with the problem of deer in numbers which the medieval forester did not experience. In many woods the most conspicuous sign of increased browsing pressure is the decline of palatable flowers like the oxlip. More serious in the long run is the loss of seedlings and saplings of trees. At Castor Hanglands near Peterborough, for example, hazel, ash saplings and brambles are in retreat and are now sparse except in places where deer have been fenced out. Coppice regrowth is particularly vulnerable, and the only solution may be to resort to expensive fencing. Large mammals have at last returned in numbers which recall prehistory, but there is a price to pay.

Wildwood birds

Relatively little is known about the woodland birds of the distant past, since few of them were of economic importance and, compared with mammals, their bones are seldom well-preserved. Various collections of bird bones from caves and rock fissures have been analysed, however, and, although it is not always possible to identify or date them, they suggest that the Wildwood shared broadly the same breeding birds as woodland today, albeit in different numbers and proportions. Bird distributions are not of course static; they have changed in living memory and will continue to do so, responding to changes in climate and food supply. The species which have ceased to breed in Britain are nearly all big birds: the eagle owl, crane, pelican, spoonbill, great auk, great bustard and sea eagle; and of these only the eagle owl sometimes nests in woods. Before the advance of the Wildwood, the birds of open tundra and scrubby northern forests included the hazelhen and crested lark. Those that first arrived with the returning broadleaved trees probably included the woodpeckers, some of the warblers and tits, nuthatch and hawfinch. Some birds were probably more abundant in managed Saxon and medieval woods than today. One would expect there to have been more raptors, owls and woodpeckers and more of those songbirds which nest in thickets, hedges and young coppice. One of the earliest English poems, significantly, is about an owl and a nightingale, and Chaucer and other medieval writers often refer to the melodious 'small fowles', which brought joy to a hunter's or a pilgrim's heart. Gerald of Wales noted that the nightingale, common in England in the Middle Ages, ceased to breed once it reached the Welsh border. This is more or less still true eight centuries later although a few pairs sometimes stray over into Gwent and Glamorgan.

The medievals sometimes recorded the nests or eyries of raptors because they were worth a great deal of money and were part of the property of the manor. In a fascinating study of the Domesday Book records for Cheshire, D. W. Yalden reconstructed the eleventh-century distribution of a hawk called *acciptris,* almost certainly the goshawk (*Accipiter gentilis*). The Domesday Book mentions twenty-four eyries scattered over the eastern half of the county which, unlike the western half, was well wooded in 1086. The position of each eyrie coincided with a large area of woodland, and indicates that each pair of birds held an average hunting territory of around 100km^2 (40 square miles). This ties in with what is known of the goshawk's requirements today. They are large birds, like outsize sparrowhawks, not given to migration and needing extensive tracts of undisturbed forest. They nest high up in tall trees and the same eyrie is used year after year by a succession of different birds, so that their position was well worth noting by medieval falconers. While the smaller (and less valuable) sparrowhawk has adapted well to the typical English countryside of small woods, hedgerows and open farmland (before the advent of pesticides anyway), the goshawk was always vulnerable to the clearance of the remaining large woods. There is no knowing how many pairs nested in Britain in 1086; Cheshire, with its twenty-four recorded pairs, was one of the more densely wooded English counties and probably contained a higher breeding density than most, but the national total might well have been in the order of 500–1,000 pairs.

By the early nineteenth century, the goshawk had become a very scarce bird and, after enduring much persecution from game interests and egg collectors, it had ceased to nest in Britain by about 1900. A small but increasing number of pairs, possibly originating from escapes, have nested since the 1950s, taking advantage of the new conifer plantations which represent the largest areas of land under trees since the Middle Ages (although there the resemblance ceases).

To attempt to reconstruct bird life further back in the past, to those once extensive tracts of virgin Wildwood barely touched by the

WOODLAND HERITAGE

**WOLVES AND
WOODPECKERS**

WOLVES AND WOODPECKERS

woodcutter's axe, we have to turn to parallels in continental Europe. Of these, perhaps the best known is the Bialowieza National Park on the Polish–Russian frontier. The Bialowieza is not completely undisturbed; it was devasted by fire in 1811 and by fellings during and after World War I, and its present structure and composition therefore owe something to human influence. But, even so, the heart of the Bialowieza is closer to a state of nature than anywhere in Britain since at least the thirteenth century. It still shelters many of its aboriginal large mammals, including wild boar, elk, red deer and wolf; reintroduced herds of European bison add a nice primeval touch and there are even some wild horses (tarpan), although they are presently confined within an experimental enclosure. Much of the Bialowieza forest consists of flat, undrained swamps, thick with mosquitoes; giant fallen trunks and unearthed root plates abound, and in places soaring limes and hornbeams form a canopy 50m (160ft) high.

Such a place, one might imagine, would teem with birds. The results of a breeding-bird census conducted in 1975–9 indicated otherwise. The average density of breeding birds at Bialowieza is about fifty to seventy pairs per square kilometre (250 acres), much less than in many English and Welsh woods. The forest-edge ash and alder stands are the most productive areas and the natural conifer stands the least. The breeding densities of most birds numbered fewer than three pairs per square kilometre, and even hole-nesters like tits, surrounded by abundant food and nesting places, numbered only between four and thirty-six pairs. Judging by these results, the dawn chorus of the British Wildwood would have been pretty feeble compared with a Wealden coppice or even a wooded park today. The main reason advanced for this tremendous disparity between abundant food and nesting space and low bird numbers is the much heavier level of predation in primeval forest. There are far more 'safe' nest sites in ancient woods today than in an equivalent area of the original Wildwood, where much greater numbers of hungry and eagle-eyed raptors, owls, weasels and other carnivores were out hunting. For this reason tits do not use nest boxes at Bialowieza and the breeding success of most birds there is relatively poor: the woodpigeon, for example, failed to fledge a single chick during the survey period. It appears that songbirds respond to heavy predation at Bialowieza by nesting at a low density, and that the 'carrying capacity' of this woodland is therefore lower than it might at first appear.

On the other hand, the actual *composition* of birds at Bialowieza is remarkably similar to that of mixed broadleaved woodlands in southern England. Bialowieza contains more species, including several kinds of woodpecker that need quantities of dead standing wood, but many of them are present at a very low density. Of the common forest birds, only collared flycatcher does not also breed in Britain. The Bialowieza contains proportionately more hole-nesting birds than most English woods as does the still extensive tracts of virgin pine-spruce forest in Scandinavia. Bird behaviour in virgin forest also differs from British woods since, in large tracts of continuous forest like the Bialowieza, most birds forage *within* the wood and do not use the surrounding farmland. Bialowiezan blackbirds are true wild woodland birds. In

Britain, where most woods are tiny by comparison, many birds use woods as refuges for nesting but feed mostly on open ground outside, especially in winter. The density of birds in small woods set amid productive farmland or well-timbered urban parks can therefore far exceed that of virgin forest since it is not limited by the food supply *within* the wood. Perhaps for that reason, our woods have a greater proportion of ground-feeding birds like thrushes, robins and dunnocks.

The commonest woodland birds today are those which have been able to exploit changing conditions most successfully. They may not have been common in the Wildwood: blackbirds and starlings were much less abundant only a hundred years ago. A few of our birds have abandoned woodland altogether: the swift nests in tree holes in parts of Europe, but in Britain it has long since adapted to using towers or house roofs. The woodpigeon once lived in deciduous forest but is now the scourge of farmland. In the end, the closest approximation to Bialowieza in Britain turned out to be the New Forest, the least modified landscape in the whole of lowland England.

Ancient woods as homes for mammals

If you go down to the woods today . . . live mammals are almost as elusive as teddy bears. You can easily spend all day in a wood and see none at all except, perhaps, for foreigners like grey squirrels and rabbits (although you will probably hear rustling in the undergrowth). It is only when you begin to look for their tracks, dung and nibblings that signs of life begin to appear. Most woodland mammals can live in quite small woods of around 5–10ha (12–24 acres), either because their territories are small or because they do much of their foraging outside the wood. Among native mammals only the red squirrel and the dormouse are more or less confined to woodland; but on the other hand woodland is an important habitat for all the others except for grass-feeders like the brown hare and the field vole (and even these can be common in open

The use of ancient woodland by wild mammals. The figures are not, of course, to scale, nor would all these species be present in the same place at the same time

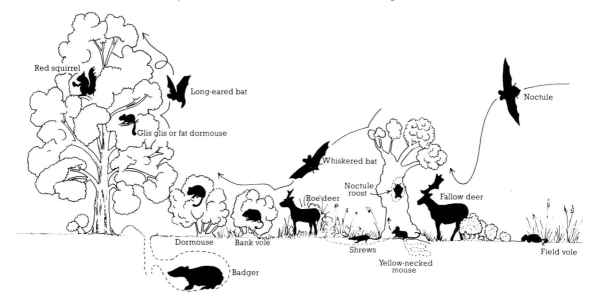

Red squirrel
Long-eared bat
Noctule
Glis glis or fat dormouse
Whiskered bat
Noctule roost
Roe deer
Fallow deer
Dormouse
Bank vole
Shrews
Yellow-necked mouse
Field vole
Badger

137

woodland). Animals with large territorial ranges, like the badger, may build their burrows in small woods but wander out at night along a regular beat using hedgerows, railway embankments and other places with thick cover. In large woods, on the other hand, badgers will forage mostly within the wood.

It would be misleading to claim that the best places for woodland mammals are ancient woods, since most British species are very adaptable. Two-thirds of the lowland mammals can breed in hedges. Structure and diversity are the key to how many mammals a wood can support, and the woods which possess these qualities to the greatest extent are generally old-established ones which are managed as coppice-with-standards. A reasonable amount of ground cover is vital for voles, shrews and hedgehogs, and open, heavily grazed woods typical of upland stock-rearing areas, or dense high forest with bare leafy floors, will usually be relatively poor in these animals. Well-structured woods also contain more food throughout an animal's active life. Most broad-leaved woods can provide a reasonably good larder of nuts, fruit and fungi at the end of the season, but in early summer, after the spring bonanza of buds, catkins and young leaves is over, food becomes much scarcer and the diversity one associates with specifically ancient woods is especially important during this lean time. Ancient woods are also likely to provide more old stumps and hollow coppice stools and trees than younger woods, offering secluded nesting sites for many of the smaller mammals, and roosts and nurseries for woodland bats.

Managed coppice benefits the majority of mammals, and their response to different stages of regrowth has been studied in several woods. The wood mouse, which is usually the commonest mammal in broadleaved woodland, is almost ubiquitous, occurring in large numbers at all stages of the coppice cycle, including recently bared ground. Common shrew and bank vole both need ground cover for their surface runs and only recolonise the clearings after a year or two. Their density peaks after three or four years, when harvest mouse, field vole, water shrew and pygmy shrew also find congenial conditions. Red squirrel and dormouse prefer more mature coppice, since hazel does not produce any nuts until it is at least six years old, and a short cycle may not suit them. Mammal numbers are much lower in old and neglected coppice, where the areas of greatest activity are likely to be along the scrubby edges of the wood, and wherever else there are quantities of brambles, hawthorns, blackthorns and other shrubs.

A surprising number of mammals can climb trees. Among the less likely ones are the bank vole, 'Cleth the Climber', which scurries about after bark and berries in the food-rich underwood, and the common shrew, which hunts grubs and insects in bushes up to about 3m (10ft) in height. The foraging of the yellow-necked mouse and wood mouse can take them far above ground, and they sometimes take over old bird's nests as food-stores and dormitories. Stoats and weasels are also nimble climbers, and the latter often raids bird's nests, especially those in holes and nest boxes (also eating any mice which happen to be sleeping there). The rare pine marten is the most acrobatic mammal of all, as much at home in the tree-tops as any bird, although in Britain it spends more time hunting and foraging on the ground.

There are few comparative studies of mammals in different types of   *Bank voles*
woodland, but most species seem to be widespread and not restricted to
particular types of vegetation. Trees with edible nuts, especially oak,
beech and hazel, are important food sources; it is said that every
mammal, apart from the pure carnivores, can make the most of a good
yield of acorns (although the red squirrel is an exception – acorns poison
it). Hazelnuts are a great favourite of squirrels, mice, voles and dormice.
Red squirrels are popularly associated with large mature pinewoods, but
in places where they have not yet been ousted by the grey, such as the
Lake District and the Isle of Wight, they also inhabit mature, broadleaved woods containing a good mixture of trees especially beech, ash,
hazel, maple and, in the few places where their ranges coincide,
hornbeam.

The Mammal Society's badger survey showed that more than half the
setts were in mature broadleaved woods and copses, and that the
animals sought places which had adequate cover, well-drained soil, little
disturbance from humans and a plentiful and varied food supply
throughout the year. Bank voles and wood mice are found in all kinds of
broadleaved woods throughout Britain but are scarce in conifer
plantations. The yellow-necked mouse is seldom found far from
woodland and hedgerows, and its disjointed distribution, centred on
East Anglia, south-east England and the Welsh Marches, suggests that
it was once more widespread. It is nowadays found mainly in districts
well populated with ancient and natural woods. In Essex, where it was

WOLVES AND
WOODPECKERS

studied by W. I. Montgomery in the 1970s, it prefers mature broadleaved woods on dry soils surrounded by arable land. In continental woods the yellow-necked mouse spends more time foraging in the canopy than the wood mouse, although this does not appear to be the case in Britain.

Apart from the squirrels, the dormouse is Britain's most arboreal mammal, rarely venturing down to the ground except to hibernate. It is also the species whose fate, more than that of any other native mammal, is caught up with the fate of ancient and natural woodland. With its big beady eyes (when awake), orangey-brown fur, long whiskers and bushy tail, the dormouse is a cuddlesome creature and used to be a popular pet. That is why all Victorian children had heard of the sleepy, stupid tall-tale-telling beast at the Mad Hatter's tea party, although few of them had ever set eyes on one in the wild. The dormouse has declined in the century since the Mad Hatter and a recent Mammal Society survey found that it has disappeared from several counties and is now common only in parts of the south of England and the Welsh borders, mainly in well-wooded districts. Fears for its long-term future have generated more scientific interest in the dormouse, and its secrets are slowly being unravelled by nocturnal naturalists working with radio transmitters and specially designed dormouse boxes.

Dormice build two kinds of nest: a summer one, which is always above ground, often deep inside a bramble thicket or in a tree hole; and a winter one on or below the ground, usually under moss, bracken or dead leaves, or in an old coppice stool, in which they sleep from October to early May. The summer nests can be found by patient searching in early winter when the leaves have fallen and the occupant is safely out of the way. Dormice are elusive and uncooperative objects to study, although once detected they can seem quite tame and unconcerned by human presence. Fortunately, to the practised eye they reveal their presence by leaving characteristically gnawed hazelnut shells and ragged, bark-stripped stems of honeysuckle. It used to be thought that they spent most of their time in the lower, shrubbier parts of the wood, but recent work has shown that they forage high into the canopy at certain times of the year, and will roost in bird boxes and tree-holes. The dormouse exploits different types of food during its period of wakefulness depending on the type of wood. In May it might climb into the canopy to seek catkins, caterpillars and birds' eggs. Later it feeds on honeysuckle leaves, generally near the ground, but in July it is back among the branches for the ash-key season before descending to the shrubbery for autumn's bounty of nuts and berries. By October it is already a plump and snoozing ball of fur on the forest floor.

Dormice used to be found most commonly in managed hazel coppice, but a multi-tangled layer of mixed shrubs and trees is likely to fit the bill just as well, so long as sufficient light can filter through the branches to the forest floor and there is a plentiful food supply throughout the season. Even in ideal conditions the dormouse never occurs in large numbers like other woodland rodents. A hectare (2½ acres) of suitable woodland might hold at least seventy each of voles and wood mice but only ten adult dormice. Because the latter live longer and have fewer young, their populations are fairly stable with a slow turnover, quite unlike the cycles of boom and crash which characterise mice and voles. Dormice are also sedentary animals, living out their lives in a three-dimensional aerial maze of around 30,000m³ (40,000cu yd). Animals like this thrive best in stable conditions, not a feature for which the British landscape is noted at present. Other factors, too, are against them. Dormice have not liked our recent cold, wet summers, sensibly electing to sleep through the worst parts of them, nor neglected shaded woods, nor bare hazels stripped of their nuts by marauding grey squirrels. Mild winters with variable temperatures, another feature of recent years, may produce unseasonal activity, thus depleting their vital reserves of winter fat.

To survive in reasonable numbers dormice may need nursing through this unfavourable period. We already know more about them, thanks to the use of electronic tracking equipment and the dormouse's own interest in nest boxes. In several woods in Devon they have grown so fond of the pied flycatcher's nest boxes, and the eggs they contain, that they pose an interesting dilemma to conservationists: what are more important, flycatchers or dormice? Dormice cannot cross broad rides unless the branches intermingle, and some woodland nature reserves are being managed so as to provide continuous aerial routeways for the mice, while nest-box schemes are being introduced or continued to help build up their numbers and to make it easier to count and study them. With the recent resurgence of interest in dormice, particularly the current study funded by the Worldwide Fund for Nature, it is likely that more woods will receive management geared to their needs.

The present sizeable numbers of the edible or fat dormouse, *Glis glis*, in the Chilterns are descended from animals liberated into woods near Tring by Lord Rothschild in the 1900s. It is a chubby, greyish animal, resembling more the grey squirrel than the native dormouse, and living a squirrelish way of life in the canopy of mature broadleaved woods, although in autumn it sometimes raids gardens and orchards for fruit. Their love of apples tempt *Glis glis* into attics where they attract attention and annoyance by the racket they make, rolling the apples about and bouncing after them with excited squeaks and twitters. About thirty are trapped and removed from attics each year by unamused officials from the public health department. *Glis glis* nests in tree-holes and forks close to the trunk and its arboreal habits may have prevented it from spreading beyond the well-wooded parts of Buckinghamshire, Berkshire and Hertfordshire. Most of its haunts are in ancient woodland, albeit much modified by beech planting, but it also flourishes in plantations like Wendover Wood in the Chilterns where it has made a nuisance of itself by stripping the bark from young conifers.

The other group of mammals most closely associated with broad-leaved woodland is the bats. All fifteen resident species hunt insects in woodland and all except the two horseshoe bats sometimes roost in hollows and holes in trees, where they find the darkness, seclusion and high humidity they need in daytime. In the Wildwood their principal roosts were probably tree-holes and they would have hunted insects over the top of the canopy and along the edges of woodland clearings, especially by rivers and lakes. At least one species, Bechstein's bat, was much more abundant in the original forest than at present. Its bones

WOODLAND HERITAGE

WOLVES AND
WOODPECKERS

have been found in quantity in the Grimes Graves flint mines in Suffolk and in limestone caves at Cresswell Crags, Nottinghamshire, where the bats roosted about 3,500 years ago. Today it is one of our rarest and least-known mammals – bat enthusiasts catch an average of one per year – centred on the New Forest, the Isle of Purbeck and south Devon, all areas notably rich in bats. It is still fairly common in well-wooded parts of Europe, where it can be seen on warm, calm evenings flying slowly over tall hedges and along woodland rides. Its rarity in Britain is thought to be due to forest clearance coupled with climatic deterioration, but little is known about its habits here since there is no reliable way of finding it.

Bechstein's bat has tremendously long ears and broad wings, features it shares with Britain's two kinds of long-eared bats and another rarity, the barbastelle. The excellent hearing and high flight manoeuvrability of these bats enables them to fly slowly around woodland trees in a characteristic twisting and tumbling way, gleaning large insects like moths and beetles from the foliage. To detect their prey their ears are attuned to the low-frequency sound of an insect about to take off and are sensitive enough to detect the echo from their (to us) almost inaudible squeak and pinpoint their prey. The common or brown long-eared bat is by far the most frequent user of artificial bat boxes in woodland (sixty-six of them were once found crammed inside a single box), and is perhaps our most characteristic species of mature broadleaved woodland. The largest British bat, the noctule, and its smaller cousin, Leisler's bat, are also woodland species in the main, but their wings are narrow and streamlined, designed for hunting insects in the air, often high above the canopy. They can also detect and catch insects on grass stems and other ground vegetation, plunging down from on high in a sudden swallow-like swoop. Noctule roosts and nurseries are usually in dead trees or mature trees with holes of sufficient size. Any species of tree will do, but an old ash tree, riddled with holes like a pepperpot, is a particular favourite. The noctule often has to compete with starlings for nest space but its tolerances are broad and it has even been known to use old woodpecker holes in pine trees. Nor is woodland absolutely necessary so long as there are some trees of sufficient age. It is often seen in parks and suburban green spaces, and even occurs in the unwooded vicinity of March in the Fens, although in this case the bats are obliged to eat not moths or fat grubs, their preferred prey, but midges. Perhaps this versatility explains why noctules are not rare, despite their dependency on that scarce and declining resource, the old tree.

Ancient woods as homes for birds

About 92 species of birds nest in woodland in Britain, and the single richest area is probably the New Forest where no fewer than 75 of them breed regularly. By contrast, native birchwoods in Sutherland commonly contain only 15 or so species of breeding birds. Large native woods in southern England and East Anglia can support between 45 and 55 breeding species, and there are also strange pockets of almost equally bird-rich woodland in Yorkshire, Northumberland, Cheshire

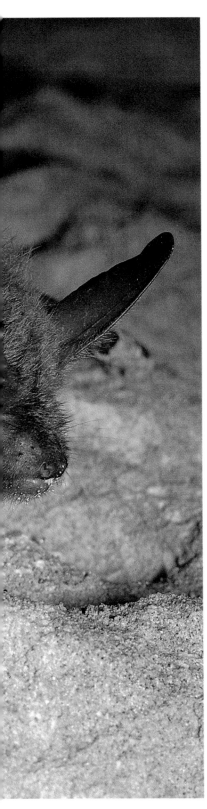

Bechstein's Bat. The rarest and least known of our native mammals, but evidently common in prehistory

and the counties bordering the Severn estuary. An enormous body of information on the birds of individual woods has been amassed in recent years by the NCC, the Royal Society for the Protection of Birds (RSPB) and the British Trust for Ornithology (BTO), much of which has been summarised by R. J. Fuller in his *Bird Habitats in Britain* and will not be repeated here.

So far, however, it is not possible to compare the birds of specifically *ancient* woods with those of secondary woodland or plantations. To an even greater extent than mammals, birds exploit suitable conditions as they arise. Ancient woodland may well account for the majority of breeding pairs of certain species with specialised requirements, such as nightingale, wood warbler and hawfinch in broadleaved woods, and the more restricted Scottish crossbill and crested tit in Caledonian pinewoods. Others, like the woodpeckers and nuthatch, are most frequent in large broadleaved woods. Woods with the greatest variety of nesting birds are likely to combine large size with a favourable geographical location, a diverse structure and a wide range of vegetation, including thickets and old trees. Continental studies suggest that the *density* of nesting birds, but not necessarily the diversity of species, is also related to the fertility of the soil, so that, other things being equal, one might expect more nests in clay or limestone woods than in woods on sandy or peaty soils.

Woodland birds can be divided roughly into three groups: those which nest on or near the ground, including underwood and scrub; those which nest in mature trees, generally in holes; and those which build nests in the tree-tops. The latter are generally large birds – raptors, crows, magpies and herons – for which tall trees offer relative safety and a vantage point, but these do most of their hunting and foraging outside the wood. Oddly enough, few woodland songbirds nest in the canopy in Britain and the rest of Europe (the hawfinch is a notable exception), by contrast with similar forests in the New World. Most of them are scrub or coppice-nesters or hole-nesters. Few are confined to woods, since the former may use suitably overgrown hedges and other areas of scrub and tangle, while the latter are often equally characteristic of parks and secluded gardens containing nest boxes.

The birds which depend most on broadleaved woods are our three woodpeckers, marsh and willow tit, nuthatch, treecreeper, redstart, nightingale, blackcap, garden warbler, willow warbler, chiffchaff, wood warbler, pied flycatcher and hawfinch. In Scotland, one could probably add blue tit and great tit, in the breeding season at least. The majority of these species feed on insects during the breeding season, and a large proportion of them are summer visitors. Thicket-nesters thrive best in woods with dense underwood, although they can crowd into patches of scrub or nearby hedgerows if conditions are unsuitable. Managed coppice is famous for its spring bird-song, and in recently cut clearings birds like tree pipit and woodlark use trees and shrubs as song or display flight-posts. As the coppice reaches its leafiest and densest stage, garden and willow warbler, blackcap, chiffchaff and nightingale are among the most characteristic birds. After ten years or so, they in turn yield place to chaffinches, robins, blackbirds and tits, and in old coppice most of the previously mentioned birds will nest in scrub at the edge of the wood.

143

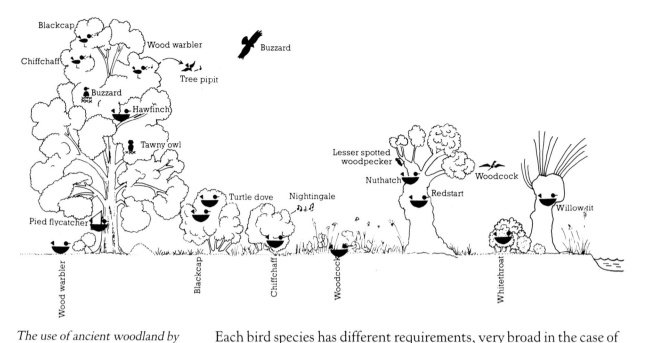

The labels in the illustration read:

Blackcap
Chiffchaff
Buzzard
Wood warbler
Buzzard
Tree pipit
Hawfinch
Tawny owl
Pied flycatcher
Lesser spotted woodpecker
Nuthatch
Redstart
Woodcock
Willow tit
Turtle dove
Nightingale
Wood warbler
Blackcap
Chiffchaff
Woodcock
Whitethroat

The use of ancient woodland by birds. Not all of them would occupy the same place at the same time: the owl would be mobbed by the songsters, and the appearance of the buzzard would silence them all!

= nest sites

= song perches

Each bird species has different requirements, very broad in the case of adaptable and ubiquitous birds like starlings and chaffinches, but much narrower in others which may depend on suitable woodland management to maintain their numbers. The nightingale, for example, needs just the right amount of shade and shrubbery to nest successfully. Nightingales build their nest close to the ground and so seek out impenetrable thickets of coppice poles which are covered with leaves all the way down to ground. The necessary density of foliage is provided by hazel and mixed coppice, but not by chestnut which is the main commercial coppicewood today. In Suffolk and Kent, where nightingales have been studied intensively, the best stage is reached about six or seven years after coppicing. Thereafter the coppice bush becomes more 'leggy', developing a hollow centre and shading out the foliage nearest the ground. The ideal management for nightingales is therefore a coppice cycle of eight to ten years, in which up to a quarter of the wood is suitable for nesting at any one time. Medieval woods, which were often managed in this way, were probably loud with nightingales. But the decline of coppicing has reduced its status to one of our rarer woodland birds, and there are now thought to be fewer than ten thousand pairs in Britain. Its prospects may improve with the revival of suitable management in many nature reserves and community woods, and with the dramatic opening up of many south-eastern woods by the gale of October 1987.

Some nineteen species of woodland birds nest in the holes and crevices of mature trees and are more characteristic of high forest or wood pasture than of coppice. In oak stands of different ages in the Forest of Dean, nuthatch, treecreeper, redstart and greater spotted woodpecker were restricted to the older parts, presumably because of their need for timber of sufficient girth and softness. Crested tits and, to a smaller extent, lesser spotted woodpeckers, prefer soft, even rotten, wood to excavate their nest-holes. In woods lacking sufficient numbers of suitable trees, the numbers of some hole-nesting species can be boosted by supplying them with nest boxes, and spectacular results have been obtained in the case of the pied flycatcher. If one puts enough nest boxes of suitable size in an oakwood in Devon or Wales, this attractive species can become the commonest breeding bird in the wood. For the pied flycatcher, natural nesting sites are evidently at a premium whereas their food supply of flying insects is almost unlimited.

Two more songbirds share the pied flycatcher's predilection for western sessile oakwoods. The wood warbler needs large, fairly open woods with a well-developed canopy and sparse ground vegetation. Its well-disguised domed nests are built on the woodland floor among grasses, dead leaves and low cover, and for this reason this warbler will not nest in the dense underwood favoured by its close relatives. The other western species, the redstart, is a hole-nester and, like the pied flycatcher, takes readily to nest boxes. It is found in a wide range of woodland, providing it is not too dense, but is another characteristic inhabitant of sessile oak woodland. A recently published map of the breeding range of redstarts in Devon shows a remarkable concentration in the valley oakwoods of Dartmoor and Exmoor. The red kite is a speciality, although sadly a rare one, of mature oakwoods on the slopes of steep valleys in central and southern Wales, and a project is under way to introduce it into suitable woods in England and Scotland where it used to breed more than a century ago.

During the breeding season, most woodland birds occupy a fixed territory. Outside the breeding season, most of those which are not migrants range more widely in search of food, flocking together like goldcrests, tits and, in more open habitats, finches such as siskin and redpoll, or visiting garden bird-tables like blue and great tits and thrushes. A few, however, remain tied to woodland throughout the year and these are some of our most sedentary species. Two of the best examples are hawfinch and nuthatch. Both need mature trees. The shy, secretive hawfinch is a specialist feeder on hard seeds, most famously cherry stones, but also those of elm, hornbeam, sycamore and maple. Although fairly widespread, it is not easily seen but it is most frequent in mixed broadleaved woods, presumably enjoying as much variety as possible within the limits of its chosen diet. The Home Counties hornbeam woods are especially good places to find hawfinches. The nuthatch also specialises in hard nuts, in this case hazelnuts, acorns, beechnuts and sweet chestnuts, which it forces into crevices in the bark and bashes open with its powerful bill. Despite its visits to bird-tables in winter, the nuthatch rarely strays far outside woodland. Perhaps its lack of mobility explains the otherwise surprising lack of nuthatches in many woods and parks which seem ideal for them.

THE NATIVE PINEWOODS

The Caledonian pinewoods of Scotland have a distinct community of birds which sets them apart from other native woods. They are the principal home of the Scottish crossbill and crested tit and are an increasingly important refuge for capercaillie and black grouse. The larger pinewoods are also among the most exciting places in Britain to see birds of prey.

The Scottish crossbill, regarded by some as a distinct species from the

'common' crossbill, enjoys the distinction of being the only British bird which is almost entirely confined to ancient woodland. There are only about 1,500 Scottish crossbills in the world, and all of them live in the native Caledonian pinewoods and some of the older Scots pine plantations nearby. This stocky, big-headed finch eats pine seeds and not much else; its entire mode of life is therefore allied to the Scots pine. Its powerful, scissor-like bill is a specialised tool for prising open tough cones and it is of little use for other purposes. Fortunately the cone crop rarely fails and is available all year round so that the Scottish crossbill has no pressing need to travel very far, except to different parts of the wood in search of fresh cones. It even nests in mid-winter to coincide with the peak of seed production. These birds have been closely studied by Dr Alan Knox in the extensive native pinewoods of Deeside where they occur in largest numbers. According to Knox, they prefer large areas of continuous forest with stands of old, widely spaced pines, and, unlike some of the other species of old pinewoods, they have been conspicuously unable to take advantage of new planting in the Dee Valley and elsewhere. The future of the Scottish crossbill, one of Europe's rarest birds and our only endemic bird species, depends on the preservation of enough *mature* native Scots pine woodland within its limited range.

The importance of the native pinewoods derives not only from the trees themselves but also from the ground vegetation which, when left undisturbed, becomes lush with hummocks of blaeberry, heather, mosses and bushes of juniper as many-shaped as cumulus clouds. Crested tits use this layer for shelter and forage and it is also important for the survival of the two largest native gamebirds, capercaillie and black grouse. All Scottish capercaillies owe their origin to nineteenth-century introductions for, although a true native, it died out about two hundred years ago when suitable pine woodland was at its lowest ebb. The capercaillie is the world's largest grouse and a full-grown cock is a magnificent creature, weighing in at about 9lb (4kg) with a wingspan of about 5ft (1.5m). A bird this size needs space to spread its wings and strong branches to bear its weight, which is one reason why capercaillies do not live in dense young plantations. It breeds most successfully in open pinewoods with a lush growth of blaeberry (bilberry), the main diet of the chick.

As recently as 1970, the capercaillie was probably as common in central and eastern Scotland as at any time since its reintroduction, but since about 1975 their numbers have fallen sharply. Dr Robert Moss, of the Hill of Brathens research centre in Deeside, has demonstrated that they breed most successfully in native pinewoods and that populations in other woods and plantations are probably sustained by the movement of birds from the native woods. Cold wet weather in early summer in 1984–7 resulted in poor breeding, and the adults have been over-shot in some woods, mainly by continental trophy hunters (British game interests show a curious lack of interest in the capercaillie, while foresters regard it as vermin). But another cause of decline is the present scarcity of suitable habitat. Capercaillies gather in the spring for displaying and mating at a lek, a fixed site in the forest from which the territories of individual cocks radiate outwards like slices of a pie. The

most impressive leks are in extensive pinewoods of at least 3– 4km² (1– 1½ square miles), about a third of which should be old forest if the bird is to maintain its numbers successfully. There are not many such woods, even in the Highlands, and so the great native pinewoods of Glen Tanar, Ballochbuie, Abernethy and Rothiemurchus form the heartland of the capercaillie and, probably, its healthiest breeding populations. The new plantations have the potential to support a low density of capercaillies once the trees are at least thirty years old, but for the capercaillie to nest successfully conifer plantations will need to be managed on a longer rotation with a wider spacing of trees and more Scots pine than is customary at present.

The black grouse shares the lekking habits of the capercaillie, and it too needs woodland with dense ground vegetation for shelter and roosting, especially in winter. It sometimes stays on in the spring to nest in the depths of open native pinewoods like Glen Tanar in Deeside. As with the capercaillie, the native pinewoods are becoming an increasingly important refuge for this declining species, since much of its erstwhile breeding habitat of birch scrub among open moorland has been cleared and/or afforested. In Scandinavia, the black grouse is a typical inhabitant of clearings in mature forests, and by nesting in pinewoods in Scotland it may be reverting to its ancestral habits. Fortunately the black grouse can also nest successfully in young plantations of spruce and larch, which in their initial stages often contain much birch.

Native Caledonian pine. This fine old tree greets walkers from the Lairig Ghru in the Cairngorms as they begin to descend towards Aviemore. The forest of Rothiemurchus lies at our feet. May 1978

147

9

SWEET SCENTS AND HOLLOW TREES

He who owns a veteran bur oak owns more than a tree. He owns a historical library, and a reserved seat in the theatre of evolution.

Aldo Leopold,
A Sand County Almanac

In summer 1935, a well-known entomologist, Claude Morley, sat down beside a large beech stump in the New Forest to record what insects were making use of it. By the time he had completed his observations, two months later, his notebook was crammed full of a bewildering variety of species which had variously buzzed around, crawled over or bored into this single, unexceptional old tree. A list of just the *rare* species he saw filled two full pages of the *Entomologist's Monthly Magazine*. Starting at the base of the trunk, he discovered various communities of insects living among the moss and gnarled roots. Above, on the bare wood, long ago stripped of its bark and now exposed to the sun, basked hoverflies and longhorn beetles, while cuckoo wasps searched the trunk for insect holes in which to lay their eggs. Beetles and micro-moth larvae nibbled the bracket fungi encrusting the lower part of the trunk, while adult carpet moths roosted among the multicoloured lichens in furrows in the bark. In the dry hollow at the top of the stump a social wasp was building its nest. And all this bustle and variety was the mere outward and visible expression of a stump which was riddled internally with a microcosm of grubs and beetles that fed on wood, mould and debris, together with their predators and parasites. Populations of many of these insects and other invertebrates go through many successive generations in the same stump, and many more will have colonised it as the trunk gradually rotted away. A long-lived and favourably placed tree like Morley's beech will have supported hundreds of different species during its life-span.

The number and variety of invertebrates supported by a wood, let alone a single stump, is simply mind-boggling. On a quiet day in mid-summer you can actually hear some of them at work, the gentle patter of caterpillar droppings hitting the woodland floor, the half-forgotten 'midsummer hum' of flowery glades. Invertebrates strip whole trees of their foliage and recycle countless tons of leaf litter and dead wood. Every acre (0.4ha) of woodland soil contains about half a ton of mixed invertebrates, including roughly 250kg (550lb) earthworms, 25kg (55lb) spiders and 40kg (88lb) slugs and snails. To put this into context, the same area contains only about 4kg (9lb) worth of birds and mammals, above or below ground. In all, about 15,000 species of invertebrates live in Britain's woods, which is roughly the same as in all other kinds of habitats, natural and unnatural, put together.

Insect statistics, like astronomical ones, are apt to leave one somewhat breathless. To find some sort of order in the numbers and lists we need to look in more detail at the particular places, such as the leaf-litter, glades, banks and ponds, where individual communities of insects live. In many cases we need to adjust the scale still smaller. A great many insects and other invertebrates live in tiny 'niches', holes in the bark or wood or inside birds' or ants' nests. Others need a variety of different places within their flight range, like certain hoverflies which need flowers as nectar sources and dead wood for their larvae. Ancient woods in general are better endowed with this innate *intimacy* of scale and variety than other woods, and therefore support far more species. Those which are poor colonisers or which have particular requirements not widely found elsewhere may be virtually restricted to ancient sites, and it is with these that this chapter is principally concerned. Such insects are attuned to long-term stability and, like the flowers on which they feed, they may have lived in the same place for hundreds, if not thousands, of years. Insects are more sensitive to change than flowers, however, for unlike them they cannot survive unfavourable periods as dormant seed. Individual insects are nearly all short-lived and most complete their life-cycle within the span of a year. If through some mischance their habitat disappears, even for just a few years, they will inevitably disappear too. And if the wood is an isolated one they may never return: the least adaptable of them are probably already extinct.

Secondary woods and plantations, on the other hand, are colonised entirely by invertebrates which have managed to fly in or have crawled from nearby woods and hedges. These woods will, if conditions permit, accumulate more species over the years, especially if they happen to lie close by an ancient wood, but even old, well-established plantations lack those characteristic species of ancient woodland which are unable to move far from their birthplaces. Their presence can therefore indicate woods which have retained some aspects of natural forest and where conditions have remained suitable for a very long time.

Our knowledge of woodland invertebrates is very uneven. Apart from those which draw attention to themselves by biting, stinging or looking dangerous, only butterflies, dragonflies and some of the larger moths are reasonably well known to the non-specialist. Most of the others lack familiar names and, as if in compensation, the smallest and least significant of them seem to own the longest scientific names. Hoverflies, slugs and snails, grasshoppers and dead-wood beetles have received a fair amount of attention lately, but there are only a handful of people who can identify with confidence a bark-louse, a psyllid bug or a pseudoscorpion, despite the important role these small animals play in natural woodland cycles.

Woodland contains four main types of invertebrate: those which feed on plants; those which feed on detritus; carnivores; and parasites. Plant-eating insects are the most numerous, and the table shows the relative importance of different native trees and shrubs. This list omits the many generalist feeders which are less fussy about what kind of leaf they eat. Most trees near the top of the list, like sallow, birch and hawthorn, have palatable leaves, while beech and ash, which are tougher and contain more tannic acid, occupy a lower place than one might expect. Oak has the richest insect fauna of any tree in the south of England, but it is overtaken north of the Humber by birch and sallow.

WOODLAND HERITAGE

SWEET SCENTS AND
HOLLOW TREES

Numbers of plant-eating insects associated with forest trees and shrubs in Britain (based on the list compiled by Kennedy and Southwood in 1984).

Sallow and willows	450
Oak	423
Birch	334
Hawthorn	209
Poplar and aspen	189
Scots pine	172
Blackthorn	153
Alder	141
Elm	124
Crab apple	118
Hazel	106
Beech	98
Ash	68
Rowan	58
Lime	57
Hornbeam	51
Maple	51
Juniper	32
Sweet chestnut	11
Holly	10
Yew	6

New Forest cicada, Cicadetta montana. *Our only native cicada, now confined to glades and scrubby places in the New Forest. Abroad it is particularly attracted to small-leaved lime, and may be a 'wildwood' relic in Britain*

No tree ever has its full complement of dependent plant-eaters, since some species are restricted in range or need trees of a particular age or siting. One would expect woods with many different species of trees over a wide range of ages to be richer in insects than more uniform woods, although the amount of evidence to support this assumption is surprisingly slight.

To cut or not to cut . . .

Many people consider that coppicing is the best way of managing a wood to benefit invertebrates. This is probably true up to a point, but much depends on how often the wood is cut and whether parts are left for the species which need mature foliage or deep shade. Some woodland nature reserves seem to be managed largely in the interests of butterflies, most of which prefer open woods on short coppice rotations. Such conditions chiefly benefit species which need masses of flowers and bright sunshine. Ground beetles do well in coppice glades, as do wolf spiders, jumping spiders, wood ants and some solitary bees and wasps. Leaf beetles, weevils, aphids and some moth caterpillars enjoy the juicy leaves of young coppice. Old coppice stools also contain a good deal of dead and decaying wood and pools of rainwater, and are notable breeding sites for rare flies. But the best coppiced woods for insects tend to be those which have been managed in this way without interruption for many years. The results of coppicing on long-neglected stands have sometimes been disappointing, probably because many of the invertebrates which would benefit most no longer live in that particular wood!

Other invertebrates flourish best in less intensively managed woods with more mature foliage. These include leaf-mining moths, crane flies, web spiders, bark-lice, many beetles, and most of the species which live in leaf-litter. Too frequent cutting can cause these to decline. Coppices sometimes have few or no large trees and not much fallen wood of any size, and are therefore poor in species which live in dead wood (considered separately below), except for those which bore into rotting roots. Short-rotation coppicing is not therefore always the ideal management for ancient woods. At worst it may encourage little of importance to conservation at the expense of damaging the existing interest. For all except the smallest woods, the ideal management is to aim at a balance between the conflicting requirements of various species, and to resist the temptation to be mesmerised by the most attractive ones, like butterflies. Conservationists ought to take some sort of Hippocratic oath to treat all species as equals.

Inside a log

About one fifth of the invertebrate fauna of natural temperate forest depends on dead or decaying wood, and these species have been dubbed 'saproxylic' from *sapros* meaning dead and *xylos* meaning wood. (It should be pronounced 'saprozylik', not 'saprok*sillik*' as uttered by many entomologists.) Among the insects, several hundred species of beetles

and flies, and a smaller number of bees, wasps and ants, breed in wood of varying states of decay. Non-insects commonly found under loose bark or fallen logs, or in hollow trees include woodlice, millipedes, centipedes, pseudoscorpions, spiders, slugs and snails. To give some idea of how abundant these species must have been in the original virgin forest, an Irish entomologist, Dr Martin Speight, estimated that a hectare (2½ acres) of undisturbed natural woodland produces about 6 tonnes of dead wood annually, which rots down to produce nutrients equivalent to half the entire annual leaf-fall. In the Wildwood, scientists believe that between three and eight trees in every hundred were dead but standing, while most of the remainder were mature or old – the complete opposite of commercial plantation woodland. These conditions can still be found in the remaining tracts of virgin forest in Sweden, Finland and Poland, where the saproxylic invertebrates are an extremely numerous and important part of the natural forest cycle. That so many of these species are now rare in Britain, and indeed throughout most of Europe, is a reflection of how modified are most woods from their natural state and how few have contained aged trees *continuously* since then.

In commercially managed woods, trees are felled before maturity and the dead wood is taken away, thus removing the entire habitat of the wood-decomposers. Many of Britain's scarcer 'saproxylics' are therefore more common in wood-pasture, especially medieval deer-parks, than in dense woods, and perhaps only two places today retain the original diversity, if not the numbers, of insects in natural woodland: the New Forest and Windsor Forest, which between them contain the largest number of old trees surviving in the lowlands. The New Forest contains between two-thirds and three-quarters of all saproxylic species found in

Wood cricket, Nemobius sylvestris. *Another New Forest denizen, but also occurs locally in sunny woodland clearings among deep leaf-litter in four southern countries. Its purring song is often mistaken for the grasshopper warbler*

151

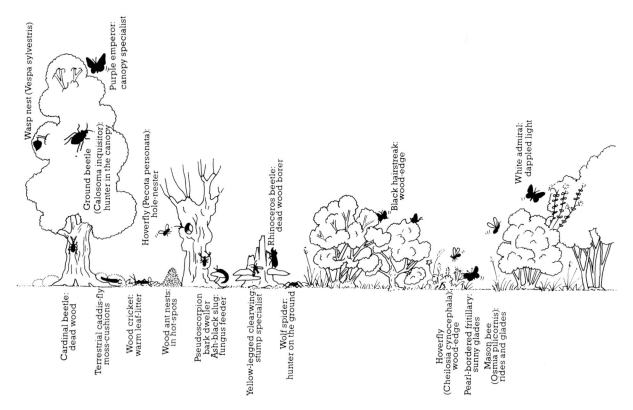

Habitat 'niches' for invertebrates in ancient woodland (not to scale)

Labels in figure:
Wasp nest (Vespa sylvestris)
Purple emperor: canopy specialist
Ground beetle (Calosoma inquisitor): hunter in the canopy
Hoverfly (Pecota personata): hole-nester
Rhinoceros beetle: dead wood borer
Black hairstreak: wood-edge
White admiral: dappled light
Cardinal beetle: dead wood
Terrestrial caddis-fly: moss-cushions
Wood cricket: warm leaf-litter
Wood ant nests: in hot-spots
Pseudoscorpion: bark dweller
Ash-black slug: fungus feeder
Yellow-legged clearwing: stump specialist
Wolf spider: hunter on the ground
Hoverfly (Cheilosia cynocephala): wood-edge
Pearl-bordered fritillary: sunny glades
Mason bee (Osmia pilicornis): rides and glades

Britain, while Windsor is reputed to be richer still. Impoverished though our fauna is, we are nonetheless fortunate compared with some European countries where old trees are even rarer; Belgian trees, for example, are not allowed to die a natural death and a recent quest to find a really old one was abandoned in failure. Old trees today have little commercial value and are frequently felled on dubious grounds – forest hygiene, public safety or an obsession with tidiness. As an American writing on European attitudes to the past wrote recently, a few old trees feed our nostalgia for good times past, but 'too many degenerating specimens become unpleasant reminders of the passing of beloved familiar landscapes'. It is no wonder, then, that many of these 'saproxylic' insects are so rare, since they often need specifically big old trees. And they would, I imagine, concur with Oliver Rackham that 'a thousand hundred year-old oaks are no substitute for one five hundred year-old oak'.

Trees need to be several hundred years old, and preferably pollards, to reach their full potential as invertebrate habitats. Oak, beech, hornbeam and Caledonian Scots pine are the most important. Old trees typically have massive trunks with cavities, swollen bosses, broad, often broken, limbs and dead wood of every description and state of decay. Looking through a hole in the sapwood into the red-rotten interior of an old oak pollard you glimpse a different world, dark, dank and sheltered like a cave, sometimes with growths of fungus and piles of gently rotting wood-mould. Once established, these conditions can last almost unchanged for centuries before the tree finally dies, its roots decay and the trunk topples down. Even the fallen log will, if left alone to rot, be used by invertebrates for many more years and it may take a further quarter-century to rot away completely. Each stage of senility and decay in a tree's protracted death possesses its own distinctive fauna. Many invertebrates breed in small-scale habitats, notably in humus or rainwater-filled rot-holes, in the powdery heartwood, under loose bark or on persistent sap-runs resulting from injury. Those which live in standing dead wood are in many instances different from those in fallen logs, and, with the exception of Scots pine which, being a softwood, has a different chemistry, the condition of the timber is generally more important than the particular species of tree.

In the remainder of this chapter, we will look in more detail at some of the invertebrates of dead wood and other woodland habitats. There is space to mention but a fraction of them, and our knowledge of their ecology is in any case limited. What we know of the distribution and habits of our woodland moths, ants, snails and spiders has been pieced together by the efforts of enthusiasts like Claude Morley, who was left sitting under his tree at the start of this chapter. Much remains to be discovered. The tree-tops of tropical jungles are better known than those of our own woods, and the first good close-up pictures of life in the canopy of British woods were apparently obtained just a few years ago by television cameras filming *The Living Isles*. What we need more than ever is for more Claude Morleys to go out and build shelters and tree-houses in our woods, and to record by patient observation the comings and goings of the vast, but barely visible, woodland city.

Beetles (Coleoptera)

Beetles are among the most numerous of woodland insects and about 650 of them are rarely found far from the food and shelter of natural woodland or old trees. Beetles like warm places and Britain's climate is too chilly and wet for a large proportion of European species. For the same reason about half of Britain's fauna is confined to the southern half of the country and so one would expect a wood in Kent or Hampshire to be a great deal richer than one in Northumberland, and open, flower-rich woods on southern slopes to be better than damp, shaded north-facing ones. Pine and birchwoods in the Highlands have much in common with Scandinavian forests and contain a number of specialities rare or absent elsewhere in Britain. Beetles are a comparatively well-studied group and much of what has been discovered about their ecology and history is applicable in some measure to less-known groups.

SWEET SCENTS AND HOLLOW TREES

The life histories of beetles are almost incredibly diverse, and there can be few potential food sources which they do not exploit to the full. Woods provide quantities of living and dead wood, pollen and nectar (hawthorn, bramble and hogweed are favourites), leaves and stems, plant-litter, dead animals, dung, toadstools and lichens, fruits and nuts and an almost limitless selection of partly decayed detritus. Some specialist beetles cultivate fungus gardens inside woody galleries, or live as scavengers inside ants' nests, or in woodland ponds and streams. Some are carnivores of varying shape, size and ferocity, and lurk wherever there are concentrations of herbivorous insects and their larvae. The handsome *Calosoma sycophanta*, for example, is a big, fast-moving beetle which hunts moth and sawfly caterpillars high up in the canopy of well-grown trees. In America, foresters rely on its efficiency in controlling potential pests. In general the more varied the structure and species composition of a wood, the more interesting the beetle fauna is likely to be.

No fewer than fourteen families of beetles in Britain consist almost exclusively of species which feed on living or dead wood in their larval stage, and among them are some of the most spectacular and well-known species, including the stag beetle and the colourful and elegant longhorns. Some of the better-known dead-wood beetles are, for some unknown reason, bright red, such as the click beetle, *Ampedus sanguineus*, the beautiful net-winged beetles (Lycidae), whose larvae feed on wood-mould in hollow trunks and stumps, and the cardinal beetles (Pyrochroidae) which exploit the warm, moist zone beneath loose bark. Among the stag beetle's relatives is the grotesque rhinoceros beetle (named after an upwardly projecting horn that sprouts from its head) which breeds in rotting wood. Wood, especially dry wood, is not a nutritious diet, and the larvae of some of these beetles therefore grow slowly. The stag beetle, whose grubs tunnel into the roots of mature trees, can take up to five years to reach the adult stage. Slow growth coupled with large size demands stable conditions and plenty of food. Largeness seems to be a liability among invertebrates today – the endangered list of British insects is full of big beetles that send the faint-hearted sprinting back indoors.

Saproxylic beetles and their habitats have been studied in detail in recent years by entomologists contracted by the NCC, and the findings were summarised in a recent publication (Harding and Rose, 1986). This lists no fewer than 196 species which are characteristic of wood-pasture containing old trees, and divides them into three groups. The first contains relatively widespread species which in certain districts, usually towards the edge of their natural range, are confined to old trees but are less fastidious elsewhere. The black-headed cardinal beetle, *Pyrochroa coccinea*, is one of these. It is fairly common and widespread in parts of the North and West, epecially in Wales, but seems restricted to over-mature timber in the South. The middle group is made up of beetles which are commonest in wood-pasture throughout their range, but are also encountered less frequently in other habitats. Most restricted are sixty-eight species which are more or less confined to wood-pasture containing aged pollards and are therefore indicators of long habitat continuity, if not primary woodland. The rarest of all are confined to Britain's best sites. The large click beetle, *Elater ferrugineus*, for example, has been found only in the New Forest and Windsor Great Park. *Hypebaeus flavipes* is confined to red-rotten oak pollards in Moccas Park, in Hereford and Worcester, and apparently ignores the numerous over-mature maiden oaks nearby. The violet click beetle, *Limoniscus violaceus*, inhabits the rotting interiors of a few hollow beeches at Windsor and is protected by law.

What ails these rare and declining beetles? It cannot be habitat scarcity alone, since rotten oaks and beeches, though lamentably uncommon, are a great deal less so than *H. flavipes* or the violet click beetle. The answer probably lies in woodland history and the poor colonising ability of the species concerned. The Wildwood teemed with beetles which are rare today or have died out altogether through climatic change or forest clearance. Out of fourteen woodland species which were present in the Bronze Age but, so far as we know, not since, no less than eleven bred in rotten wood. In more recent times the pace of change has quickened, and the past 150 years have seen the extinction of at least twenty more old forest beetles, including spectacular specimens like the hairy longhorn *Leptura virens* and the metallic-blue stag beetle *Platycerus caraboides*. Beetles confined to a handful of old-forest sites are probably on the last stage of a long slow decline from original abundance that has lasted thousands of years. Even relatively widespread old-forest species may be too scattered and isolated within their oases of woodland for any possible interchange between sites. Their future is linked to the wider problem of preserving the remaining

SWEET SCENTS AND HOLLOW TREES

Black-headed cardinal beetle, Pyrochroa coccinea. *Fond of flowers and old stumps where its carnivorous larva hunts smaller invertebrates beneath the bark*

SWEET SCENTS AND HOLLOW TREES

The table below lists the British woodland butterflies, their foodplants and their habitats.

Association with ancient woodland:
**Strong, ie more than half the colonies are in and around ancient woods.
* Moderate, ie a preference for ancient woods, but more widespread.

Open sunny rides and glades
Meadow brown (grasses)
Gatekeeper (grasses)
Scotch argus (grasses)
Dark green fritillary (violets)
Small pearl-bordered fritillary (violets)*
Marsh fritillary (devil's-bit scabious)
Red admiral (stinging nettle)
Small tortoiseshell (stinging nettle)
Peacock (stinging nettle)
Comma (elm, stinging nettle)
Duke of Burgundy (primrose, cowslip)
Holly blue (holly, ivy)
Common blue (bird's-foot trefoil)
Small Copper (sorrel)
Brimstone (buckthorn)
Grizzled skipper (wild strawberry)*
Dingy skipper (bird's-foot trefoil)
Chequered skipper (moor-grass)*
Small skipper (grasses)
Essex skipper (grasses)
Large skipper (grasses)

Lightly-shaded rides and glades
Ringlet (grasses)
Wood white (vetches)*

scraps of medieval wood-pasture and old forest in an era when anything without commercial value is liable to destruction. When insects like the violet click beetle become extinct the loss is not confined to science; we are taking an axe to our own prehistoric roots.

We do not know whether woodland beetles range far beyond their breeding sites. Strong-flying beetles, like the bigger longhorns, have the ability to do so in theory but are nevertheless seldom seen outside their natural habitat, except in stackyards of logs and other stores of recently felled timber. A few beetles, such as some of the weevils, are flightless and are presumably poor colonisers. Others require hot sunshine or warm still evenings to summon up enough energy to fly, which may be one reason why beetles like the lesser stag beetle are more tied to ancient woods in the cooler northern parts of their range. Evidence that some woodland beetles are unwilling to leave the shelter of the trees was deduced from observations made in Scottish oakwoods during the 1960s by R. A. Crowson. He noticed that many species of beetle were restricted to ancient oakwoods which had not been subjected to frequent felling. Neighbouring nineteenth-century oak plantations provided an apparently suitable habitat but lacked a large number of the ancient woodland species. Crowson suggested an explanation in terms of the limiting conditions needed for flight. Most beetles fly only in warm, still, humid air, and then only in certain seasons with a peak in late-spring and early summer. In central Scotland at that time of year the temperature is warm enough only at midday, when the beetles are restricted by prevailing wind or by their crepuscular habits to the shelter of the trees. They are therefore unable to cross wide stretches of open ground and can colonise only adjacent woods. Crowson recorded similar beetle behaviour in the Lake District. In southern England, temperatures are high enough to permit mass evening flights of beetles, when individuals may be caught up in air currents and whisked some distance away. The ability of beetles to colonise isolated recent woods may therefore be greater in the South than further north.

Butterflies

One of the saddest signs of change in our woods has been the decline of most of the woodland butterflies. This was first brought home to me in the early 1960s when I started to visit local woods in Cambridgeshire hoping to find what I had been led by books to expect. True, the more ubiquitous wayside browns, orange-tips and peacocks were common enough, but where were all the fritillaries, hairstreaks, white admirals and other species which breed only in woodland? By contrast, a century ago, the young F. W. Frohawk, later to become a well-known naturalist and illustrator, had this to say about his own local wood near Ipswich:

It was in July 1872 I first saw the great Fritillaries sucking nectar from the bramble blossoms and thistles . . . As many as five Purple Emperors I watched playing about around the top of a large oak. The White Admiral was in abundance everywhere. In that year the Large Tortoiseshell was to be seen everywhere, commonly seen sitting on tree trunks with expanded wings in the sun.

Sixteen years later, Frohawk made his first visit to the New Forest:

> I shall never forget the impression it made . . . Insects of all kinds literally swarmed. Butterflies were in profusion, the Silver-washed Fritillary were in hordes in every ride and the beautiful variety *valezina* was met with at every few yards, as were both the Dark Green and High Brown Fritillaries. The elegant White Admiral were sailing about in quantity everywhere. On a bank under a sallow was a large female Purple Emperor with its wings expanded, evidently washed out of the sallow by rain. The Large Tortoiseshell was a frequent occurrence and the Brimstone in every ride.

He would probably be astonished if he could revisit these places today. Few of the above-mentioned butterflies remain in any numbers and some have disappeared altogether. In the eastern half of Britain the main places to see butterflies in woods are along broad sunny rides, roadsides and adjoining bramble thickets, but in most places those seen will be typical of wood-edges and sheltered grassland rather than woodland interiors. Of the latter, only the speckled wood and, to a lesser degree, the white admiral, have profited from the increased shading of formerly open woods. Climatic deterioration, and in particular the recent succession of dismal summers, has contributed to the decline, but butterfly numbers have always been subject to the dictates of the weather. The New Forest, for example, was much poorer in butterflies at the turn of the century than in the 1880s, but most species had returned in their former numbers by 1919 and remained common for at least two more decades. The fear among butterfly lovers today is that nearly everywhere numbers are now so greatly reduced that the decline may well prove permanent.

The richest butterfly woods used to contain about forty species – two-thirds of the total number breeding in Britain. A few large woods, such as Bentley Wood in Wiltshire and King's Park Wood in Sussex can still support almost as many, but most woods, including classic ones like Monks Wood in Cambridgeshire, Abbots Wood in Sussex and, alas, the New Forest, can no longer be considered prime butterfly sites. Western woods on poor soils have retained more butterflies than eastern woods, perhaps because they are naturally more open and less isolated from other natural vegetation. This openness is important as most woodland butterflies not only need sunshine for flight but also lay their eggs on herbs of the forest floor, such as violets, vetches and primroses, or on sallows and blackthorn along the forest edge. They therefore thrive best on regular cutting and felling, which supply glades and 'flushes' of spring flowers. Butterflies which feed as caterpillars on trees, shrubs and woody climbers are on the whole better adapted to contemporary forest management, although they too thrive best in woods with numerous clearings.

The black hairstreak butterfly is perhaps the best-known ancient woodland insect and, although its story is well known, it may be worth retelling it since here is an insect whose present distribution can be explained in terms of woodland history. The black hairstreak feeds on blackthorn and is restricted to woods and adjoining hedges and thickets on the belt of heavy clay soils between Oxford and Peterborough, where its foodplant grows in profusion. Since its discovery in 1825, about sixty

**SWEET SCENTS AND
HOLLOW TREES**

Moderate or dappled shade
Speckled wood (grasses)
Green-veined white (cresses)
White admiral (honeysuckle)*
Silver-washed fritillary (violets)*

Newly cut woodland and ride margins
Pearl-bordered fritillary
  (violets)**
High brown fritillary (violets)*
Heath fritillary (cow-wheat
  etc)**
and some of the glade species

Tree or shrub-feeders, mostly in the canopy
Large tortoiseshell (elm, sallow)
Purple emperor (sallow)*
Brown hairstreak (blackthorn)*
Purple hairstreak (oak)
White-letter hairstreak (elm)
Black hairstreak (blackthorn)**

Dense shade
Nothing

colonies of the black hairstreak have been found on the Oxford clay. All are localised along sheltered, sunny rides, glades and wood edges, and the adults do not seem to stray very far from their circumscribed breeding grounds. Like the other woodland hairstreaks, these butterflies are quite elusive, and when glimpsed they are usually flying close to the foliage in a characteristic tumbling manner, or at rest feeding on honeydew (aphid droppings) or on the flowers of bramble, privet or hogweed. Since it is not a wanderer, the black hairstreak can survive only in places where there is a continuous supply of blackthorn. Dense scrub is a symptom of neglect, and short coppice rotations, which were the norm in the Middle Ages, failed to allow sufficient time for old blackthorn thickets to establish. The black hairstreak was probably a rare and local butterfly even then.

The clue to the hairstreak's odd distribution lies in the history of the woods of the East Midlands clay belt. Since the early Middle Ages much of this region has been protected from extensive clearance as chases and Royal Forest. These wet sticky clay woods were usually managed on a long coppice cycle, and not very efficiently at that, so that there was time for dense stands of scrub to grow up, each of which lasted for at least twenty years. In these conditions, which were seldom encountered to

Black hairstreak butterfly,
Strymonidia pruni. *An elusive insect of blackthorn thickets in and around East Midland forests*

the same extent elsewhere, the black hairstreak could flourish. Modern forestry techniques are much less favourable to it, but fortunately naturalists made a fuss about the butterfly in good time and some of its best sites have been preserved in plantations as special refuges. Other sites have been acquired by Country Trusts and managed in a suitable way, so that the outlook for the black hairstreak is much more favourable than it might otherwise have been; indeed it still occurs in about half of its recorded sites which, compared with the fate of some other rare butterflies, ranks as a major success story.

The habits of the black hairstreak make it one of the easier butterflies to protect. The heath fritillary offered what in some ways was a greater challenge. The range of this attractive butterfly, which has russet, chequered forewings and an underside like stained glass, has shrunk over the past hundred years and, by 1980, it was restricted to a large block of ancient woodland near Canterbury and a few scattered woods, old meadows and sheltered valleys in the West Country. In its Kentish haunts, the heath fritillary lays on cow-wheat in open, sunny spaces within the wood. In former days it used to follow the woodman around like a faithful dog, sometimes appearing in great plenty a year or two after cutting, only to disappear a few years later as the regrowth shaded the ground. In consequence this butterfly occurred only in woods where new clearings were being created continually, usually on a short-period coppicing rotation. Like the black hairstreak, the heath fritillary has poor powers of dispersal and there is no record of it ever having

Heath fritillary, Mellicta athalia. A slow flying butterfly of coppice glades in Kent and Essex, plus several scattered sites in open woodland and heath in the West Country

159

Possible ancient-woodland-
indicator species of butterflies
and larger moths and their
larval foodplants

*Most if not all breeding sites are
ancient woodland.
Brackets around the name of the
species mean it is found outside
ancient woodland over some of
its British range.

*Associated with mature trees or
high forest*

Yellow-legged clearwing (oak)
*Welsh clearwing (birch)
*Triangle (oak, beech)
*Scarce hook-tip
  (small-leaved lime)
Oak lutestring (oak)
Satin lutestring (birch)
(Pauper pug) (lime)
*Marbled pug (oak)
*Blomer's rivulet (wych elm)
  (Brussels lace) (lichens on oak,
  blackthorn and palings)
*Dotted carpet (lichens on oak)
Square spot (various trees)
*Great oak beauty (oak)
Great prominent (oak)
Four-spotted footman (lichens
  on oak etc)
*Orange footman (lichens on oak
  and beech)
*Small black arches (probably
  oak)
*Scarce merveille du jour (oak)
*Rannoch sprawler (birch)
(Angle-striped sallow) (birch)
*Heart moth (oak)
*Light crimson underwing (oak)
*Dark crimson underwing (oak)
*Common fanfoot (withered
  leaves esp. oak)
Olive crescent (withered leaves
  of oak and beech)
*Clay fanfoot (oak)
Purple emperor (goat willow)

*Associated with ancient
hedges and wood edge habitats*

Maple mocha (maple)
Maple pug (maple)
Pinion-spotted pug (hawthorn)
Plumed prominent (maple)

colonised an isolated wood. It is slow-flying and 'lazy', spending its entire annual life-cycle within a few acres of open woodland. At the Blean Woods near Canterbury, the local market for hop poles and chestnut palings ensured the continuance of commercial coppicing, thus preserving fairly large populations of this butterfly at a time when it was dying out elsewhere. Now that its needs are better understood, and more particularly because conservationists think it sufficiently important, some woods in Kent are being managed to encourage the heath fritillary, and it has also been successfully reintroduced into Essex. At the Blean Woods National Nature Reserve the warden has succeeded in building up its numbers by linking regularly coppiced strips with permanent rides and glades. One can now visit some nature reserves in late June in the confident expectation of seeing scores, if not hundreds, of what is still perhaps Britain's rarest resident butterfly.

Butterflies attract attention and cash because they are popular and attractive, and because they are rightly seen as symbols of wildlife in decline. Successes like the conservation programmes for the black hairstreak and heath fritillary have a therapeutic value, and also a wider message. People used to assume that, if you protected a wood from the grosser forms of exploitation, then the insects would look after themselves. This is a fallacy and the disappearance of butterflies from numerous woodland nature reserves proves it. Insects, even rare ones, are versatile and resilient creatures within limits; otherwise they would not have survived. But their world and its climate is a miniature one and within it insects lives can be quite complex. A day in the life of a heath fritillary might include spells of feeding, sunbathing, sleeping, fighting, prospecting, mating, egg-laying and all kinds of interactions with other insects, and at different times the butterfly might seek tall herbage, flowers, sunlit bare ground and stumps, shrubs, and, of course, the vital patches of cow-wheat. Insects like this do not thrive on uniformity. They need rather an intimate mixture of light and shade, different states of growth and natural surface irregularities, and they cannot withstand wholesale change and intensive production. To conserve them we not only need to preserve their larger woodland habitat but to try to see their world from their point of view.

Moths

Woodland moths outnumber the butterflies by more than twenty to one, but most of them, in their adult state at least, are secret creatures of the night and their ecology is surprisingly little known. Moths need foodplants for their caterpillars, suitable areas for pupating, nectar sources for those adults which feed (many do not) and dark, humid places to hide by day, such as dense thickets, accumulations of leaves, or bark crevices. Unlike butterflies, a large proportion of Britain's moths feed as caterpillars on forest trees and shrubs. A table shown on page 162 sets out the numbers of species supported by different trees and shrubs, omitting those which feed on a wide range of plants. It tallies quite well with the table of plant-eating insects on page 149 but needs some qualification. Many moths which feed only on oak are confined to the

South, and in Scotland birch and sallows probably have the richest moth fauna. Oak leaves quickly become tough and tannic, and many oak-feeding caterpillars are therefore active early in the year, feasting on the buds and tender young leaves. The more palatable leaves of sallow, bramble, roses, hawthorn and blackthorn are important foodplants as well as nectar sources for the adult moths. Wych elm, maple, juniper and aspen have highly distinctive moth faunas, with a large proportion of rare species.

One would expect the best moth woods to combine a wide mixture of native trees with a well-developed underwood, and field experience tends to bear this out. The richest wood for moths in Britain is said to be Orlestone Forest in Kent ('Ham Street Woods' in the entomological literature) which lies on wet Wealden clay and is mostly managed coppice-with-standards with a very diverse range of natural vegetation, interspersed with heathy clearings and grassy rides rich in flowers. Equally important, it is beyond question an ancient wood, containing massive hornbeam stools, wild service trees and Midland hawthorn bushes, and a notable bryophyte flora. It is the home of delectable moths like the clifden nonpareil, the scarce merveille du jour and the lesser belle, and on summer nights the collectors' lamps shine like street lights.

Good moth woods are generally, but not always, ancient; recent mixed scrub can also be productive, especially in well-wooded areas, but few species thrive in conifer plantations (although those few that do can strip the trees bare). Detailed moth records for the past century or more are available for certain classic sites, and can be compared with recorded changes in woodland management. This has been attempted recently by Mark Hadley for Abbots Wood in Sussex where most of the stands of tall oak were felled during World War II, and afterwards the rest was 'coniferised' so relentlessly that it now stands, in Hadley's words, 'as a monument to the softwood industry'. Since 1934, the number of species of larger moths recorded there has fallen by a third from 330 to 230, while only five new species have colonised the wood. The losses include all the rare species for which the wood was once famous although, to be fair, the downturn in climate this century may have influenced their fall as much as any physical change. One new rarity, the white-banded carpet, colonised the wood in the 1960s, centred on the one remaining patch of original broadleaved woodland. The planting of birch and other broadleaves along the edge of the wood to soften its appearance has also resulted in the return of certain species not recorded for many years, such as the alder moth and alder kitten.

On the whole, woodland moths seem to have weathered the twentieth century better than butterflies but they too have suffered severe declines, especially those which need clearings and rides. One familiar example is the broad-bordered bee hawk-moth, which used to buzz around bugle flowers in bright sunshine in many woods, but suddenly became very scarce in the 1950s. For a really spectacular fall, it is hard to beat a moth called the common fanfoot, which needs renaming the rare fanfoot. Its caterpillar has unusual habits, evidently preferring withered oak leaves attached to sickly or fallen boughs, but whether or not that has something to do with its present scarcity is unknown. Some moth collectors believe that overall numbers of woodland moths have

Associated with managed coppice, glades and broad rides

(False mocha) (oak)
(Argent and sable) (birch)
Lead-coloured pug (cow-wheat)
Bilberry pug (bilberry)
White-banded carpet (rosebay willowherb)
*Drab looper (wood spurge)
Orange moth (various trees and shrubs)
Little thorn (bilberry)
(Barred umber) (hazel, sallow, birch)
Broad-bordered bee hawk (honeysuckle)
(Green arches) (honeysuckle, bilberry and others)
Blossom underwing (oak)
(The starwort) (golden-rod)
*The cudweed (golden-rod)
*Orange upperwing (oak)
(Slender brindle) (various woodland grasses)
(Mere wainscot) (wood small-reed)
(Concolorous) (wood small-reed)
*Lesser belle (aspen)
Pearl-bordered fritillary (violets)
(Heath fritillary) (cow-wheat)
(Duke of Burgundy) (primrose, cowslip)
*Black hairstreak (blackthorn)
(Wood white) (various vetches)

Extinct woodland or hedgerow species

New Forest burnet (England only) (various vetches)
Speckled beauty (lichens on oak and beech)
Scarce dagger (oak)
Marsh dagger (hawthorn, blackthorn)
Union rustic (various grasses)
Lunar double-stripe (temporary colonist) (aspen)
Clifden nonpareil (temporary colonist) (oak)
Chequered skipper (England only) (various grasses)

SWEET SCENTS AND HOLLOW TREES

The numbers of butterfly and moth species, supported by tree and shrub foodplants
(based on Emmet, 1979; Skinner, 1984; and Thomas, 1986).

Oak	131
Birch	133
Willows and sallows	111
Hawthorn	80
Poplar and aspen	66
Blackthorn and cherry	63
Alder	43
Rowan and whitebeams	37
Hazel	35
Scots pine	35
Bramble	32
Elm	31
Wild roses	30
Beech	26
Hornbeam	22
Maple	19
Buckthorn	18
Ash	16
Juniper	15
Lime	11
Chestnut	10
Spindle	6
Yew	4
Holly	3

also fallen, pointing to the once fruitful custom of searching trunks, which most now regard as a waste of time. The reasons advanced have varied from the fatal attraction of car headlights to the virtual disappearance of the English spring. Evidently something is amiss, but until moths receive more scientific study we are left guessing at what it might be.

Some work on how moths respond to different types of management in an ancient wood has been carried out at Bernwood Forest on the Buckinghamshire/Oxfordshire border by Paul Waring, who is currently the NCC 'mothman'. His researches indicate that caterpillars are most abundant in the more open parts of the wood, especially on the shrubs and overhanging boughs of trees lining the warmer rides and glades. In areas managed as coppice, the stools bearing two or three years regrowth supported greater densities of caterpillars than any other stage. However not all species preferred young growth and many were found only on older foliage, their numbers falling after cutting. Mature hazel coppice proved especially rich in moth caterpillars. Thus dense overgrown coppices retain their value for the many moths which feed on trees, shrubs and climbers, although increased shading can prove disastrous for the species which feed on herbs on the ground.

A great many of our butterflies and moths are more common in ancient woodland than anywhere else, although probably few of them are restricted to ancient woodland throughout their range. The more widespread species may be strictly confined to ancient woods in certain areas but are more adaptable elsewhere. In Derbyshire, for example, argent and sable, maple pug, seraphim and nut-tree tussock seem to be restricted to ancient woods and wooded parks, but all four occur in other habitats in some counties. In Oxfordshire the maple prominent seems to be a reliable ancient-woodland indicator, but not in Northamptonshire, where it is a regular visitor to my non-woodland garden moth trap, and still less in East Anglia where it occurs all over the place and is increasing (which is odd, because its foodplant, field maple, certainly is not). Some years ago, Charles Gibson of the Oxford University Zoology Department and I drew up a list of butterflies and moths which in central southern England seem to be found mainly in ancient woodland and which might be useful when evaluating woods for conservation purposes. The list has received a measure of concurrence from experienced entomologists and it is therefore reproduced here (see pages 160-1). We observed that, while it seems to work reasonably well in England east of Dorset and south of the Humber, many of the species are more widespread further west, where many, if not most, woodland butterflies and moths are also found on heaths, sheltered sea cliffs and along well-vegetated lanes. In the Highlands there appears to be no butterfly or larger moth which is confined to native pine or birchwoods, although among the micro-moths there are some dwellers in strange places – like *Archinemapogon yildizae* in large decaying bracket fungi and *Myrmecozela ochraceella* in wood ants' nests – which might be.

The moths listed have very varied requirements. Some, like the yellow-legged clearwing and the great oak beauty, need well-grown trees; others, like the drab looper and the lead-coloured pug, lay their

eggs on woodland herbs. A few feed on lichens and may be as vulnerable as their foodplants to atmospheric pollution. I suspect that many of these moths need large woods. Nearly all of the listed species have declined in the past forty years, although this did not influence their choice. If we are right in asserting that these are the moths that are most strongly associated with ancient woodland, it is reasonable to suppose that they are poor colonisers, even though some of them can fly fast and far. The distribution of moths like the scarce hook-tip, the crimson underwings and the triangle certainly ties in closely with large concentrations of ancient woodland.

Yellow-legged clearwing, Synanthedon vespiformis. A moth which looks like a wasp – it lays its eggs in the bark crevices of oak stumps and appreciates regular small-scale felling

Bees, wasps and ants

The order of Hymenoptera has more than six thousand species and recently overtook the true flies or Diptera as Britain's largest order of insects. The majority of them are inconspicuous, their larvae living as parasites inside the bodies of their unfortunate fellow insects. Some of them parasitise wood-boring insects and depend on the same habitat conditions as their victims. But the best-known woodland Hymenoptera are the aculeates, better known as the bees, wasps and ants. These are of great interest to biologists since they have the most complex adult behaviour patterns of any group of insects. Woodland bees and wasps need a wide variety of habitats within their flight range: they may breed, feed and mate in separate parts of the wood, and at different times may need bare ground, dead wood, foliage and flowers, often confining much of their activity to warm sunny places. Some are double-brooded and use different flowers in each brood. Perhaps

SWEET SCENTS AND HOLLOW TREES

because they are so choosy, populations of solitary bees and wasps tend to be small and often fluctuate from year to year. All of this makes them very sensitive to changes in their surroundings. It is not altogether surprising, therefore, that more than a quarter of Britain's native bees, ants and wasps are presently categorised as rare or endangered. Theirs is a high-risk life-style based on the natural diversity of traditionally managed woods, and is not well-suited to modern silvicultural methods.

Many woodland bees and wasps burrow into logs, stumps and old fence-posts, notably the digger wasps *Crossocerus* and *Ectemnius*, eumenid wasps such as *Symmorphus* and the megachilid bees *Anthidium*, *Megachile* and *Osmia*. The frequent removal of dead wood may have contributed to the apparent extinction of *Crossocerus vagabundus*, which used to nest inside old beetle galleries in rotten logs. The mason bee *Osmia pilicornis* burrows into coppice stools and discarded poles and branches, and it probably depends on regular coppicing or ride management for suitable nesting places and flowers. Some species need standing timber of considerable girth. The ant *Lasius brunneus* builds its nests in old, partly decayed but still living tree-trunks, especially oak and hornbeam pollards, since these provide both wood pulp for nesting material and a large store of aphids to feed on. Its nests are also inhabited by a large number of other insects, especially beetles. The hornet also needs old trees, nesting inside dry hollow trunks and often hibernating beneath loose bark. It seems to be remarkably good at finding suitable nesting places since, although it is no longer the familiar, frightening insect that Dante consigned to Hell, it is holding its own in natural wood-pasture and mature woodland, and has successfully explored the possibilities provided by birds' nest boxes, roof cavities and even unused letterboxes.

Nearly a quarter of British bees and wasps lay their eggs in the nests of their fellows and are known as cleptoparasites ('clepts') or, more prosaically, as cuckoos. The young cuckoo larva subsists on its host's food store, after first eating the original occupant. Many cuckoos raid the nests of wood-boring bees and wasps. The best known are the Chrysididae, known as ruby-tailed wasps or jewel-wasps from their brilliant metallic colours, but others include solitary cuckoo bees in the genera *Stelis* and *Coelioxys* and the bumble-bee genus *Psithyrus*. Cuckoos are normally scarcer than their hosts – they have to be or else their host would die out. They also tend to decline more quickly than their hosts when things start to go wrong with their habitat, and so, paradoxically, woods noted for insect cuckoos are probably good for wildlife in general.

The places to find bees, wasps and ants are warm, sunny, flower-filled rides, glades and banks. Most of them feed on flowers to some extent and blossoming shrubs are particularly important for the spring species. Brambles are a rich source of nectar and pollen later in the year. Too frequent cutting and mowing or the over-grazing of rides and clearings deprive these insects of their main food resources. Many woods used to have a flower-rich border of natural grassland which was always well used by flying insects; the ploughing of the surrounding land right up to (and sometimes beyond) the wood-bank probably reduces the woodland insect fauna even when the wood itself remains unchanged. Bees and wasps are also more vulnerable than most insects to the drift of poisonous sprays from surrounding crop fields. In counties like Suffolk and Lincolnshire it is hard to be cheerful about their future.

Ants, social bees and social wasps often build large and elaborate nests. Particularly conspicuous are the great piles of the wood ant *Formica rufa* and its northern relatives *F. lugubris* and *F. aquilonia*, which are always carefully placed to trap solar heat and maintain the nest interior at a fairly constant high temperature. They need unshaded or only partially shaded bare ground and thrive best in undisturbed places – partly because some people seem unable to resist prodding the nests with sticks. These complex constructions, among the largest nests of any animal in Britain, are also home to numerous 'paying guests' and scroungers, and how the latter manage to avoid being bitten, stung or eaten is something of a mystery. Certain rove beetles secrete sweet substances which are much enjoyed by the ants, who put up with them on that account despite the beetles' regrettable habit of eating young ant larvae. Various beetle and fly larvae, springtails and woodlice scavenge about the nest living on debris, and the ants seem to ignore them.

It must be difficult, however, to ignore the great fat grub of a chafer beetle *Potosia cuprea*, which lives on decaying chips of wood deep inside wood ants' nests in Scotland and northern England. *P. cuprea* eventually grows into a handsome bronzy-green beetle which emerges hastily from the nest and flies away to spend most of its remaining life immersed in the flowers of thistles and umbellifers, gorging on pollen and nectar. The small buff-coloured moth *Myrmecozela ochraceella*, however, spends virtually all its life inside the nest, emerging only at dusk for brief nuptial flights. In daylight hours it can be summoned by gently tapping the nest. I have done this myself and have a vivid memory of moths shooting out like flying fish amid the acrid stench of excited wood ants. There is even another ant, the tiny *Formicoxenus nitidulus*, which builds its own nests in small twigs deep inside the wood-ant mounds.

Nests of social wasps and bees also house various insect guests, welcome or otherwise. The hornet has a particularly rich nest fauna, including a magnificent rove beetle, *Velleius dilutatus*, which pays its way by preying on various fly maggots, which in their turn feed on nest debris. Thus the honest-living aculeates of a wood support a much larger number of assorted parasites and scroungers. When one adds the numerous mimics of bees and wasps, like the very odd daddy-long-legs *Ctenophora ornata*, which does its best to look like a hornet, it is clear that a great many insects depend, one way or another, on aculeates for their survival. They are a vital part of a healthy woodland insect fauna.

The two-winged flies (Diptera)

Woodland flies, of which there are at least a thousand, have Gothic tastes. Many a Hammer film redolent with slimy, fungus-covered stumps, stagnant pools and sinister old trees presents perfect breeding grounds for endangered flies. They are, in popular belief at least, insects of decay and charnel-house odours. The *Insect Red Data Book* hints at

WOODLAND HERITAGE

SWEET SCENTS AND
HOLLOW TREES

their immense variety: ancient woods are homes for rare crane flies, hoverflies, fungus gnats, soldier flies, snipe flies, robber flies, stiletto flies, flat-footed flies, and stilt-legged flies, among others too numerous to mention. Many of these are exceedingly local. A dipterist friend, Dr Neil Bayfield, once pointed out to me the broad mossy stump of a Caledonian pine. 'That', he said, 'is where I go to look for the robber fly, *Laphria flava*' (a furry and somewhat intimidating bumble-bee look-alike). Either side of the stump the native pinewood stretched to the horizon, but *L. flava*, for inscrutable reasons of its own, apparently prefers this particular stump to any other.

The behaviour of flies varies so much that it is difficult to generalise about them. Some, like the fungus gnats, are shade-lovers, often needing permanently humid places such as the underhangs of banks, seepages and pond margins. Alderwoods are ideal places, especially for woodland crane flies that breed in mud and litter. One specialist group, the Sciomyzidae or snail-hunting flies, are parasites of slugs and snails, and frequent the same moist places as their prey. Other flies, by contrast, congregate in the warmest and sunniest parts of the wood, sunbathing on bark or feasting on nectar and over-ripe fruit. The flies one notices most in woods are unfortunately often those which force their attentions on you. The ones that cover your face and sandwiches in summer are sweat flies. There are fewer of the biting kinds than in marshes or fens (deer often lie up in woods to escape their attentions), but woodland flies do include an alarming horsefly, *Tabanus sudeticus*, the size of a queen bumble-bee. These have given the group as a whole an undeserved reputation. Most flies are a great deal more secretive, and some are more easily found as larvae than as adults; indeed the adults of a few woodland species have never yet been seen in the wild.

Like beetles, bees and butterflies, adult flies may have quite different needs from their young stages. Many have a sweet tongue and are most plentiful in open woods which are rich in flowers throughout the growing season. Sallow catkins and blackthorn flowers are important nectar sources early in the year, followed later by hawthorn blossom whose rather sickly scent has a great attraction for flies. Umbellifers, especially hogweed and angelica, are also popular, while late in the season ragwort, ivy flowers and rotten blackberries are much visited. Some flies show little interest in flowers, however, preferring honeydew and tree sap.

Fly larvae have much more precise habitat needs than the adults and a few are confined to ancient woods by their foodplant. The tiny scathophagid *Parallelomma vittata* mines the leaves of woodland lilies, especially Solomon's seal, herb paris and lily-of-the-valley, and one of the less conspicuous hoverflies, *Portevinia maculata*, develops in the basal leaves of wild garlic. Another hoverfly, *Cheilosia semifasciata*, used to mine the succulent foliage of orpine in open woods but now appears to have virtually died out except in North Wales, where it has sensibly chosen to rely on a commoner non-woodland plant, wall pennywort. Like beetles, many flies breed in what entomologists call 'dead-wood situations'. But unlike beetles, some of which can live in almost bone-dry wood, flies generally prefer damp or wet wood in shaded places. Isolated trees in parks are less suitable unless they are

Habitats of saproxylic insects

Above left: *The stump of a giant beech, bearing spore-powdered tiers of the bracket fungus,* Ganoderma applanatum. *Windsor Forest, 1988.* (Right) *A copious sap-run resulting from injury to a beech trunk. Dynevor Forest, 1988*

Right: *A large rot-hole, high up on a beech at Duncombe Park. This one was being used by a rare hoverfly,* Pecota personata

Left: *The fallen hulk of a once-mighty oak, red-rotten from within, gently crumbling into humus. New Forest, 1987*

167

SWEET SCENTS AND
HOLLOW TREES

kept moist internally by sufficient quantities of living sapwood. Favourite places are damp, well-rotted logs and stumps, rot-holes part-filled with humus, and the syrupy 'gunge' formed from sap flowing from insect bore-holes and other wounds on the trunk. Oak, ash, elm, beech and aspen are the most productive forest trees, but few flies are confined to one or the other. Mature elms used to contain particularly fine larders of rotting matter and flowing sap, and Dutch elm disease must have made an impact on flies and their ilk.

The richest localities for woodland flies in Britain are the New Forest and Windsor Great Park, emphasising once again the superlative conservation value of these places. Some flies are restricted to just these two, such as the handsome green-and-yellow-striped hoverfly, *Caliprobola speciosa*, which breeds in wood-mould inside beech and oak stumps of great girth. Native birch, pine and aspen in the Highlands also support numerous rare species, and most of these seem to be more effective colonisers than their English counterparts, even occurring in plantations, as long as the latter contain dead wood and reasonably old trees. Although the special Highland flies have a northern distribution many occur only at low altitude in relatively sheltered river valleys, especially the Spey.

Being colourful and reasonably easy to identify, hoverflies have received more attention than most other families of flies. The adults are all fond of sunshine and flowers but their early stages embrace many contrasting ways of life. Some larvae are voracious predators of aphids, while others feed on vegetation or, like the familiar rat-tailed maggot, on decomposing matter in pools. Many breed in wood or related habitats like rot-holes and sap-runs. Alan Stubbs and Steven Falk, the authors of the standard work on hoverflies, list forty-seven species which are found mainly in ancient woodland, twelve of which they regard as reliable indicator species. They include the most striking of the bumble-bee mimics, *Pocota personata*, which breeds in rot-holes, usually high above ground, and the much commoner *Xylota sylvarum*, which is able to utilise a wider range of dead-wood conditions including dead boughs on living trees, as well as wet sawdust and decomposing bark. The large hoverfly *Volucella inflata*, is associated with the borings of the goat moth larva, although, since good 'goat moth trees' are few and far between, large beetle borings are probably used as well. The larva of this species is probably a scavenger but those of *Ferdinandea* species and *Brachyops insensilis* develop in the sap oozing from the wound in the trunk.

Slugs and snails

One of the earliest investigators of the ecology of British slugs and land snails, A. E. Boycott, divided them into two roughly equal groups. Those which are widespread, often occurring in gardens, he called 'man-lovers'. The others, which seem wedded to their ancestral way of life in woods, are the 'man-haters'. Needless to say we are concerned with the latter, much less familiar, group. There are about fifty man-haters, and the best woods, like Selborne Common in Hampshire and Hayley Wood in Cambridgeshire, contain up to four-fifths of them. Most slugs and snails are sensitive to drought and their favourite woods are moist and shady, with fallen logs or boulders, deep accumulations of litter and lush ground vegetation. They prefer north-facing slopes to south-facing, and ash and beech to oak, probably because the former are more often found on chalk or limestone. Many woodland snails are restricted to lime-rich soils.

Boycott observed that many woodland slugs and snails were confined to areas of old forest and were evidently poor colonists. He noted that slugs and snails eat a wide range of vegetation and decaying matter and therefore have no problems in finding food. For this reason they tend not to form well-defined communities of species closely associated with particular habitat conditions. The ash-black slug, *Limax cinereoniger*, for example, occurs in woods in the Highlands and the lowlands, on both acid and lime-rich soil and under a wide range of trees from Cotswold beech to Caledonian pine. What its sites do have in common is that they are nearly all large natural woods with an abundance of this slug's favourite diet, toadstools. It shows little inclination to stray from such places and is regarded as one of the indicators of ancient woodland, except in high-rainfall districts. Boycott noted that some of the slugs and snails of older woods on the South Downs and the Cotswolds had failed, even after two hundred years, to spread into neighbouring beech plantations. An NCC booklet by Kerney and Stubbs (1980) lists nine species which seem unable to colonise new sites and are therefore good indicators of the stable environment associated with ancient woods.

More recent comparative studies of woods in Cambridgeshire and Somerset indicate that ancient woods usually contain many more species of mollusc than secondary ones, and that woods with a variety of different types of soils and vegetation are likely to be richer than those which are more uniform. Disturbance can rapidly eliminate the more sensitive species and ancient woods have been known to lose three-quarters of their molluscs after being clear-felled and replanted with conifers. The effect is more severe in the East than in the North and West where more humid conditions enable many woodland molluscs to live in sheltered habitats outside woodland such as hedgerows, old walls and scree, and to colonise well-established secondary woods and plantations.

Some species now regarded as local and rare were evidently common and widespread in the wet Atlantic period, judging from the frequency of their fossils. The cheese snail, *Helicodonta obvoluta*, for example, was widespread and common in southern England four thousand years ago, but is now confined to steep north-facing escarpment woods on the South Downs in places where there are abundant fallen boughs and logs. The bulin snail, *Ena montana*, and the plaited snail, *Spermodea lamellata*, equally common as fossils, are also confined today to a few southern woods. The cheese snail and the bulin snail are still common hedgerow species on the other side of the Channel and the cause of their decline in Britain is unknown. It cannot be woodland clearance alone since the shells of the bulin snail have been found in Bronze Age settlements already stripped of their original woodland cover, and, to confound the woodland ecologist further, one of its surviving sites is a rubbish-filled roadside ditch!

WOODLAND HERITAGE

SWEET SCENTS AND
HOLLOW TREES

Spiders and pseudoscorpions

The sheltered, humid space between loose bark and the wood beneath is a favoured zone for minute forms of life, including small molluscs, bark-lice, woodlice and mites, which feed on decaying wood, fungal mould and other debris. Pseudoscorpions are among the predators in this miniature world. Although never more than 0.5cm (which is less than ½in) long they are quite impressive-looking animals with long scorpion-like claws. *Dendrochernes cyrneus* is the largest of them and it also has the most exacting needs, being confined to the underside of old dry bark subjected to the full glare of the sun. It also crawls further into the interior of the trunk along cracks leading into the heartwood. It is found mostly on over-mature oaks in wood-pasture, notably at Burnham Beeches, Windsor Great Park and Sherwood Forest, although in some of its sites it also occurs on old beech and elm pollards. Within its localised haunts, *Dendrochernes* can be very numerous and this is probably the best ancient woodland indicator species in the group. Others which favour bark on over-mature trees are *Chernes cimicoides*, *Allochernes wideri* and *Lamprochernes chyzeri*. Many pseudoscorpions also exploit other woodland habitats, including leaf-litter, squirrel dreys and the nests of birds and ants.

Spiders are much bigger and more mobile animals. All of them are predators which catch their prey by hunting, web-spinning or, in the case of the colourful crab spiders, by lurking in ambush. Spiders have relatively soft skins and are vulnerable to drying; so woodland provides an ideal environment for them. At least sixty species are rarely found outside woods, and most of them live among foliage in the trees or in the leaf-litter below, or both. A few specialists live under stones or loose bark or in the nests of birds and ants. One of these, *Tuberta macrophthalma*, lays its eggs in ants' nests, usually, but not always, in and around old tree stumps and dead wood. It appears to be confined to wood-pasture and the only recent observations of it are from Charnwood Forest and Sherwood Forest in the Midlands where it is quite common, although it used to occur in widely scattered places in southern England and South Wales. Another rare spider, *Lepthyphantes midas* lives in old nests of pigeons and jackdaws, again usually in wood-pasture, and there are several related species with a similar life-style. In general, mature beechwoods and oakwoods seem to be the richest places for spiders. Few of them seem to be associated with particular plants, but one, *Hyptiotes paradoxus*, is usually found on yew or box, and two others have an unexplained liking for dog's mercury. Some specialise in particular parts of trees, such as *Thyseostenius parasiticus* which hunts along dead boughs on living trees. These spiders, and no doubt many others, are more likely to be found in ancient woodland than elsewhere, but much remains to be discovered about these relatively little-known animals.

10
WHITHER ANCIENT WOODLAND?

Loss

What does it feel like to return to a much-loved wood just in time to catch the JCB pushing over the last stump? The sense of loss at the passing of a familiar landmark, a favourite primrose bank or a dell where orange-tip butterflies used to gather, is a feeling not easily shared, for these things are part of our intimate private world. They do not have a market value, may indeed be commonplace even in conservation terms, but they mean something to us because they are a treasured part of our daily lives. Just over a century ago Gerard Manley Hopkins expressed his own pain when the aspens of Binsey were felled, in lines drenched in grief:

> My aspens dear, whose airy cages quelled,
> Quelled or quenched in leaves the leaping sun,
> All felled, felled, are all felled;
> Of a fresh and following folded rank
> Not spared, not one
> That dandled a sandalled
> Shadow that swam or sank
> On meadow and river and wind-wandering
> Weed-winding bank.

Never mind that the Binsey aspens were not strictly 'his' at all, that they belonged to someone else who was fully within his legal rights in chopping them all down. In a private sense, they were shared by Hopkins and everyone else who had taken delight in them.

    Oliver Rackham suggested that we experience four separate kinds of loss when a familiar ancient wood comes to a sudden, brutal end. There is the obvious loss of beauty: one less 'melodious plot of beechen green' for the midsummer nightingales, one more parish without carpets of anemone, the sudden replacement of an individual place full of variety and colour with yet more cereals, conifers or tarmacadam. Then there is the loss of somewhere to wander away from the late twentieth century into a place of quiet and solitude, where you can listen, watch, think and relax. Too many of our woods, famous ones among them, are private places in the wrong sense, with 'Keep Out' notices nailed to the tree-trunks. Thanks to the Enclosure Acts and the pheasant, English people have less freedom to wander in their own country than the Scots or the Irish, and one of the main delights of a holiday in Sweden or the

I think that by retaining one's childhood love of such things as trees, fishes, butterflies and toads, one makes a peaceful and decent future a little more probable, and that by preaching the doctrine that nothing is to be admired except steel and concrete, one merely makes it a little surer that human beings will have no outlet for their surplus energy except in hatred and leader worship.

    George Orwell, 'Some thoughts on the common toad' (1946)

'Go away'

WHITHER
ANCIENT WOODLAND?

Austrian Tyrol is precisely that sense of unfettered movement. It is of course nice to know that gamekeeping has preserved many a copse and covert that would otherwise have been lost, but for most of us the benefits are confined to the view from our passing cars. Bill Adams put it very well in *Nature's Place*: the naturalist today 'is in rather the same position as the farm labourer in the countryside two hundred years ago. He has few legal rights in the countryside, but very real interests in the way the land is managed'.

If the reader has come to this chapter last, I hope there is no need to labour Rackham's third and fourth kinds of loss: of historic vegetation and wild animals, birds and insects; and, above all, of *meaning*, the wood as a living record of natural and human evolution. A book the size of this one could be written about every one of the thirty thousand ancient woods in Britain.

All natural habitats in Britain, including woods, have declined in the lifetimes of everyone over twenty. In 1984, the NCC published a book called *Nature Conservation in Great Britain* which gave the full chilling statistics of the price we have paid in beauty for our home-grown timber and cereals. Ancient woodland has declined less than natural grassland and marsh, which are much easier to get rid of, but the loss since 1945 is nonetheless unprecedented. We have lost 10 per cent of our traditional woods to agriculture, quarrying and urban developments, and a further 30 per cent have been converted to plantations with the loss of some, or most, of their original wildlife. More ancient woodland has been lost in the past forty years than in the previous four hundred. The loss has been greater in some counties than others, and proportionately greater in large woods than small ones. Most ancient woods that retain nearly all their natural vegetation are smaller than 10ha (25 acres). This decline went largely unnoticed, and 'after-comers cannot guess the beauty been'. Occasionally, however, when a much-loved local wood was threatened with destruction there was a popular outcry and press campaign, as at Bradfield Woods in Suffolk in 1969, Sladden Wood in Kent in 1978, Abernethy Forest in Speyside in 1980 and Brockenhurst Copse in Hampshire in 1988. As for the flora and the beasts, there has been, on the whole, a greater decline amongst woodland insects and 'primitive' plants like liverworts and lichens than amongst birds, animals or flowers. The press notices national extinctions, like the large blue butterfly, but not the equally significant loss of once familiar objects of 'ordinary' woods, yesterday's commonplaces become today's rarities, and maybe tomorrow's extinctions. In parts of Britain you will now have to visit a nature reserve to have much chance of finding things like butterfly orchids, scarlet elf-cups, stag beetles or dormice.

This book is not about the hard-nosed political climate that encouraged state agencies and private owners to destroy or convert their ancient woods in the 1950s and 1960s; indeed that tale has yet to be fully told. Nationwide statistics have their uses in the world of conference tables and free lunches, but it is with our own parish or county that most of us are chiefly concerned. I am therefore going to write about two districts in which I have lived and worked, and which I particularly care about. The first, Rockingham Forest, contains what is left of the medieval forest of that name. Many of its woods are still owned by the Crown, and are therefore subject to national trends. Deeside in Aberdeenshire, on the other hand, is a place of large private estates, where natural birchwoods on the valley sides and on former moorland soften and add colour to the landscape. Both examples suggest that to understand what is really happening we need to peer behind the bland assertions of statistical tables.

Rockingham Forest stands out from the Ordnance Survey map of north-east Northamptonshire as a patchwork of green, representing a mixture of large, medium-sized and small woods between Kettering and Stamford by contrast with the comparatively woodless countryside to the immediate west and south. It was traditionally a place of coppice-with-standards woods on heavy soils, of large country houses and their parks, and pretty brookside villages with large churches nestling in the vales between the softly swelling hills. Comparative newcomers to the landscape are airfields, ironstone quarries and trunk roads. The management of the Crown woods in the Forest, about two-fifths of its total woodland, is the responsibility of the Forestry Commission who have a district office in the heart of the woods at Fineshade.

In 1974, George Peterken, no stranger to these pages, produced a detailed comparison between the Rockingham Forest of 1946 and that of 1972, using a combination of aerial photographs and foot-slogging. In that time the *amount* of woodland had changed hardly at all. Give or take a few new quarries and fields, an extra plantation here and there, there was little apparent change – so long as one stayed indoors and looked only at maps. But *inside* the woods change had indeed taken place, and that on a scale unparalleled in Rockingham Forest's nine-hundred-year history. In 1946, four-fifths of the Forest woods were of native broadleaves, and more than half of them were ancient and natural. About 1,000ha (2,500 acres) were still managed as coppices. Twenty-five years later, only half the native woods remained, and coppicing was confined to about 90ha (220 acres) of ancient woodland near Pipewell, where there was a local market for stakes and binders for hedging. The rest had been converted to 'productive' woodland, mainly of conifers blended with a few spindly oaks, by felling, underplanting and the poisoning of the indigenous trees. Certain 'compartments' were allowed to retain more of their native vegetation but had been converted from coppice-with-standards to dense high forest of considerably lower wildlife value. The best remaining ancient woods were in private ownership, except in the special case of Bedford Purlieus, which attracted quarrymen as a possible source of ironstone and had defied previous attempts to turn it into a plantation through the sheer vigour of its underwood.

In 1972 there were no nature reserves in Rockingham Forest, but eleven Sites of Special Scientific Interest(SSSI), scheduled by the then Nature Conservancy. The Conservancy had no authority to interfere with forestry plans, however, and in practice the SSSI woods changed along with the others. Of the eleven, two were replanted, one was ruined by quarrying and rubbish dumping, and another was nibbled around the edges by a Corby housing estate. Others seemed likely to be quarried away in the near future. George Peterken expressed pessimism about the future: not one of the 1946 coppice woods remained in a good

WOODLAND HERITAGE

WHITHER
ANCIENT WOODLAND?

condition for, even when spared the axe, they had fallen into neglect and their rides became over-shaded. As if to symbolise all this, the chequered skipper butterfly, a notable and attractive local resident, suddenly disappeared.

The prospects for ancient woodland were at their darkest in 1972. Shortly afterwards, the Forestry Commission, under pressure from government review bodies, began to broaden its approach to encompass landscape and amenity matters as well as timber production. Fifteen years on, more of the old Rockingham Forest has survived than then seemed likely. Bedford Purlieus is now receiving treatment sympathetic to its standing as one of Britain's premier ancient woods. Short Wood, the subject of our woodland walk nine chapters ago, was saved from destruction at the eleventh hour when the Northamptonshire Wildlife Trust purchased it with the help of a grant from the World Wildlife Fund and funds raised by a medieval fair. And King's Wood, Corby, shows that ancient woodland can survive complete encirclement by houses if the will is there to preserve it. Seventeen years on, Peterken now has this to say:

> The ancient woods of Rockingham Forest seem more likely to survive now than at any time in the last forty years. Ironstone mining has ceased, and (at the time of writing) the Forest is being considered as the nucleus of a great new Midlands forest. Many of the best remaining medieval woods are either nature reserves, or managed under agreements with the NCC, and the Forestry Commission are growing more native broadleaves in their plantations. Although hedges are still staked and bound, coppicing remains very uncommon. The woods will not be preserved in their medieval form, alas, but are now being more gently moulded to modern conditions.

Birchwoods account for about half of Scotland's natural broadleaved woodland, and nearly all of them are privately owned. Visitors to the Dee and Don Valleys in Aberdeenshire will find all stages in the birch cycle, from the vigorous bushy stubble on overgrown grouse muirs to elderly woods near the tree-line, full of splintered stumps and bracket fungi, and well on the way to becoming open moorland. Since, in silvicultural terms, birch is considered a short-lived, worthless weed, it is valued lightly with little thought for the future. It is simply part of the landscape, apparently as eternal as the river and the crags. Because of our very British disregard for the birch, no one took a hard look at what was happening to these woods until 1986, when two members of the Aberdeen University forestry department, Ian Brown and Andrew Wightman, published an account of the changing fortunes of Deeside and Donside birchwoods over the past forty years. As George Peterken had found for Rockingham Forest, the total area of birch woodland in the two valleys remained about the same, but, and this was the big surprise, less than a third of it still grew *in the same place* as it did in 1947. The birch landscape is in continual motion, for birch, though shedding seed as abundant as Highland rain, does not regenerate well under its own shade. At present the birch is colonising the neglected moors and pastures and wartime felling sites at one end of the valley, but declining through stock-grazing and red-deer browsing at the other.

Even so, at first sight all seems reasonably well with the birch. But if

one goes beyond the figures to look at the state of individual woods, the picture is less reassuring. Of the mature birchwoods, which include most of the really interesting ones, Brown and Wightman judged more than half as moribund. Unless they are fenced they have no long-term future. Similarly many of the young birch sites will never mature: they are not regarded as woods but waste, and improved pasture or spruce plantations will be their fate, depending on the swing of the agricultural pendulum. And so, the authors conclude:

> . . . despite the fact that deer and domestic stock benefit from birchwoods at present by their provision of browse, some grazing and shelter, it would appear from the lack of sensible management that the tenants and proprietors of this land see no future need for birchwoods. Or is it that twenty or thirty years appears to be a long time to non-foresters? In the course of one generation our old birchwoods, half of which are already moribund, will be gone.

But who is to preserve the birchwoods if not their owners? Action is needed now, but, 'how is this to be done in Donside and royal Deeside with their beautiful public landscape but fiercely defended private ownership?'

The birch-dominated scenery of Deeside as seen from Crathie Wood near Balmoral Castle. Many of these woods are recent, and the hillsides were barer a century ago. They may be barer still fifty years from now. May 1977

175

WHITHER
ANCIENT WOODLAND?

Discord

A small book on the history of forestry in Scotland by John Davies, a former Forestry Commission Conservator, affirms that foresters are at least as alive to the beauty and atmosphere of old woodland as anyone else:

> To come down from the high tops of the Cairngorms into the shelter of Rothiemurchus and smell the pines and junipers is an experience that I have never felt elsewhere. Words like scent and smell seem coarse, but there is a marvellous air in the pinewoods – clean and delicate. I have felt awe and a sense of unease and prehistory on the windswept Prescelly mountains in Wales where some of Stonehenge was quarried, and I have drunk of the richness in the shadows of the great beechwoods in Sussex, but the old Speyside pinewoods satisfy me far more.

'But', the author concluded, rather reluctantly (for he well knew what actions his words implied), 'if left to their own devices these woods would slowly disappear.'

The conviction that trees cannot grow without the aid of foresters is not recent, but it has become so powerful as to set aside all evidence to the contrary. Forestry policy in Britain is a planter's policy, and, until the recently revised grants scheme, it set little store by our native trees, except oak and beech. Its literature seems to take little account of the difference between planted trees, which have to grow where they are put, sometimes with part of their rootstock missing, and natural trees, which grow where they please. Modern forestry tends to treat indigenous trees in ancient woods as weeds, to be replaced by planted conifers, plus a few oaks and a fringe of 'amenity' broadleaves to soften the impact on the landscape. True, the Forestry Commission inherited woods devastated by the fellings of two world wars and tangled through neglect, but to restore them to productivity the nation chose to wipe them bare and start again rather than manage the existing vegetation. The discord between modern forestry in its harshest phase and the traditional husbandry of woods could hardly have been greater.

Tree-planting for amenity and, at first, even nature reserve management was influenced by forestry ideas and attitudes. Some of the staff of the old Nature Conservancy were themselves foresters and thought their first National Nature Reserve, Beinn Eighe, was being improved when they planted square blocks of pine and spruce in it. One still comes across advisory leaflets which treat tree-planting and nature conservation as though they were synonymous. Farmers are encouraged to plant field corners or waysides with sycamores or oaks in the belief that this somehow helps nature, but half the saplings thrust into indifferent soil and then neglected promptly die and even if successful they may well end up smothering something much more interesting that happened to be there already. 'Plant a tree in '73' was the catch-phrase of that year. Politicians and other important people were photographed as, jacketless and grinning, they stuck copper beeches into Highland birchwoods and ash poles into hedgerows already bristling with ash poles. The Post Office did their bit by bringing out a postage stamp bearing a picture of that fine native of Albania, a horse chestnut. 'Plant some more in '74' we sang, as well-meaning officials lovingly planted conifers in medieval deer-pasture, apparently oblivious to the landscape around them. Then came two glorious summers: 'Barely alive in '75'. 'All dead sticks by '76'. It was all so disappointingly bone-headed. An estimated half of the ten million 'amenity trees' planted each year at a pound each were dead five years later.

We have forgotten how wild woodland trees work. Broadleaved trees are supposed to be stubborn, slow-growing brutes, but a coppice pole of hazel or ash will easily outstrip a Sitka spruce. Traditional woodmanship had more or less died out by the 1950s, and there seemed to be only a small and uncertain market for hardwoods. It coincided with the post-war faith in scientific progress, the beckoning glitter of technology, plastic and tower blocks to solve problems of manufacture and social deprivation. These attitudes transferred themselves to the way we treated woods. Foresters were encouraged to believe that their skills lay in making two trees grow where but one had grown before (and that a useless coppice stool). Wild trees, with their independent wilful ways, belonged to the past. Planted trees, carefully nurtured throughout their brief lives (for they are struck down while still adolescents), are under human control and therefore trustworthy, like pets and garden roses.

Worst of all are old and misshapen trees, Parson Kilvert's 'grey, gnarled, low-browed, knock-kneed, bowed, bent, huge, strange, long-armed, deformed, hunchbacked misshapen oak men'. Such trees are not merely the object of scorn to the woodland manager; they are actively *disliked*. Even Parson Kilvert was afraid of them. We mistake stag-headed crowns or hollow trunks, natural events in the lives of trees and not only at the end of them, for sick trees that need felling. Perhaps they remind us uncomfortably of our own mortality, not to mention disease, decay and other nastinesses. Clearing out old stumps, logs and other useless objects has been part of the forester's work since the Middle Ages, but modern heavy machinery enables him to make an unprecedently thorough job of it. The law favours precautionary felling, for landowners are held liable for any damage caused by falling boughs. The Forestry Commission issues an advisory leaflet on how to recognise a hazardous tree which, in the manner of gardening books, is illustrated by a tree suffering from every imaginary kind of ailment. This is exactly the kind of tree that interests naturalists, rare insects and woodpeckers.

The result of all these preconceptions and prejudices is that commercial management in ancient woodland no longer favours wildlife in the way it once did. Today's emphasis is almost wholly on production for sawing and pulping, and woods are managed as crops of timber to be harvested every seventy years or so. There is little interest in the underwood, or even, until recently, in natural regeneration. This might be justifiable, at least in economic terms, if these woods were nonetheless well managed, if all this effort of conversion made some significant difference to Britain's timber trade balance. But they are not and it does not, and much of the destruction of our ancient woods has been a waste of time and money. To quote Oliver Rackham:

WOODLAND HERITAGE

WHITHER
ANCIENT WOODLAND?

Hangman's Wood, Essex. The understorey has been cleared to discourage lurkers, and the wood has thereupon been transformed into a mere collection of trees with the loss of much of its interest and meaning. January 1982

Britain is dependent on imported timber and wood which cannot be appreciably reduced by sacrificing wild vegetation to grow more at home. There is not the space. If all our woods . . . were to be transformed overnight into the most productive plantations, this would not be noticed by the user of timber: the extra amount grown would be less than is now wasted in sawdust.

I will not weary the reader with more than one example of modern forestry at its most wilfully destructive; examples are not hard to find. Today the unenclosed woods of the New Forest are managed to satisfy a consensus of interests, and foresters, naturalists and commoners have become allies. It was not always thus. Between 1950 and 1970 the Forest suffered from a concatenation of events of gathering stridency, all in the name of supposedly helping the common woods to regenerate. It culminated in a declared policy of sacrificing the Forest's ancient (but healthy) trees, those very trees which we go there to admire, to satisfy the forester's dream of a more 'balanced' age-structure. What the 'regeneration fellings' achieved in practice was to reduce parts of old woodland to quagmires, replace the natural uneven-aged structure with dull uniform stands of oak and beech and invite ponies to graze the ground flat (the woods were supposed to be pony-proof, but the animals seemed to have no difficulty getting in). It was an unmitigated disaster. Fortunately ministerial intervention in 1971 came just in time to save the Forest from its foresters.

This is no doubt very unfair. Foresters are not mindless vandals, and the public mood of the time seemed, on the whole, apathetic, even if it did not support what was happening. What kind of woods do we, the public, want? Richard Mabey suggested that 'our ideal wood is green and snug, light and roomy, with a few secret glades and dark corners to add a hint of romance, but not so big that we cannot find our way out'. No fearful, shadowy wildwoods for us then; perhaps a few old trees for their picturesque appeal, but not too many. But much of the interest of woods is in what grows, scampers and flies *between* the trees, not just in the trees themselves. A wood is more than a collection of oaks: we expect it to be vibrant, colourful, loud, full of puzzles and surprises and things to excite our sense of wonder. We should not be stigmatised for preferring the old woods to the new, nor accused, wrongly, of continually harking back to some imaginary golden age. Ancient woods are frequently compared with ancient monuments, and to the extent that they deserve the same attention the analogy has its uses, but it should not be pressed too far. Ancient woods are part of the present and, let us hope the future as well as the past; were once useful to the commoner and the woodman and may become so again. Ancientness implies deep roots, but there is life in the sapwood yet and the trees are still growing.

Storm

The cover picture of the Countryside Commission's 'action pack', *Task Force Trees*, is an arresting portrait of a storm by Jean François Millet. An oak is caught in the process of being literally shredded alive: severed branches fly past ducking peasants, the earth heaves and roots and limbs knot and twist as if in mortal agony. It seems that in a second or two the wind will not only tear the tree from the earth but send it hurtling through the dun grey sky and out of the picture.

Until the small hours of Friday, 16 October 1987, Millet's picture would not have been thought suitable to illustrate an *English* landscape. Its subject matter was in any case the daily life of the rural poor in nineteenth-century France, not a scientifically accurate portrait of a tree. But the wind that blew in southern and eastern England that Friday made an impact on people's minds as well as on the landscape. People think differently about trees and woods now. Things may never be quite the same again, for we have experienced a shocking reminder of the mortality of the landscape. If we continued, after Dutch elm disease, to take trees for granted, we do so no longer.

On the face of it, then, the great storm was a natural disaster. Southern England had experienced nothing like it since 1703, although Scotland, a much windier place, received two blows almost as severe as recently as 1953 and 1968. Suffolk, Kent and Sussex, three of our most thickly wooded counties, received the brunt of the storm, but woodland and hedgerow trees lay like straws, or in tangled heaps, west as far as Dorset and north to Norfolk. Living a mile from the Lincolnshire border, I heard nothing worse than a window banging loose in the night, though my way into Peterborough was blocked by one of the cathedral limes. But, in the worst-hit woods, there was a raw saw-mill smell, trees laid across one another like pick-a-sticks, great root-plates pointing heavenwards, leaving gaping craters to turn into ponds. Sevenoaks in

WHITHER
ANCIENT WOODLAND?

The Storm (after Millet)

179

WHITHER
ANCIENT WOODLAND?

Kent had only one oak left. In all, about fifteen million trees had blown over, including a fifth of all the trees in the three most stricken counties. At least five thousand ancient woods suffered some damage. Twelve of the NCC's National Nature Reserves and no less than sixty-eight woods belonging to the Woodland Trust were badly knocked about. People stared from their windows in disbelief at a changed landscape.

The oddest thing about the storm was its patchiness. Some woods had been virtually flattened whilst others nearby, apparently equally vulnerable, were left almost unscathed. Others still had experienced localised knots of destruction within their interiors, as if swiped by a gigantic fly-swat of the gods, leaving the surrounding trees still upright. Shock was, understandably, the order of the day on 16 October, coupled with relief that the storm was at its height when most of us were tucked up in bed. As people began, gingerly, to clamber into the wrecked woods, a pattern of sorts did begin to emerge: the damage was not random. South-facing woods and those on exposed ridges were the most badly hit, not unexpectedly, but the wind had also funnelled along narrow valleys and ghylls shredding the trees as it went. Even-aged plantations were turned into head-high mattresses of broken foliage for, once the wind exceeded the tree's breaking strength, down they went, pins hit by an invisible ball. Ancient natural woods experienced mixed fortunes. Top-heavy pollards and standard trees in coppices proved vulnerable, yet many old trees, judged decrepit and moribund, survived this storm as successfully as they survived the 1703 one. With notable exceptions like Scords Wood in Kent, complete devastation was rare, and there are very few, if any, natural woods that will not recover completely by natural regeneration, if we allow it to happen.

Woods, after all, are made to survive natural catastrophes. Our oldest woods have probably recovered from a score or more storms of equal ferocity, and should survive a few more yet, though probably not in our lifetimes. The structure of natural woods, and even some of their individual trees, like the stag-headed oaks of Birkland in Sherwood Forest, bear the imprint of past storms. There are woods in Scotland blown sideways by the 1968 storm that are growing up again, with skewed trunks to mark that event. Thanks to the great storm, we have an unprecedented opportunity to find out more about how wild woods work, if only enough owners can be persuaded not to opt for wholesale clearance and replanting. In the meantime, we are already witnessing some of the *benefits* of great storms. Dark woodland floors, denied daylight for years, have suddenly received a sunburst of light which has set nature's clock ticking once again with saplings, flowers and butterflies.

Despite the terrible damage and loss of life caused by the great storm, it may, on balance, prove a blessing in disguise to our ancient woods. The South East lost 40 per cent of its ancient woods in the previous fifty years and hardly anybody noticed. But, in the words of *Task Force Trees*, 'After the storm millions of people woke up to the value of trees in the landscape of both town and countryside.' We have become a more tree-conscious nation, and, it is to be hoped, are more aware of the differences between natural and manmade woods than were the previous generation of 'Plant a tree in '73'.

Hope

Pepper Wood, between Bromsgrove and Stourbridge in Worcestershire, is a remarkable place. Go there on a bright Sunday afternoon in winter and you will find its clearings and glades full of people busy cutting coppice-wood, gathering brushwood into heaps and, turning polewood on makeshift lathes. This is a community wood, maintained and cared for by volunteers in their spare time. The cut wood is converted on the spot into products like pea and bean sticks, thin rods for weaving into the tops of newly laid hedges, clothes props, tent pegs and birch brooms, all of which are sold locally. Most of this 134 acre (54ha) ancient wood is cut over as coppice every ten to fifteen years, but the west side is managed as high forest, thinned occasionally to leave the best oaks and ashes with enough space to grow to maturity, while the north side is left completely undisturbed. In summer, this warm, open wood is a haven for wildlife, including local specialities like the white admiral, lesser spotted woodpecker and a peculiar terrestrial caddis fly. But the heart-warming message of Pepper Wood goes beyond the mere preservation of nature. It has reunited the parishioners, heirs of the medieval commoners, with their wood and symbolises the special place of traditional woodland in our history and culture.

Pepper Wood is owned by the Woodland Trust, who, at the time of writing, own 360 woods, most of them ancient ones, and are currently spending a million pounds a year acquiring more. The Trust sets out to rehabilitate woods, for example by removing conifers and encouraging traditional skills like coppicing and hedge-laying. They have a policy of unrestricted access to their woods. Thought has gone into the design of their woodland walks leaflet, each of which fits into a weatherproof sleeve for taking with you into the wood and replacing inside its ring binder afterwards. The remarkable success of the Woodland Trust reflects the growth of popular, *participatory* nature conservation in the eighties, compared with the science-orientated spectator sport of the sixties and seventies. Much of the dynamic of woodland conservation is now coming from small-scale or local enterprises, grant-aided by bodies like the NCC and the Countryside Commission (there is a separate body in Scotland), who recognise that the best way to bring neglected or misused woods back into beneficial management is to develop markets for traditional produce like hazel hurdles or thatching spars. That this approach is entirely compatible with nature conservation objectives is demonstrated by the famous Bradfield Woods in Suffolk, which have one of the richest floras in the country but also supply a local firm with wood for making rakes, scythe handles, mallets, tent pegs and other products. The one actually *depends* on the other.

Local markets for traditional woodland produce can often be found by those who combine persistence with a certain creative flair. Coppice wood from the Swanton Novers woods in Norfolk, bundled into faggots at a pound each, supplies Anglian Water with material for coastal and river defences and a local brick kiln with fuel. My enterprising friend Peter Wormell is hoping to encourage new markets for oak coppice in Argyll by providing fuel for smoking the salmon from nearby fish farms. Local woodland projects like 'Woodland Care' in East Sussex and

WOODLAND HERITAGE

WHITHER
ANCIENT WOODLAND?

After the Storm: fallen boughs at The Thicks, Staverton Park, Suffolk. A smell of raw timber, and venerable trees leaning at drunken angles. March 1988

'Project Sylvanus' in Devon and Cornwall are moving towards financial independence by entering mainstream woodland consultancy work. At another level, Common Ground, established in 1983 to promote enthusiasm for natural and historic places and things close to home, has already helped people to rediscover their parishes *themselves* via the Domesday parish maps project, and published a charming book on woodland care, *In a Nutshell*.

There are, unfortunately, serious problems facing those who would like to make a living from traditional woodland crafts. In these unstable times, markets are uncertain and they present more of a financial risk than the permanent ready outlets for softwoods. Many of the practising craftsmen are elderly and their skills, with a lifetime's experience behind them, cannot be learned overnight. Their kind of work perhaps appeals most to committed but unmaterialistic young people, who often lack the means for the initial outlay for a vehicle, chainsaw, storage yard and good-quality tools, even when helped with a government enterprise grant. Moreover there is still a serious need for a rehabilitation grant for

restoring neglected, deer-devastated coppices to a state where commercial coppicing is even possible. Nevertheless there *is* a living to be made from ancient woodland. Walter Lloyd, for example, runs a small business burning coppice wood from Lake District woods for charcoal, most of which is sold for barbecues at a local petrol station. The demand always exceeds the amount he can supply, and the woods benefit from the renewed cutting. When it rains, he makes cleft oak tent pegs and wattle hurdles made from hazel and willow rods. It does not make a fortune, 'but it's a good living compared to a forester or an agricultural labourer's wage. It's not like a job on the Stock Exchange, but it's more sure'.

Sometimes the task facing woodland managers is truly formidable. The wildwoods of Wales are a case in point. There are virtually no large woods left in Wales other than plantations, but many a small one lies shrunken and forlorn far inside its original woodbank. And they go on shrinking because their value to farmers lies mainly in the shelter they offer to grazing animals on the open hill, not in their wood or timber. There are about 30,000ha (75,000 acres) of native broadleaved woodland left in Wales, most of it scattered in tiny fragments and nearly all have a different owner. In 1985 various bodies interested in preserving and revitalising these woods got together to begin the Welsh Wildwood Campaign, Coed Cymru, with a small paid staff financed by

A scene of traditional woodmanship in the late twentieth century. Workers cleave ash poles to make fencing rails and gates, at Treswell Wood, a nature reserve owned by the Nottinghamshire Trust for Nature Conservation

WHITHER
ANCIENT WOODLAND?

grants from the Countryside Commission, Forestry Commission and others. To date Coed Cymru has encouraged owners of 1,574ha (3,889 acres) of neglected ancient woodland to fence out livestock, create small clearings to encourage natural regeneration, and, when that is not sufficient, plant native trees. In the circumstances this is quite an achievement, but until grant-aid is attractive enough to persuade Welsh hill farmers to fence their woods, further erosion of the remaining woodland is inevitable. As a colleague put it, 'They are not going to fence woods so long as their future lies in more sheep.'

Hope, then, but much uncertainty also, lies ahead for our heritage of ancient woodland. For the present we can take some comfort from the official protection they receive, which is much stronger now than ten years ago, while farmers and woodland owners are less ready to invest money in grubbing them up. By area, about two-fifths of our ancient and natural woods (by number it is less than one fifth) are Sites of Special Scientific Interest, which receive a measure of protection from the Wildlife and Countryside Act, and, equally important, attract grant-aid from the NCC and the Heritage Trust. The Forestry Commission has affirmed that all ancient woods qualify for their special broadleaves or native pinewoods grants, and it uses the NCC's ancient woodland inventories when deciding whether or not a particular wood qualifies for grant. But the grant schemes still have some way to go before they can protect ancient woods adequately. They require too high a level of intervention, and are still grounded in the old clear-fell and replant philosophy, albeit mollified by insisting on relatively small felling 'coups' rather than the familiar lunar tracts of bare earth. Neither do they take much account of regional differences in woodland, although this may soon be rectified. We can at least take some reassurance from the beginning of a convergence between the hitherto separate paths of forestry and woodmanship allied to nature conservation. To continue on this favourable course we must hope for a continued warm breeze from public opinion, and a corresponding current from government.

There is, as they say, no room for complacency. Purchasing woods at current land prices is an extremely expensive way of conserving them but it is the only certain way. We may love old woods but we have no control over their future unless we own them. The most dangerous time for an ancient wood is shortly after it is sold on the open market to someone interested in making money out of the site. Developers will pay more to destroy woods than conservationists can to preserve them, and a government committed to individual enterprises may be tempted to overrule its protective safeguards by invoking 'national interest'. Woods and other wild habitats are only safe so long as no one wishes to use them for anything else. And new pressures on ancient woods spring up almost daily. At the time of writing, the problem of the day is the growing sport of war-gaming, in which grown men apparently use woods as cover from which to squirt each other with paint in organised mock battles. Such profitable pastimes are forcing up the market values of woods beyond the reach of conservationists and timber growers alike.

In the European elections of 1989, 15 per cent of those who bothered to vote voted Green. The 'green' issues that received most attention in the media were invisible things like the hole in the ozone layer, and the greenhouse effect and its twin apocalyptic head, acid rain. Or else they were about far away places like the Amazon rain forest and the Sahara desert, respectively dwindling and spreading. I do not recall any speeches about newt ponds, primrose banks or bluebell woods. Are these really peripheral matters, Disneyesque entertainments rather than serious subjects for 'debate' or have the new generation of green politicians missed an important point, that concern for the environment begins at home? The common ground is no longer enshrined in law or custom, but so long as coppice shoots spring from the stumps and the nightingale returns to nest in the hazel bush, we will all continue to find solace and inspiration in these wonderful, secret places.

WOODLAND HERITAGE

WHITHER ANCIENT WOODLAND?

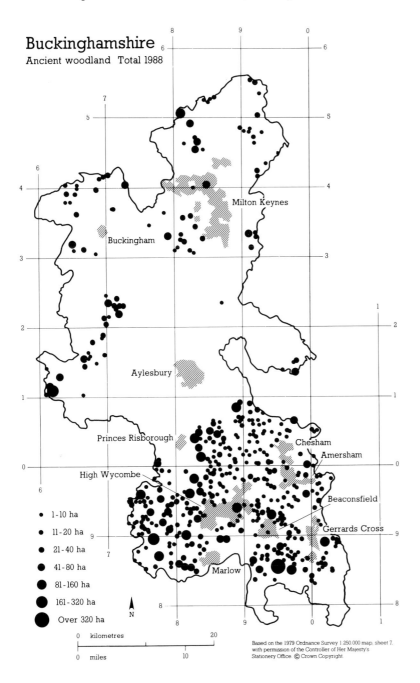

Buckinghamshire
Ancient woodland Total 1988

Milton Keynes

Buckingham

Aylesbury

Princes Risborough

Chesham

Amersham

High Wycombe

Beaconsfield

Gerrards Cross

Marlow

- • 1-10 ha
- • 11-20 ha
- ● 21-40 ha
- ● 41-80 ha
- ● 81-160 ha
- ● 161-320 ha
- ● Over 320 ha

N

0   kilometres   20

0   miles   10

Based on the 1979 Ordnance Survey 1:250,000 map, sheet 7, with permission of the Controller of Her Majesty's Stationery Office. © Crown Copyright.

Ancient woodland in Buckinghamshire. Note the dense concentration of ancient woods in the Chilterns and their contrasting absence in the Vale of Aylesbury (details from the NCC ancient woodland inventory).

BIBLIOGRAPHY

This is not a full reference list but a chapter-by-chapter guide to further reading on some of the main topics covered by this book, and also a source for quoted passages in the text.

INTRODUCTION

Among the many books in print about Britain's trees, woods and forests, relatively few are specifically about ancient and natural woodland. But this is a field which Oliver Rackham has over the past fifteen years made very much his own, beginning with *Trees and Woodland in the British Landscape* (Dent, 1976), elaborated in the weighty (and expensive) *Ancient woodland: its history, vegetation and uses in England* (Arnold, 1980) and summarised and updated in *The History of the Countryside* (Dent, 1986). Rackham's style combines scholarship with literary elegance and a rare donnish wit; the theme of all of his books is the way in which today's ancient woods are formed by nature and past human activity acting in combination. At the core of his books are his own researches, which, though remarkably wide, are centred on botany, Saxon and medieval history and East Anglia. His books about particular woods act as detailed illustrations of the theme, but also have a wider relevance; so far these are *Hayley Wood. Its history and ecology* (Cambridgeshire and Isle of Ely Naturalists Trust, 1975), *Woods of south-east Essex* (Rochford District Council, 1986) and *The Last Forest. The story of Hatfield Forest* (Dent, 1989). I recommend them highly.

My other favourite modern books on the ancient woods of a county or a place are Phil Colebourn's volume on *Ancient Woodland* (Hampshire County Council, 1983) in the *Hampshire Countryside Heritage* series, Colin Tubbs' book, *The New Forest* (Collins, 1986) in the New Naturalist series, and, at a rather more technical level, *The Native Pinewoods of Scotland* (Oliver and Boyd, 1959) by H. M. Steven and A. Carlisle. Indispensable as a guide to woodland nature conservation is George Peterken's *Woodland Conservation and Management* (Chapman and Hall, 1981).

TREES AND SHRUBS

There are a great many books, of varying quality, devoted to British native and non-native trees and shrubs. Skipping the purely botanical ones, I found much to enjoy in Gerald Wilkinson's *Trees in the Wild* (Stephen Hope, 1973) and in the unsurpassed pen portraits of trees in Geoffrey Grigson's *The Englishman's Flora* (Paladin, 1975). On particular trees, oak has a book to itself, *The British Oak*, (Classey, 1974), and so does (mainly non-woodland) elm in R. H. Richen's *Elm* (Cambridge University Press, 1983). Birch is the subject of a symposium published in the Proceedings of the Botanical Society for Edinburgh in 1984. The classic account of hornbeam is Christy, M. (1924), The hornbeam, in the *Journal of Ecology*, Vol. *12*, 39-94, which, unlike some of the more recent papers in that journal, is beautifully written. The quote about sycamore is from Esmond Harris (1986), The case for sycamore, *Quarterly Journal of Forestry*, Vol. *81*, 32-36. For more about the whitty pear, see Norman Hickin's *The Natural History of an English Forest. The Wild Life of Wyre* (Hutchinson, 1971). Classification of British woodlands: the references are: A. G. Tansley, *The British Isles and their Vegetation* (Cambridge University Press, 1939), George Peterken, *op. cit.*, R. G. H. Bunce, *A Field Key for Classifying British Woodland vegetation* (ITE, Cambridge), Parts 1 (1982) and 2 (1989) and J. Rodwell, *National Vegetation Classification. Woodlands and Scrub* (University of Lancaster, unpublished report to the Nature Conservancy Council). For a good popular account with wonderful illustrations, see the woodland chapter in Phil Colebourn and Bob Gibbons', *Britain's Natural Heritage. Reading our countryside* (Blandford, 1987). References to Evelyn are from his classic, *Sylva, or a discourse of forest-trees*, first published in 1664 and regarded as the foundation of modern forestry.

WILDWOOD

The literature on woodland prehistory is large and becoming larger by the day. The most readable general account is probably still Winifred Pennington's *The History of British Vegetation* (English Universities Press, 1969), but the standard work is Sir Harry Godwin's *History of the British Flora* (Cambridge University Press, 1975). At a local level, the *Regional Histories of England* (Longman, 1987 onwards) contain a great deal of up-to-the-minute information on woodland archaeology. There are good things too in two collections of papers published as *Archaeological* aspects of woodland ecology, Volume 146 in the BAR International Series (Oxford University, 1982), and Archaeology and the Flora of the British Isles (Oxford University, 1988). On the elm decline, I have largely followed Rackham (see his History of the Countryside), and on lime a series of scientific papers by C. D. Pigott. On human attitudes to trees and woods, see Keith Thomas' very readable study, Man and the Natural World. Changing attitudes in England 1500-1800 (Penguin, 1984). The quotation by T. H. White is from The Once and Future King (Fontana, 1962, p 91). Willow Garth is the subject of a paper in Nature No 239, The age of the British chalk grassland by M. B. Bush and J. R. Flenley (1987).

MEDIEVAL WOODS

For the geography of medieval woodland in England, see The English Medieval Landscape, edited by Leonard Cantor (Croom Helm, 1982). The Royal Forests are dealt with at length by C. R. Young in The Royal Forests of Medieval England (Leicester University Press, 1979), N. D. James in A History of English Forestry (Blackwell, 1981) and J. M. Gilbert in Hunting and hunting reserves in medieval Scotland (Donald, 1979). For medieval woodland in Wales see W. Linnard's excellent Welsh Woods and Forests: history and utilisation (National Museum of Wales, 1982). English medieval parks are enumerated in Cantor's The Medieval parks of England: a gazetteer (Loughborough, 1983). For the botanical aspects of medieval woodland, see Oliver Rackham.

The history of Wychwood has been traced by Beryl Schumer (1984) in a Leicester University occasional paper, The evolution of Wychwood to 1400: pioneers, frontiers and forests, and also in unpublished manuscripts by B. P. Petchey and V. Wickham Stede. There is a more accessible summary in Frank Emery's The Oxfordshire Landscape (Hodder and Stoughton, 1974), and a good paper about Woodstock Park by James Bond in the Arboricultural Journal, Vol 5, pp. 201-13. Shotover Forest is the subject of David Steel's Shotover – The Natural History of a Royal Forest (Pisces, 1984). My notes on Staverton Park are based on a paper by George Peterken (1969), Development of vegetation in Staverton Park, Suffolk, in Volume 3 of Field Studies, pp 1-39. The end piece quotation is from the NCC's Nature Conservation Review (Cambridge, 1977), edited by D. A. Ratcliffe.

WOODMANSHIP

For an account of woodland crafts, a treasury of lost skills, see H. E. Edlin's Woodland Crafts of Britain (Batsford, 1949). Linnard's Welsh Woods offers fascinating insights into past Welsh woodmanship, while M. L. Anderson's posthumous A History of Scottish Forestry (Nelson, 1967) presents a mass of raw

information, full of anecdote and detail, but it is a quarry, not an edifice. For more about Neolithic trackways, see B. Coles and J. Coles, Sweet Track to Glastonbury: the Somerset Levels in prehistory (Thames & Hudson, 1986); for Star Carr, see Excavations at Star Carr, edited by J. G. D. Clark (Cambridge, 1954); for Roman ironworks, H. Cleere (1976), Some operating parameters for Roman ironworks, in Bulletin of the Institute of Archaeology, 13, 235-46. The book about Flag Fen lies in the future, but an interim account is by F. Pryor and others in the Proceedings of the Prehistoric Society, Vol 52, 1-24.

There are numerous papers about coppicing, barking and other commercial practices in the forestry literature, particularly the Quarterly Journal of Forestry. I commend the historical researches of J. M. Lindsay, summarised in his chapter, Commercial use of woodland and coppice management, in The Making of the Scottish Countryside (Croom Helm, 1980) and History of oak coppice in Scotland, Scottish Forestry, Vol 29, 87-93. My details on tan-barking are from A. Gilchrist (1874), On the treatment and management of oak coppice in Scotland.

Sources for the three woods: Hobson's P. M. (1988), Methven Wood (Almondbank, Perth), the history of its management, in Scottish Forestry, 42, 104-12; the unpublished estate papers of Glen Tanar and the proceedings of a seminar held in 1983 (NCC, 1985), and A. Tittensor and R. Tittensor, Natural History of the Mens, Sussex (Horsham Natural History Society, 1977). For another heavily exploited native pinewood, see P. E. O'Sullivan (1973), Land-use changes in the forest of Abernethy 1750-1900AD, Scottish Geographical Magazine, Vol 89, 95-106.

FLOWERS

For a celebration of woodland wild flowers, see Richard Mabey's The Flowering of Britain (Hutchinson, 1980); for their distribution, The Atlas of British Flora (Nelson, 1962), edited by F. H. Perring and S. M. Walters, and for details of the ecology of the common species, Comparative Plant Ecology. A functional approach to common British species, edited by J. P. Grime and others (Unwin Hyman, 1988). For ferns, the New Naturalist volume, Ferns (Collins, 1988), by Christopher Page is first rate.

Other references mentioned in the text:
H. Beevor (1925) Norfolk woodlands from the evidence of contemporary chronicles, Quarterly Journal of Forestry, 19, 87-110
G. H. Knight (1964) Distribution of the bluebell in Warwickshire, Journal of Ecology, 52, 405-21
R. D'O Good (1944) On the distribution of the primrose in a southern county, The Naturalist, No 809, 41

T. R. Peace and J. S. L. Gilmour (1949) The effect of picking on the flowering of bluebell, *New Phytologist*, 48, 115-17

G. F. Peterken (1974) A method for assessing woodland flora for conservation using indicator species, *Biological Conservation*, 6, 239-45

G. F. Peterken and R. C. Welch (Eds) (1975) *Bedford Purlieus: its history, ecology and management*, Monks Wood Symposium, Vol 7 Monks Wood Experimental Station, Abbots Ripton

G. F. Peterken and M. Game (1981) Historical factors affecting the distribution of *Mercurialis perennis* in Central Lincolnshire, *Journal of Ecology*, 69, 781-96

R. Hornby and F. Rose (1986) *The use of vascular plants in evaluation of ancient woodland for nature conservation in Southern England*, Unpublished NCC report.

MOSSES, LICHENS AND FUNGI

The relevant literature is thin and most of it scattered in specialist publications. Two important references are *Pasture-woodlands in lowland Britain. A review of their importance for wildlife conservation* by F. Rose and P. T. Harding (ITE, 1986) and D. A. Ratcliffe (1968), An ecological account of Atlantic bryophytes in the British Isles in *New Phytologist*, 67, 365-439. On toadstools, I made use of two unpublished NCC reports, *The fungi of Gait Barrows NNR*, by P. D. and L. A. Livermore (1987), and *Some ideas on the conservation of fungi* by P. D. Orton and D. Minter (1985).

BIRDS AND BEASTS

Contrariwise, there is a huge literature on British woodland birds, and a smaller but still substantial one on mammals. Important general sources are R. J. Fuller's *Bird Habitats in Britain* (Poyser, 1982) and *The Atlas of Breeding Birds in Britain and Ireland*, edited by J. T. R. Sharrock (Poyser, 1976).

There are no modern, scholarly works devoted to extinct animals, but J. E. Harting's *British animals extinct within historic times* (Trubner, 1880) is still a good read, and L. Harrison Matthews' *Mammals in the British Isles* (Collins, 1982) a useful update. On Gerald of Wales and the beavers, see an interesting correspondence in *The Countryman*, Autumn 1988 and Spring 1989. My notes on the goshawk are taken from D. W. Yalden (1987), The natural history of Domesday Cheshire, *Naturalist*, Vol 112, 125-31. For the birds of primaeval Poland, see L. Tomialojc and others (1984), Breeding bird community of a primaeval temperate forest, *Acta Ornithologica*, Vol 20, 241-310.

Of today's woodland mammals, the dormouse is presently very much under the spotlight. The Mammal Society survey 1975-79 is summarised in *Mammal Review*, 14, 1-18, and for a lively account by a dedicated dormouse watcher, see Steve Whitbread's

The aerial dormouse in *BBC Wildlife* December 1986. The yellow-necked mouse was the subject of an ecological study by W. I. Montgomery in *Mammal Review*, 8, 177-84.

INVERTEBRATES

The matter of this chapter is based on a wide scatter of sources in specialist journals and, particularly, by unpublished NCC reports. Claude Morley's beech figures in A beech-tree's insects and their parasites, *Entomologist's Monthly Magazine*, April 1935, 90-91. The other main quoted references are:

C. E. J. Kennedy and T. R. E. Southwood (1984) The number of species of insects associated with British trees: a re-analysis, *Journal of Animal Ecology*, 53, 455-78

M. Speight (In press) *Saproxylic invertebrates and their conservation*, Council of Europe Nature and Environment Series, Strasbourg

F. Rose and P. T. Harding (ITE) (1986) *Pasture woodlands in lowland Britain*, ITE, Huntingdon

R. A. Crowson (1962) Observations on Coleoptera in Scottish oak woods, *Glasgow Naturalist*, 18, 177-95

J. Heath, E. Pollard and J. Thomas (1984) *Atlas of butterflies in Britain and Ireland*, Viking, London

A. E. Boycott (1934) The habitats of land Mollusca in Britain, *Journal of Ecology*, 22, 1-38

CONSERVATION

The conservation book for our time is Richard Mabey's *The Common Ground. A place for nature in Britain's future?* (Hutchinson, 1980), in which ancient woodland is given due prominence. I based my notes on Rockingham Forest and Deeside on:

G. F. Peterken and P. T. Harding (1974) Recent changes in the conservation value of woodlands in Rockingham Forest, *Forestry*, 47, 109-28

G. F. Peterken (1976) Long-term changes in the woodlands of Rockingham Forest and other areas, *Journal of Ecology*, 64, 123-46

I. R. Brown and A. D. Wightman (1988) The birch woodlands of Deeside, 1947-1985 – A declining resource? *Scottish Forestry*, 42, 93-103

The quotation describing a forester's joy over the Speyside pinewoods is from John Davies, *The Scottish Forester* (Blackwood, 1979). For New Forest woodland history, see Colin Tubbs' *The New Forest* (Collins, 1986). Articles on markets for traditional woodland products appear at an increasing rate in forestry literature, for example, C. Driver (1985), Charcoal – another market for neglected woodland, *Quarterly Journal of Forestry*, 79, 29-32 and R. C. C. Tabor (1989), A role for hazel in woodland conservation, *ibid*, 83, 177-82.

INDEX

Numbers in *italic* indicate main references; those in **bold** indicate illustrations

Sweet chestnut coppice in Challock Forest, Kent. Later this
flowery scene will become deeply shaded. May 1987